Peary at the North Pole

Robert Edwin Peary

DENNIS RAWLINS

PEARY

at the

NORTH POLE

Fact or Fiction?

Robert B. Luce, Inc.   Washington — New York

Contents

Acknowledgements

The following persons are among the many* whose aid, encouragement, advice, cooperation, and wisdom have made this history possible.

Florence Ward Wood, Alison Wilson, Anne Wilde, Virginia Wheaton, Carlton Wells, Dorothy Watson, Mabel Ward, M. Ian Stuart, Aloha South, Richard Lee Smith, Edward A. Shackleton, Harry Schwartz, Buford Rowland, Gloria Root, Bruce and Lillian Robinson (deceased), Charles Ritter, Sylvia Reynolds, Mary Revere, Bill Rawlins, Ralph Plaisted, Giggina Pietrangeli, George Perros, Bill Perkinson (deceased), the staff of the Peabody Library, Erika Parmi, Chas Panati, Patricia Palmer, Charlotte Palmer, Lynn Mullins, Sarah Mueller, Dick Montague, Linda Merriken, S.S. Meigs, Ted Manekin, Curtis MacDougall, Larry Kirwan, Martha Kelsey, Christine Keller, Mary Johnson (deceased), Kathy Jancuk, Brad Jacobs, M.T. Hughes, Ludvig Hertzberg, Bobby Headley, Edie Goodall, Lucy Geckler, Martin Gardner, Herman Friis, Charles T. Fitzgerald, Roy Fentress, Wilma Fairchild, Joseph Ernst, Bridget Engelmeyer, Helen Egan, Henry Edmunds, Elaine Eberly, David Eaton, George Dennis, Jr. (deceased), Ethel Demuth, George Curtis, Gary Christopher, Alicia Brex, Jim Bready, Joseph Binns, Clay Barrow, Wayne Barrett, Bernt Balchen, John and Barbara Avirett, C.B. Allen — and, most patient of all, my wife.

*Some have asked that their anonymity be protected.

1. Dream and Ambition

Excerpts from the diary of Robert Peary, entered under the fateful date, April 6, 1909:

On the trail before midnight [from April 5 camp, at 89° 25' north latitude, hundreds of miles from land, out on the treacherous drifting ice floes of the central Arctic Ocean] . . . A dense, lifeless pall of gray overhead, almost black at the horizon, and the ice ghostly chalky white with no relief . . . Striking contrast to the glittering sunlit fields over which we have been traveling for [the last] four days, canopied with blue and lit by the sun and full moon. The going better than ever; hardly any snow on the hard granular last summer's surface of the old floes, the [frozen] blue lakes larger. The rise in the temperature to minus 15 degrees has reduced friction of the sledges 25 per cent and gives the dogs [an] appearance of having caught the spirits of the party . . . short barks and yelps. Twelve hours on a direct course (thirty miles). Can I wait to cover those other five [miles]? Not a sign of a lead [open water which might block sledge progress over the ice] in this march. The thick weather gives me less concern than it might, had I not been forehanded yesterday, and fearing a cloudbank in the south took a latitude sight [noon sextant observation of sun's altitude] (89 degrees 25 minutes). This [figure] is two miles ahead of my dead reckoning [estimate of distance from place of previous observation, c.100 miles back] and [so] indicates that I have been conservative in my estimates,

7

as I intended, or that the ice has slacked [north] or both
. . . [After noon sight: 89° 57′N.]: The Pole at last!!! The
prize of three centuries, my dream & ambition for 23
years. *Mine* at last. I cannot bring myself to realize it. It
all seems so simple and commonplace. . . .

In fact, as things were to turn out, nothing could have
been *less* simple — sensational claims seldom are, when they
rest on shaky credentials. Thus the foregoing account of the
final attainment of the North Pole — for all the hundreds of
thousands of dollars it attracted — gave Admiral Peary no
end of headaches, both during and after its construction.
Indeed, unlikely as it may seem at first sight, the reader of this
book may rest assured that he will, before its end, be able to
recognize no less than a half dozen curiosities just in the above
quotation.

And this is quite aside from the rest of Peary's remarkable 1909 report — a tale of such prodigious accomplishments as has never been fully appreciated by a hitherto un-
informed public.

The reader will not only marvel at these and further
miraculous claims and gyrations, he will ultimately be presented with the first unifying and non-conspiratorial explanation ever proposed for them — outside the supernatural. He
will even see why April 6, 1909 became the immortal date of
discovery — and will learn the year in which the diary entry of
that date was finalized.

As the nineteenth century closed, the international race
for the North Pole had increasingly become a focus of public
interest. American, British, and Norwegian entries predomi-
nated, with ships, sledges, dogs, ponies, and even balloons
being employed in attempts to reach the geographical ends of
the earth. Growing personal and national rivalry impelled explorers — who, in those days, usually organized the expeditions they led — to risk their fortunes, reputations, and lives
in the far North and South, while wealthy individuals and
nations invested huge sums in these explorations in hopes of

8

sharing high-latitude prestige and claims to new lands discovered.

The actual Poles, however, remained inviolate from each successive thrust, a situation that served only to heighten challenge and thereby goad civilized man all the more.

Suddenly in the late summer of 1909, came the startling announcement that the highest possible latitude — 90° north — was touched at last.

"Stars and Stripes nailed to the Pole."

On September 6, 1909, Commander Robert E. Peary, America's foremost Arctic explorer, cabled to the world his achievement of the geographical goal sought by scores of the greatest explorers of all nations. The man "who refused to fail," whose motto had become "find a way or make one," had succeeded at last after eight expeditions over (as he reminisced):

twenty-three of the best years of a man's life; years filled with brute hard labor, cold, darkness, and hunger, and punctuated with a broken leg, with mutilated feet, with such days of physical hell and nights of agony of disappointment and deferred hope, as few can realize or imagine.

He was now to be honored by the world's geographical societies, made rich by a hero worshipping public, and — after the House of Representatives' acrimonious Peary Hearings of 1910-1911 — promoted by special act of the Congress to Rear-Admiral. From 1909 on, commanding at least $1,000 per booking, Peary lectured across the nation in his clipped, authoritative voice to hundreds of audiences on his "attainment of the North Pole for the prestige and honor of the United States of America":

The discovery of the North Pole stands for the inevitable victory of courage, persistence, experience over all obstacles. In the discovery of the North Pole is written the final chapter of the last of the geographical stories of the Western hemisphere which began with the discovery of the New World by Columbus. Here is the cap and

9

climax, the finish, the closing of the book on 400 years of history. The discovery of the North Pole on the sixth of April, nineteen hundred and nine, by the last expedition of the Peary Arctic Club, means that the splendid, frozen jewel of the North, for which through centuries men of every nation have struggled and suffered and died, is won at last, and is to be worn forever, by the Stars and Stripes.

In 1920, Peary was buried in Arlington Cemetery before the nation's most eminent statesmen, geographers, and explorers. One of the latter was to write: "He will stand for all time as the discoverer of the North Pole."

On Sept. 6, when Peary's news reached the N.Y. *Times*, the claim was by then five days stale. Dr. Frederick A. Cook, veteran of both polar regions, and Peary's predecessor as President of the New York Explorers' Club, had, on Sept. 1st, already announced the discovery (April 21, 1908) as his own. On learning this, Peary simply called Cook a gold-bricker and so touched off the bitterest, most scandalous controversy in the long history of exploration claims. Cook, initially gracious toward Peary while merely accusing him of thievery, eventually came to portray him as a murderer as well as a degenerate, orgiastic debaucher of eskimo girls, declaring that Peary "deserved to be hanged for his actions in the North." Peary left eventual destruction of his competitor to others, but privately wrote of Cook as "a cowardly cur of a sordid imposter," a description whose metric malice is matched only by its utter aptness.

In December of 1909, some time after Peary's claim had been approved by the prestigious National Geographic Society, Cook's was rejected by even his friends at Copenhagen University (where he had submitted copies of alleged evidence), and he fled into seclusion. And so, after a quick fiscal cleanup of about $100,000, Cook was exposed, discredited, and verbally pilloried. A N.Y. *Times* editorial characterized him as, "monster of duplicity," "shameless swindler," "sneak thief," and "the greatest imposter of all time."

Historically, the North Pole has been associated with controversy, misunderstanding, and fraud. Why? Partly the

10

explanation is geographical; the North Pole seems in some ways virtually designed for hoaxery. There is no fixed land at the spot — only impermanent ice, ever-drifting over a deep ocean (this having been thought probable well before 1909); thus no claimant's marker left at the North Pole would remain there long, to be checked by later visitors. The scenery is no different from that for hundreds of miles around, so no surface description of it can provide a decisive basis of judgment of claims.

These facts occasionally produce one or both of two reactions: "then what does it matter who got there first?" and/or "anyway, how could you prove a claimant didn't get there?"

Coming from non-scientists, these are understandable — and not unrelated — questions. But, as will be seen (and as holds true for all exploration in all ages), there was much specific and valuable scientific knowledge to be gained on a trip to the North Pole in the early twentieth century. (Indeed, Peary's southernmost 1909 soundings are still used on most official maps of Arctic Ocean bathymetry. If actually taken far from the indicated meridian, as is highly likely, they are thus distorting depth contours on modern charts of dangerous waters — another indication that the controversy is not merely academic.) To say that the truth about the 1909 trip does not matter is simply to brush off exploration and science — not to mention accurate history — as being of no account.

The rest of the explanation of the controversy involves the state of the geographical community, in particular its polar-exploring section, a lesson-rich chapter of the history of science which has never previously been delineated unflinchingly. Such a review is embarked upon in the following pages with mixed feelings on the part of the writer, who, while having friends in and admiring some aspects of organized geography, sees, nonetheless, the need there for a long overdue reform in the area of frankness — an end to the placing of friendship and political expediency ahead of honest disclosure.

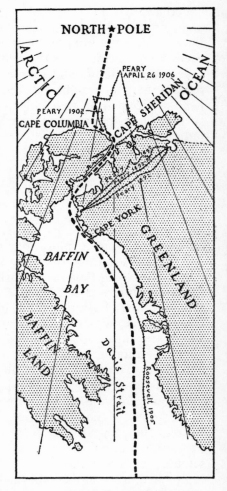

90° N. Lat. (North Pole
April 6" 1909

I have today hoisted
the National Ensign of
the United States of
America at this place
which my observa-
tions indicate to be
the North Polar axis
of the earth..., & have
formally taken posses-
sion of the entire
region + adjacent
far, + in the name
of the President +
the United States of
America.
I leave this record
+ United States flag
in possession
Robert E. Peary
United States Navy

Left, Peary's handwritten original copy of one of the two records allegedly left at the North Pole. In his final story, observations did not occur until April 7. Right, the only depiction of the 1909 path that Peary ever drew. His uncertainty (never compensated for at any time en route) as to his left-right position throughout the trip is well illustrated by the fact that, only 50 miles out from land, he already shows himself on his map to be 20 miles to the left of the Cape Columbia meridian — which he wrote the U.S. Coast and Geodetic Survey was the path he assumed he had taken to the Pole.

2.   The White Grail

The attraction the hostile unknowns of the far North have held for centuries of explorers may be incomprehensible to the warm and satisfied. The naturally curious and adventurous required no lure but that of hitherto unseen vistas. Nonetheless, the seemingly barren Arctic offers material rewards as well — for thousands of years booty and glory have been the lot of those robust adventurers who did not reap ruin or miserable death in the icy Arctic. Yet for many times that span, Eskimos have lived off the region — presumably wondering the while at the difficulty supposedly superior invaders of their habitat have so often exhibited in the performance of such a seemingly elementary feat.

The earliest records of exploration are sketchy at best — for obvious commercial reasons. A sea captain who sailed beyond Gibraltar's Pillars of Hercules and did not find legendary monsters there — or fall over the edge of a flat earth — had no interest in encouraging competition by becoming the village agnostic on his return; and before Gutenberg, he could hardly live off royalties of a book about his adventures.

A rare exception to the rule was the Marseilles astronomer and sailor Pytheas who wrote of visiting a land far to the North, where — incredibly to the ancients — it was still daylight at midnight and the ocean's water "curdled" (sea-ice). His major works failed to survive the Dark Ages, Strabo's *Geography*, for example, being thought worthier of immortality; thus, we know of Pytheas' travels only because of

13

other writers' (e.g.: Strabo, Polybius) comments on them — often denunciatory. It is ironic that the very points that Strabo brought forth as evidence that Pytheas was a wild liar not only provide a kind of preservation of the explorer's otherwise lost writings, but are now seen as the surest proof that he truly visited the Arctic. Thus, the best certification of an exploration tale's truth is its discovery of data *not previously known* and which later proves to be correct (via repeated observations by independent witnesses).

In medieval times, Viking longships doubtless pierced the Arctic circle often en route to Iceland, Greenland, and North America, evidently navigating via the sun even in cloudy weather by utilizing the polarization properties of light.

Crucial to the whole development of Arctic exploration, the centuries of searches for Northeast (north of Siberia) and Northwest (north of continental Canada) Passages to the Orient were the result of a forced diversion. The shortest route — right over the North Pole — was pointed out to Henry VIII in 1527 by merchant Robert Thorne (who incidentally noted the sailing advantages of continual day during the far North's summer). This route formed part of the exploring plans of a variety of British sea captains during the Tudor period, expeditions which in the event became the first searches for the Northwest Passage.

The growth of trade in the Renaissance led not only to the voyages of Columbus but — in the latter half of the next century — to explorations of Arctic Canada by the Elizabethan captain Martin Frobisher. Claiming to have made the Northwest Passage to Cathay and to have found gold there, Frobisher brought back an "Oriental" who was merely an Eskimo, plus tons of fool's gold — and thus bankrupted his backers, the Cathay Company of London.

At the same time, due largely to the establishment of the Russian port of Archangel and the search for a Northeast Passage to Cathay, new lands north of Europe were discovered (or rediscovered), the largest finds being the remote, glaciated, mountainous isles, Spitzbergen ("Sharp-mountains") and Novaya Zemlya ("New Land").

The first modern explorer of any of the Svalbard group (mainly West Spitzbergen and North East Land) was a Dutch navigator, Willem Barents. Barents is usually credited with the first definite "farthest North" records, his highest latitude being attained and determined on June 19, 1596, Gregorian calendar, where he also found the direction (the "variation" from true north) of his magnetic compass needle — a crucial aid to his navigation, and previously unknowable data.

Barents also led the first substantial modern exploration of Novaya Zemlya. But his ship was trapped there in the late summer ice in 1596, and so, beneath its bleak northeast slopes, his expedition became the first European one to suffer through the Arctic winter at 76° north latitude. During next June's escape around Ice Point (the northern tip of Novaya Zemlya) Barents took one last look at the scene which he had been the first to see. Four days later he was dead.

The waxing force — and proportional cost in life and ethics — of civilization's drive to the north, northeast, and northwest is personified in the early 17th century career of the English explorer, Henry Hudson. Hudson tried the Northwest Passage in 1607 but was stopped at Greenland and returned to England via Spitzbergen where he accurately reported lucrative whaling possibilities. The following year, his attempt at the Northeast Passage produced little besides a description of an inhabitant of the Barents Sea:

> a mermaid . . . from the navill upward, her backe and breasts were like a woman's . . . skin very white; and long haire hanging downe behinde, of colour blacke . . . her tayle . . . like [that] of a porposse, and speckled like a macrell.

After surviving a near-mutiny near Novaya Zemlya in the spring of 1609, Hudson was exploring the Hudson River for the Dutch late that summer. For a British company, he sought the Northwest Passage in 1611 in the British ship *Discovery* and died near the Hudson Bay's southern extremity as the result of a mutiny triggered by a dispute over the equity of food-distribution (shortages having followed his alienation of the usually helpful natives) — a recurrent source of friction in exploration.

Ironically, neither Hudson Bay, Hudson Strait, nor the Hudson River were first explored by Hudson. The Arctic island which he is said to have discovered in 1607 between Iceland and Spitzbergen, is now called Jan Mayen Island.

Both Barents and Hudson claimed to have exceeded 80° north latitude, (a feat never before accomplished in European reports), near northwest Spitzbergen; and both claims are accepted by most modern authorities, though neither is at all certain.

The only astronomical observation (the sun's altitude above the horizon, measured by naked eye with cross-staff) by Barents supposedly placing him north of 80°N. (at 80°11′N.) was computed with an arithmetic error — and thus should be 79°49′N. And none of the nearby land Barents reached is north of 80°N.

Hudson's claim of 80°23′N. (by cross-staff July 23, 1607, Gregorian), is now near universally repeated (the *Brittanica* being a creditable exception). But in 1900, Sir William Martin Conway (the first explorer to cross Spitzbergen), in the best British gentleman supra-national tradition, showed in detail the preferability of accepting the Hollander Barents' farthest North over that of his countryman Hudson's — in which he found signs of falsification (probably by Hudson's companion and chronicler John Playse).

The Hudson 1607 Spitzbergen latitudes are almost worthless on a number of counts. Setting aside random errors, erratic bearings, and misprints, we find repeated claims of the discovery of land at about 81°N. or further north. (More damningly consistent than Conway knew — he wrongly follows the authorities in not noticing that Hudson used the Julian calendar, and this affects Conway's reduction of Hudson's solar data quite drastically.) Yet no part of northwest Spitzbergen exceeds .80°N., and the whole Svalbard group is south of 81°N.

The resulting 1607 description (and 1611 map) of the

northern contour of northwest Spitzbergen is a remarkably close copy of Barents' 1598 chart — including not only its correct features but its temporary *errors*. (Corrected only in 1612 from a more careful re-examination of the deceased Dutchman's log.) The 1598 Dutch map had, for example, wrongly shown the north coast of northwest Spitzbergen trending northeast to roughly 81°N. — and the Hudson account (and map) claims to have observed this first hand.

Such blunders, along with the ease with which a competent navigator can fake solar observations, suggest that we here have history's first fraudulent farthest North.

Apparently, such pranks soon became the vogue: by the middle of the century, Dutch merchant marines were pulling any available leg with stories of their having sailed through a warm, ice-free open polar sea about the North Pole. Convincing faked observations of the sun's altitude proving impressive latitudes were produceable in force — a particularly tall instance being the attainment on Aug. 1st, 1655, of 88°56′N. latitude!

Navigated by Englishman William Baffin, the *Discovery* sailed again in search of the Northwest Passage in 1615. Baffin explored between Canada and Greenland (the semi-navigable channel to the Arctic Ocean later known as "the American route to the Pole") as far as Smith Sound, 78°N., but was stopped by ice not far from what is now the Thule U.S. Air Force Base. Baffin's records set new navigational standards in their extensive attention to magnetic measurements (especially valuable near the North Magnetic Pole). His longitudes were unusually precise, since (in a day long before reliable mobile chronometers) he scrupulously determined Greenwich Mean Time (critical for knowing one's longitude relative to Greenwich) by astronomical methods (lunar distances).

The obvious great circle simplicity of Thorne's 1527 suggestion recommended it over 200 years later when the ongoing interest in the elusive Northwest Passage to the East was rekindled after a lull throughout most of the 1600's. The eminent Scotch mathematician Colin MacLaurin, in the middle of the 18th century, expressed his displeasure at the detour implicit in the Northwest Passage proposal to go around the North Pole on the left side, suggesting instead a shorter voyage from Greenland to the Pacific straight over the Pole itself. In a day of non-airborne travel this was a fine example of a plan attractive on paper which proved quite impracticable in fact — prototype for a crowded tradition in polar history.

In apparent response, the Royal Society (London) sent out, in 1773, two ships under their own Commodore Constantine Phipps, to go over the Pole to the Orient. Phipps crossed the 80th parallel on July 12. His highest recorded latitude was made July 27, at 80°47'N, 21°E. longitude, just west of Svalbard's Seven Islands — a very accurate placement of this island group. (The error in longitude is due to a clock uncertainty scrupulously noted and checked.) Though Phipps naively accepted Hudson's claim to have reached 81°½N. and so had no thought of a record for himself, we now see that his is the first of the traditional list of farthest Norths which exceeds 80°N. and is believable.

(One of the young officers on the Phipps expedition was Horatio Nelson who showed his legendary ignorance of the meaning of the word "fear" during a run-in with a polar bear.)

At about this time, the Bering Strait passage (probably discovered in 1648 by Semen Dezhnev of Russia) from the Pacific Ocean to the Arctic Ocean was explored by the Dane Vitus Bering in 1728, and again in 1777 by that unique navigator-explorer-scientist Captain James Cook. (His protege, William Bligh, learned his extraordinary navigational skills from Cook and thus survived the 1789 *Bounty* mutiny, though he was, as Hudson before him, set adrift by his crew in a lifeboat, thousands of miles from civilization.)

Early 19th century polar sailing, Arctic and Antarctic, was largely in pursuit of the whale, the single major source of oil in a pre-petroleum world.

The expedient of offering a crass fiscal prize had been proven successful in the cracking of the age-old problem of

18

longitude in the late 18th century. So in 1818, on the recommendation of a Cook voyage veteran (now Royal Society President), Sir Joseph Banks and his former pupil, whaler-scientist William Scoresby, Jr., Parliament offered a reward of 5000 pounds sterling to the first sailor who crossed 110°W. longitude north of Canada, or who achieved 89°N. latitude.

The first attempts to capture the prize were commanded by some of the premier names of Arctic exploration in the first half of the last century: Edward Parry, John Franklin, John Ross and his nephew James Ross. In the summer of 1818, the elder Ross suddenly retreated while poised at the entrance to Lancaster Sound (which subsequently proved to be the key opening to the Northwest Passage) and was privately accused in geographical circles of having gotten cold feet at the edge of the unknown.

Parry, his second-in-command, returned with his own expedition the following year and patiently drove his ships, the *Hecla* and *Griper*, through most of the Northwest Passage along the route north of Victoria Island (finally achieved during the recent Alaskan oil rush, by the *Manhattan*, in 1969), as far west as Melville Island, longitude 110°W. After wintering, he received the Parliamentary prize on his return in 1820. Franklin's simultaneous expedition in north Canada barely survived to return to England in 1822.

While John Ross followed interests in instrument invention and pure science (e.g.: observing the moon's occultation of the then-remotest known planet Uranus with his Scottish observatory's reflecting telescope in 1824), Parry — already a public hero of the first magnitude — planned more spectacularly than ever. In the summer of 1827, he and James Ross assaulted the Pole itself, leaving his ships north of Spitzbergen to head across the ice with an amphibious plan: a combination of sledges for ice and longboats for leads of open water between ice floes. Fighting cold, storm, and a southerly drift of the floes, he made at least latitude 82°44'N. — a record North which stood for nearly half a century and ensured his instant knighthood upon his return. A major lesson of Parry's attempt was not lost on John Ross who later

19

proposed (an idea often mistakenly credited to Peary) a similar expedition, not leaving land in June: "the spring should have been the season chosen" for the sledges to start, after a winter in Spitzbergen, in order to lengthen the time spent traveling over relatively firm ice.

John Ross pioneered the paddle steamship's attack on the Greenland-Canada Arctic in 1829 with the *Victory* (also providently equipped with sails). He returned in 1832 to a world that had thought him dead — his scientifically inclined nephew James having discovered the North magnetic Pole (in 1831, at 70°N., 97°W.) on a side-expedition from the ship in the interim. A decade later, James Ross was to achieve a farthest South at the great Ross Ice Barrier (stepway to the South Pole), accompanied (in the admirable British science-naval tradition) by botanist Joseph Hooker (subsequently a key heretic in the Darwin controversy).

At this very time, the long frustrated search for the Northwest Passage culminated in the 1845 Franklin expedition of seven-score men commanded by the daring but aged Arctic veteran, Sir John Franklin, in the steamships *Erebus* and *Terror*. The ships were trapped in the ice and abandoned. The crew starved, perishing to a man. Encouraged by a 20,000 pound prize offered by the Admiralty (and later much financed by Lady Franklin) the search for a clue to Franklin's fate triggered two-score expeditions over three decades costing 20 million pounds — and this incidentally led to unprecedented exploration of the North Canadian archipelago. In 1850, William Penny, R.N. found the first graves. In 1850-1853, the combined expeditions of Robert McClure and Richard Collinson from the West (Bering Strait) traversed the Northwest Passage at last — though partly by man-hauled sledges over ice. Only years later was it deduced that the Franklin expedition had itself discovered the Passage in late spring 1847, just as John Franklin expired.

The Franklin episode also initiated the first serious United States involvement in Antarctic exploration, financed by Henry Grinnell, founder of the American Geographical Society (N.Y.), the foremost U.S. institute of geographical scholarship. The first Grinnell expedition (1850-1851) was minor: Edwin de Haven poked about Franklin's area of disappearance, was caught in the ice and drifted out of the Arctic. The surgeon of that venture, Elisha Kent Kane, then led the second Grinnell expedition, 1853-1855, taking the ship *Advance* a few miles north of the 1852 farthest of another Franklin searcher, Edward Inglefield, R.N.

The Kane expedition brought the genuine survey of the western and southern sections of the Kane Basin (discovered by Inglefield) extending the American route to the Pole and of the great Humboldt glacier in west Greenland. Also claimed was the attainment of farthest north land by William Morton, Kane's steward, on June 24, 1854, and the discovery of a supposed open polar sea, navigable to the Pole.

The highly popular writings of Kane romanticized Arctic adventure and made exciting reading in ante-bellum America, where polar fascination had long been whetted by the crank writings, lectures, and U.S. Congressional petitions (1818-1819) of John Symmes. Symmes hypothesized vast unseen openings ("Symmes Holes") into the Earth's interior at the Poles and his writings may have helped trigger the fantastic South polar tales of novelist and pseudoscientist Edgar Allen Poe.

Some of Poe's imagery could have inspired Kane's books' evocative illustrations, which — like his written reports — tended to exaggeration. From Poe's *Ms. Found in a Bottle,* 1831 (for a touch of chill in any clime, read to the third movement of Ralph Vaughan Williams *Sinfonia Antartica*):

> All in the immediate vicinity of the ship is the blackness of eternal night, and a chaos of foamless water; but about a league on either side of us, may be seen, indistinctly and at intervals, stupendous ramparts of ice towering away into the desolate sky, and looking like the walls of the universe.

A hundred thousand dollars richer on royalties from his tales, Kane died in Havana in 1857 at the height of his heroic fame — while the nationally mourning U.S. public was unaware of another side of Kane's career.

Though knowing otherwise, Kane claimed that his expedition had attained (to quote the 1972 Kane biography by the head of the American Philosophical Society, which sponsored Kane's journey): "the northernmost land ever trodden by a white man." The exaggerated latitudes on which this claim was based were mainly due to Kane's indefensibly transparent expedient of averaging mere estimates (dead-reckoning) with precise sextant (astronomical) data's positionings. Dead-reckoning is notoriously unreliable — and only to be fallen back upon in one's total deprivation of any other means of finding position. Despite the usual boastful explorer's assurances of his party's dead-reckoning precision, the Kane expedition's dead-reckoned latitudes were invariably higher than reality — the effect of detour-mileage and typical explorer's optimism. Moreover: even Morton's northernmost sextant readings (at 80°26′N., five miles north of Cape Jefferson) were in error, on the high latitude side, by 15 miles, due to non-recording of chronometer time for the "noon" altitude of the sun — data not really taken at local apparent noon. Long before the actual latitudes of the various west Greenland capes supposedly reached by Morton were checked by later explorers, his story was doubted (in the *Journal* of the Royal Geographical Society) on various grounds by the Danish authority on Greenland, Dr. Henry Rink. In any case, Morton's actual farthest-north land reached was Cape Constitution, which Kane placed at 81°22′N. (he wanted to ignore the sextant data altogether and make it 81°⅔N.!) The true figure is 80°34′N. The "enhancement" of latitude is thus virtually a full *degree* and Kane's maps are worse than Barents' 16th century work.

Kane's later promotion of the saleable (if unsailable) open Polar Sea was against the sage advice of his own expedition-colleague, the experienced Johan Carl Petersen, who wrote bluntly that "none of us has seen any Polar Ocean." Naturally, it has long since been proved a fantasy — a development which could hardly have surprised Kane, who arbitrarily expanded his Open Sea's area by 40% between reports to the Secretary of the Navy before publication, and illustrated it in his book by an astronomically impossible engraving.

Yet even today, over a century later, seemingly authoritative sources reproduce this picture without comment. The 1970 June *Explorers Journal* states in addition that the venture discovered Ellesmere Island (found by Baffin, 1616; named by Inglefield, 1852) and attained "the northernmost latitude ever reached at that time."

Kane's Arctic personal relations with the men of his expedition have been obscured or hidden over the years. Whole sections of Kane's original log have been removed and much of his private journal is missing.

However, we now know that in August, 1854, after Kane's incompetence and anglophobic patriotism had resulted in ill-planned forced sledge-drives northward, costing two lives and two permanent cripplings, half the company mutinied. They fled under Petersen, making a late-season, abortive try to reach civilization in a small open boat. Expedition-surgeon Isaac Israel Hayes' 1860 book on this episode, *An Arctic Boat Journey*, reports the trip as being undertaken with Kane's blessing — a falsehood (tacitly assented to by Kane's book) still generally believed. Indeed, five years after the 1965 publication and analysis by key Kane chronicler Oscar Villarejo of the explorer's long-hidden private accounts of mutinies under Kane, one still may read in the journal of the Explorers Club:

> There was never a question of maintaining discipline or yielding to authority. [Kane] had the utmost confidence in his associates, and they trusted their leader with a devotion and dedication seldom recorded under like circumstances.

Ironically, after the rebellious group was forced back to Kane's quarters by winter, Kane cared for his lost sheep and personally amputated some of Hayes' frostbitten toes. Combining intelligence and a strong stomach, he kept himself singularly free of scurvy through a diet of rat soup, with occasional boiled puppy.

Exploration ceased after Kane's final attempt at a sally

north ended in mutiny within 24 hours of setting out, despite his threat to execute the mutineers on the spot. The surviving members of the expedition gratefully escaped south in 1855 to Upernavik, Greenland.

With Kane dead, it was left to Hayes to parlay the fictional Open Polar Sea as a way to the Pole and to fiscal backing. In pursuit of the latter goal, Hayes denied rumors of his joining a mutiny against Kane and meanwhile stole genuine Arctic explorer Charles Francis Hall's ship's-captain and American Geographical Society support. (Hall's private journal-entries on the treacherous Hayes are as enraged as those of Kane.) Hayes' assurances that he was the best man to reach the North Pole were very convincing to the 1860 American scientific community, which backed him unanimously:

> the distance, in a direct line from my proposed starting-point at Cape Frazer, to the North Pole, is only about seven hundred miles,—scarcely greater than that travelled by myself and companions, going and returning, in 1854.

Thus was Hayes enabled to lead an expedition in the ship *United States* up the American route. At about the time Fort Sumter was falling, Hayes sledged across the Kane Basin ice from his Greenland base to mid-Ellesmere, which he had first reached and (with Kane) had named Grinnell Land in 1854. Hayes drove northward along this coast and allegedly achieved on May 18, 1861, his own farthest North land, which his astronomical data put north of 81°½N. From here he *too* saw far out onto the non-existent Open Polar Sea.

Anticipating Kanine glory, he returned to the U.S. to find instead wartime gloom and massive personal debts — which he, typically, met with the patriotic gesture of naming his farthest-seen land: Cape Union.

Though Hayes' claims are now taken seriously only by the credulous, his farthest was, in its day, accepted without question by professionals, and he was awarded a gold medal in 1867 by the Royal Geographical Society of London.

24

Decades later, the American Geographical Society was proudly displaying a case full of Hayes' medals.

According to a signed cairn-record Hayes supposedly left at his farthest North, his May 18th astronomical observations (sextant measurements of the sun's altitude) taken three miles south of the spot, at 81°32'N. placed him and his sole companion George Knorr on Ellesmere's east *coast* at 81°35'N., 70°30'W. on May 18 and 19; however:

1. The signed record has never been found, anywhere.

2. The geographical coordinates given in its text correspond to a position deep within Ellesmere, not coastal — except on Kane's erroneous earlier map (based on Morton's rough sightings of land from Cape Constitution in 1854).

3. Hayes' chart of the entire Ellesmere east coast north of 80°N. is an obvious copy of Kane's inaccurate chart's general shape.

4. Despite a calendar confusion (farthest was actually May 17, it later turned out), Hayes' eventually disclosed data yielded the same latitude originally published (with the record) for May 18! (The calendar correction should have lowered the farthest latitude by 13', to 81°22'N. — setting back Hayes into a possible tie with the Kane-Morton 1854 farthest. The demotion never took place.)

5. Hayes' record refers to observations, but his final story provided only *one* single-limb datum (not sufficient for the complete position provided in the record) from the day the record was written. (This slip we will see repeated on the April 6, 1909, original record of another explorer.)

Hayes' report returns him south from the farthest at very roughly 50 miles per day for the first two days, a fantastic speed under the conditions, especially for an explorer missing some toes. Hayes' actual 1861 farthest was probably 80°03'N., Cape Collinson. His field-diaries for the suspect period are gone. The AGS archives' 1971 examination of Hayes' copy of his data found: a leaf has been *scissored* out at the farthest.

Wise old Clements Markham, who directed the Royal Geographical Society for many years, privately recognized Hayes as "a regular impostor" — but nothing of this was said publicly and none of Hayes' official awards and recognitions was dropped.

Hayes' 1867 popular volume closed with a glowing vision of science and Christianity, "the only true religion," overcoming with unselfish zeal, "ignorance" and "ancient superstitions." The book was titled *The Open Polar Sea*.

It is the discreditable opposite of Pytheas' glory to report observing geography one expected would exist, but which is later proved not to be.

In 1871, C.F. Hall finally realized the dream Hayes had cheated him of in 1860 (and had tried to do again in 1870). In late August, Hall's expedition, in the steamship *Polaris*, was forcing its way up Robeson Channel — Hall's discovery, the northernmost link in the American route, opening onto the Arctic Ocean itself. Of course, no open polar sea was found, but a Western Hemisphere farthest-north of 82° 11'N. was accomplished nonetheless — before retreat to Thank God Harbor (Greenland) at 81°38'N., 62° W., planting the American flag north of any other on land.

In October, Hall sledged to 82°N. On returning to the ship, he was served a cup of coffee which was coincidentally followed by violent sickness. In two weeks he was dead, and the drive of the expedition died with him. While embarking for the return, half the crew was stranded during a gale. However, the lost party, commanded by George Tyson, actually managed to drift south back to civilization on an *ice-floe*, without any loss of life. Tyson's instruments and journals are today among the most precious relics preserved at the new Center for Polar Archives, U.S. National Archives, Washington.

Despite a swirl of dark rumors, an official board of inquiry concluded that Hall's death was natural. However, an exhumation and autopsy by writer Chauncey Loomis in 1968 found that Hall had ingested large quantities of arsenic in the fortnight before his death.

After the ghastly charts of Kane and Hayes the maps which Emil Bessels, Hall's physician and chief scientist, published in 1876 from the *Polaris* journey are a pleasure to en-

26

counter for their accuracy regarding points attained. Bessels may have had a fine hand at other arts as well as he is now considered the major suspect in Hall's demise.

Despite the Hall fiasco, polar fever accelerated as the 1870's progressed. An 1872 Austrian expedition led by Karl Weyprecht and Julius Payer was attempting to test one of the misguided notions of the eminent German geographer August Petermann, when, drifting helplessly icebound in the ship *Tegethoff* it stumbled upon and explored the archipelago they named Franz Josef Land, which includes the northernmost land of the Eastern Hemisphere (mostly north of 80°N.). In 1874, Payer sledged to land he placed at 82°05'. (None of Franz Josef Land is north of 81°51'N.) The ice-trapped ship was then abandoned; the Austrians escaped to Novaya Zemlya, where they were rescued by Russian fishermen.

In 1875, British sailor-scientist George Nares led a Royal Geographical Society inspired expedition up the American route in the ships *Alert* and *Discovery*. Surprisingly, the *Alert* made it all the way through Robeson Channel to the shores of the Arctic Ocean, achieving a record ship's-farthest-North which (without drift or icebreaker) hasn't been bettered by more than a few miles since. The ship wintered at Floeberg Beach (82° 27'N.) near Cape Sheridan, north Ellesmere Land.

Extensive explorations in the spring of 1876 led to the surveying of hundreds of miles of new coast line. All the dogs brought along having died, exploration was accomplished entirely by man-hauling sledges, a British specialty. Scurvy was a further source of discouragement, affecting about half the expedition. Lt. Pelham Aldrich (having briefly held the farthest record, beating Parry's old 1827 mark on Sept. 27, 1875, at 82°48'N. near Cape Joseph Henry) determined the north end of Ellesmere Land; Lewis Beaumont explored northwest Greenland; and Albert Markham led a party off Ellesmere to a new Farthest North on May 12, 1876 at 83°20'N., where Her Majesty's health was toasted, only 400 miles from the Pole itself.

In 1879-1880, a sledge-trip financed by the New York *Herald's* head, James Gordon Bennett, and led by Lt. Frederick Schwatka (U.S. Army), closed the long series of searches sent specifically to clear up the Franklin mystery. Schwatka, like Hall, in contrast to the naval regulation conscious British, deliberately adopted Eskimo ways: food, shelter, transportation — realizing that Eskimo customs were the filtrate of centuries of experience and survival.

The same year, the Swedish Baron Adolf Nordenskjöld, with government support, took his ship *Vega* north of Siberia through most of the Northeast Passage in one season. After wintering, Nordenskjöld broke free of the gripping ice and reached the Bering Strait in two days, on July 20, 1879.

Almost immediately, the largely uncharted Polar Sea north of Siberia was invaded again — but far more aggressively — by another Bennett-backed expedition: the ship *Jeanette*, commanded by George W. de Long, U.S.N., attacked and was caught in the ice late in 1879 and drifted about powerlessly until mid-1881, when it was crushed. The crew retreated south in three open boats (carried at first), landing en route at their discovery, tiny Bennett Island; two finally reached the Lena River Delta in north Siberia. There half of the survivors died of starvation and cold. De Long did not return, but his companion George Melville lived to become an admiral.

New polar disasters were not long in obliging the press and a bloodthirsty public. In 1881, as part of The First International Polar Year 1882-1883, the United States sent an expedition to Fort Conger (northeast Ellesmere, across the Hall Basin from Polaris Promontory) under Lt. Adolphus W. Greely, U.S. Army. The major purpose was unsensational; Greely recalled:

> It was no adventurous pole-seeking voyage . . . but a single unit in an elaborate system of international scientific research in which eleven nations and fifty scientific observatories worked in concert. For America it marked a forward movement toward fellowship with other countries. Indeed, it was the first instance in which the United States, acting under Congressional and Executive

28

authority, practically entered the family of nations, an entrance neither for war nor for commerce, but for the increase of human knowledge.

Greely himself explored inland and another party under James Lockwood exceeded Beaumont's Greenland distance and Markham's latitude, achieving in northwest Greenland on May 13, 1882, the United States' first and only non-suspect farthest North: 83°24'N. (41°W.) A cairn-record was left at the spot.

Poor financing had merely hampered work in the North thus far; but the successive bunglings of the relief expedition, on which Greely's return depended, left the men (after a retreat down the Ellesmere east coast) starving and freezing in tents on Cape Sabine, where the majority died. After repeated offenses, a hoarder was ordered shot by Greely. The remaining men ate clothes, shoes, then shoelaces — and finally each other.

At last, on June 23, 1884, a rescue team under Winfield S. Schley, U.S.N., "hazarding the safety of their ships, along the rocky cliffs of Pim Island, during a gale of unusual violence" (Greely) raced toward Cape Sabine on the outside chance that — after three years without word — a day's difference might matter. Incredibly, it *did*. Six near-dead men were saved. Despite their skeletal condition when found, they recovered normal health, and Greely and David Brainard (of the farthest party) lived out long and creditable careers.

The Greely-Lockwood farthest North is not only the sole sure U.S. niche in the latitude competition — it is the most indubitable of all farthests of all nations, since it was set on land. In 1900, the cairn-record Lockwood left at the spot was recovered by none other than Greely's loudest detractor, America's foremost polar explorer, Robert Peary.

An engraving from a sketch by Dr. Kane. Below, Captain Sverdrup's sketch map 1898-1902. Heiberg Land here appears to stretch as far north in azimuth as about 30° to 40° west of north.

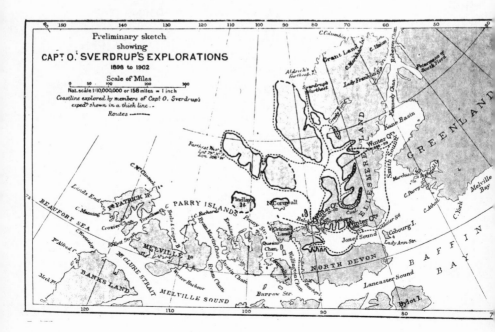

3.   Glory and Decay

Robert Edwin Peary was born in Cresson, Pennsylvania, on May 6, 1856. Upon the death of his father, his mother returned with him to the family home-state of Maine, where young Peary grew to adulthood.

Peary developed into a young man of intelligence in academic fields from mathematics to literature. He was tall and athletic, not to mention mischievous, adventurous, skeptical, romantic, persistent, original, well-spoken — and, above all, ambitious. This is not yet the place for a closer look at Peary's mixed character, yet there is no missing an early lust for fame and fortune — for something out of the ordinary. Considering his obscure origins, it is remarkable how far he went.

After his excellence earned him a degree in engineering at Bowdoin College, Maine, Peary joined the civil engineering corps of the U.S. Navy. (He was thus not an "officer of the line" and was never fully accepted by the regular Navy of his day.)

But within a few years his ambition was making everyday work intolerable (1880):

I don't want to live and die without accomplishing anything or without being known beyond a narrow circle of friends. I would like to acquire a name which could be an open sesame to circles of culture and refinement anywhere, a name which would make my mother proud and which would make me feel that I was the peer of anyone I might meet.

31

But — at least before experiencing the real Arctic — he was also driven by romanticism (1881):

I never come under these glorious influences of Nature, the sound of a rushing stream, the dash of waves, the sigh of the wind in deep green boughs, or a glorious landscape losing itself in the distant sunshine, but my thoughts turn to those first few views which have turned themselves into the eye of Columbus, Cortez, Livingstone . . . Balboa, De Soto, and all the host of travelers and explorers. And sometimes I can feel something of the thrill and blended aroma of all such first views since the world was in is infancy. . . . think of the nights and their thoughts of the morrow — what will it bring? Some new strange sight, the realization of some wild dream — or will it bring disappointment, disaster and perhaps death?
Then there is the constant expectation of some new strange sight. You struggle on with feverish anxiety to see what is beyond this mountain or that turn in the river, or if you are sailing on some unknown sea you rack your imagination to fill the unknown region just beyond the misty horizon. . . . Tis a glorious life but, ah me! the poetry of the world in this respect is rapidly fading. I am glad that my lot is cast upon the world now rather than later when there will be no new places, when every spot will have felt the pressure of man's foot, and earth and air, and fire and water, the grand old primal elements and all that is in them, will be abject slaves. . . .

Peary's youthful empathy with Columbus and Balboa led remarkably quickly to the specific ambition to conquer the grandest prize left to explorers: his first sight of San Salvador in 1884 triggered the reaction:

Birthplace of the New World, land which first gladdened the eyes of Columbus, purple against the yellow sunset as it was nearly four hundred years ago when it smiled a welcome to the man whose fame can be equaled only by him who shall one day stand with 360

32

degrees of longitude beneath his motionless foot, and for whom East and West shall have vanished; the discoverer of the North Pole.

Aggravation with regular work, and the lure of the unknown, first showed their future course with Peary in 1886 when he and a Danish friend made a serious attempt at becoming the first to cross Greenland. He failed, but as always — the mark of intelligence — he learned from failure.

On Peary's return, he met his man Friday, Matthew Henson, a young and resourceful black ex-seaman. Henson was soon with him as a manservant in the jungles of Central America, where Peary's desire for exploring pre-eminence was then expressing itself in surveying work for the proposed Atlantic-Pacific canal across Nicaragua. Henson accompanied Peary on every expedition and almost every sally north to the end of their mutual exploring career.

In 1889, Peary was disappointed to hear that the Greenland icecap had been crossed (at a relatively narrow width east-to-west) the previous year by a University of Oslo professor, Fridtjof Nansen. Nansen and five companion skiers including another future Norwegian hero, Otto Sverdrup, had burned their bridges by ordering the drop ships away from their starting point, making their attempt literally do-or-die. Peary's comment:

. . . I bought Nansen's book while in New York recently and we have been reading it. It is a pretentious affair in two thick volumes, with numerous illustrations and maps. The original material in it is, however, hardly greater than I obtained four years ago . . .

Nansen profited much by my experience, and frequently refers to me in the book. His maps show my work and he named a mountain after me and gives a picture of it.

Peary's reaction was more creditable than his remarks. He resolved upon a far more important, dangerous and pioneering venture than Nansen's, nothing less than the crossing of northwest Greenland, over the ice-cap, into the unknown region north thereof. In 1891, with his wife Josephine, Henson and a party including an amiable young Brooklyn doctor, Frederick A. Cook, Peary arrived in west Greenland for the second time, camping just north of Inglefield Bay. Over this and succeeding winters he absorbed many valuable Eskimo ways, including the crucial skill of driving dogsledges. On Sept. 12, 1893, Marie Ahnighito Peary was born to Jo Peary — a farthest North of a new sort.

When Peary broke a leg, Dr. Cook set it so well that he was skiing normally before long. When, on a winter outing, Dr. Cook was in danger from a snowstorm as they slept, Peary protected him from the wind and kept vigil over him until the storm died.

In the spring of 1892, Peary, Eivind Astrup of Norway, Cook, Henson, and another set out to the northeast over the high, featureless, windswept glacial ice-cap. Before long, only he and Astrup were pushing "into these unknown regions, dependent only upon [our] own resources and health for a safe return. . . ." After two months of travel they arrived at low coastal land (named Independence Bay) populated with animal life — including life saving musk-oxen.

In 1895 Peary and Henson repeated the journey. On the return, a failing third companion, Hugh Lee, told Peary to go on and save himself. Peary's response: "We will all get home or none of us will." The entire party narrowly survived.

The novelty, daring, and fruitfulness of the 1892-1895 journeys make them among the most admirable in polar annals. On their basis alone, Peary would merit remembrance as an exploring immortal. He had, largely by the adoption of the Eskimo dog as his main motive force — and with the deliberate *plan* to use dogs as food — developed rapid, light weight, long-range surface travel in the polar regions to a point far beyond his predecessors. He experimented on and improved his pemmican, the compact grease and meat staple food. He built igloos instead of carrying heavy, ice-accumulating tents. He introduced the practice of wearing one's "sleeping bag," namely, the Eskimo style fur outfit he and his men wore continuously.

34

His thinking is revealing in its understanding and application of Darwinist natural selection:

> The fur costume of the Eskimos, which is the costume I always use in my parties, is the evolution of generation after generation of experience right in that region, and that costume is made from the furs of animals which live in that region, and is presumably nature's best protection against the cold.

It is part of Peary's wise idea of doing things the easy way in a sense: "The engineer does not attempt to change the course of Nature — he simply conforms to her and by his skill enables her at the same time she is following her laws, to aid him." It is clear that he was one who planned meticulously against every eventuality, believing in absolute efficiency, since exploring was an occupation in which margins of error regarding position, time, and provisions literally determined life or death.

Up to this point, all of Peary's drives for the Pole had not even gotten him a farthest North. Moreover, as he returned to the U.S. in 1895, Fridtjof Nansen was far out in the Polar Sea itself, making the greatest single leap of north latitude ever. Convinced by the finding of the *Jeanette* relics in Greenland some years after the near Siberian loss of deLong's ship, Nansen had proposed in 1891 the building of a ship designed to rise above crushing ice-nip and the deliberate sailing of it into the ice of the Arctic Ocean north of Siberia, in the expectation that it would be carried by a trans-Arctic ice drift across to Greenland. Nares, Greely and virtually every other authority declared the plan suicidal. From 1893 to 1896, Nansen's special ship *Fram* drifted icebound across the Arctic basin as hoped, though somewhat to the left of the North Pole, and reached about 86°N. in autumn of 1895. Soundings — often two miles in depth — gave the profile of the Arctic Ocean bottom, in opposition to the popular theory of a shallow Polar Sea. Eclipses of the Sun and of Jupiter's satellites checked the accuracy of the ship's chronometers, and magnetic observations were taken at regular intervals.

On March 14, 1895, Nansen and his most durable skier, Lt. Hjalmer Johansen, left the ship at 84°N., heading for the Pole by dog sledge over the ice. The ice of the central Arctic Ocean is — contrary to popular image — far from smooth going, and the incessant detouring and portaging of supplies over hummocks, combined with the terrible cold to wear down the two adventurers. In early April, at 86°12'N. latitude, they gave up and turned south, having attained a farthest North not to be convincingly bettered for a generation. A series of remarkable escapades over shifting ice floes brought them to northeast Franz Josef Land in late July. After wintering, they were rescued at the end of the following spring by an expedition sent out to explore Franz Josef Land by the British newspaper tycoon Alfred Harmsworth (later Lord Northcliffe). Late summer saw Nansen and the *Fram* welcomed back in Oslo after their unique adventure — which had combined science and romance at their very finest.

For the next few years after his Greenland crossings, Peary lectured, and during summer excursions took three meteorites off Greenland's Cape York region, including "Ahnighito," the largest ever found, which was placed on permanent display at the American Museum of Natural History in New York City. The museum's major founder, philanthropist Morris K. Jesup, began to take a proprietary interest in furthering Peary's work.

That same year (1897) high Republican party influence got Peary five years Navy leave. Shortly afterward, Jesup and Herbert Bridgman of the Brooklyn *Standard Union* formed the Peary Arctic Club with some wealthy businessmen. Membership was $1,000 a year and its purpose was to get Peary and the American flag to the North Pole ahead of any others.

The flowering of the superpatriotic Club was yet to come in 1897, when Peary received his next expedition's ship from the foreigner Northcliffe, the sail and steam vessel *Windward* which had rescued Nansen in 1896. The same year saw his first two gold medals from the premier societies: the American Geographical Society of New York and the Royal Geographical Society of London.

36

It is at this time, as he became an official institution, that Peary's character began to be visibly affected.

Early intimations of the change, from the man who selflessly saved companion Hugh Lee only two years before, appear in an obscure unpublished account by young Charles G. Fitzgerald, father of an old girlfriend of this writer. (It is only by such odd chances that one circumvents the biased filter of history. The Lee incident is much preferred for official biographies.)

A passenger on the ship *Hope* as Peary brought back the great Cape York meteorite to the U.S., Fitzgerald remarks on Peary's hoarding of fresh meat (which could have cost a professor on board his blood-poisoned hand). Also:

The water which was taken aboard in Greenland is fearful and it makes everyone who drinks it very ill. . . . Peary is all right, so is the rest of the "after guard," for they evidently knew of the bad condition of the water since they laid in a private supply while the ship was anchored at Cape Haven. I saw them doing it one day and wondered, never dreaming of the real state of things. It seems to be criminal carelessness on the part of Peary not having taken in a fresh supply while waiting for the boys to arrive; however, Stickney and I got even with them one night, for while prowling around the decks . . . [we] found a beaker lying outside the after companion. We didn't do a thing but pick it up and carry it forward, where you may be sure that everybody had a good drink of the pure water. It was the only one we got during the home stretch. Next morning Peary wanted to know if anyone had seen a beaker of water on deck; it goes without saying, that nobody had seen anything of it, - Oh no ! One day Peary sent us down a very foolish note in which he requested us to promise on our honor, not to write or say anything about what we had seen or heard of the happenings north of Wilcox Head. It was all foolishness for we had never been near the blessed place. White refused to sign and by way of an inducement, Peary gave him a couple of fine walrus heads - then he signed.

Next year, Peary's first book appeared. An admirably literate and informative account of all Peary's expeditions 1886-1897, it was unfortunately marred by inclusion of some doctored photographs, one depicting an astronomical impossibility.

In 1898, just as his great four year expedition was getting set, the battleship named for his home state, the *Maine*, exploded in Havana harbor, Feb. 15, 1898. In the light of Peary's later gung-ho propagandizing for U.S. military preparedness after his own retirement from active duty, for wars in which other, younger men would do the dying, it is of some interest to observe his other oriented reaction to the only major conflict he himself had a chance to fight in. His comment to his wife was, "Well, Jo, last time they staged a silver panic to keep me from going [north]. Now they're going to have a war!" The two standard adult Peary biographies by Professor William Hobbs (1936) and John Weems (1967) have some difficulty handling this episode in the life of their hero.

War was duly declared on April 21, but Peary equally duly persuaded himself that civil engineers would not be crucial to the Navy in a mere armed conflict, and so never let first things lose their place. Happily for the U.S.' fortunes in the Spanish-American war, Adolphus Greely, the Chief Signal Officer of the Army, did not share Peary's well-timed belief in the uselessness of technical science in war and so was responsible for obtaining the vital intelligence that ended this conflict.

In any case, Peary was concerned at this time with heading off a more serious defiler of the Monroe Doctrine than a modern Spanish Armada, as a handful of Norwegian Arctic explorers prepared to invade the Western Hemisphere in the little *Fram*.

Peary's 1898-1902 plan was to sail up the American Route to the Pole as far as possible, establish a base, and make spring drives for the North Pole from that point. However, it happened that Otto Sverdrup, of Nansen's expeditions, was simultaneously planning to take the *Fram* into the same area for exploration there. Sverdrup evidently had no thought of the Pole — but Peary could not understand such a person, so he simply didn't believe it. Peary's reaction is still reflected in the chronologies presented in the Peary biographies. According to Hobbs, Peary was "greatly cast down" on learning of Sverdrup's project, "almost identical with his own. . . . To have a rival expedition operating within the same region was contrary to the best traditions and would almost to a certainty introduce difficulties." Hobbs is, as usual, sure of Peary's priority:

> Peary's plan, announced in January, 1898, before the [AGS], was fully covered in the February issue of the *Geographical Journal* [RGS] . . .; while Sverdrup's announcement appeared first in the July issue of the same journal. . . . Sverdrup states that he initiated the plan as early as September, 1896, but apparently it did not become known in Europe before the summer of 1898.

Small wonder, then, that Peary "felt that Sverdrup was thus guilty of poaching." (Weems) However, Hobbs' chronology (as well as the implicit ones of Peary's and Weems' accounts) is incomplete. The fact is that Peary learned of Sverdrup's intentions *before* his own were published (which indicates that both plans were independent creations), since he refers to the former in a letter of January 1898.

Peary's official account of his 1898-1902 work deleted a reference to meeting Sverdrup on Oct. 7, 1898, though it is in the original report. His only published allusion to the Norwegian expedition is in the preface to the printed version, "the introduction of a disturbing factor in the appropriation by another of my plan and field of work . . ."

This bridled language masked a hidden furious reaction on first hearing of Sverdrup's intentions. In a January 1898 letter to Jesup, marked "Confidential," Peary referred with fantastic venom to Sverdrup's "unprincipled attempt . . . to appropriate my route, my plans, and my objects. . . ." — even suspecting that so noble a soul as Nansen would join Sverdrup's scheme "out of spite, if for no other reason."

It is typical of paranoids that they, upon imagining malevolent secret designs against themselves, feel it is only fair to *counter*plot — thus deceit really does ultimately enter an initially open situation. Though announcing his own departure for July, for the benefit of the unsuspecting Sverdrup, Peary now planned secretly to be ready to leave within 48 hours after the *Fram* sailed. (Ironically, he ended up leaving in early July anyway, the unmentionable one having not gotten away until late June). He also initiated private negotiations to obtain a better ship, the *Terra Nova*, with no mention of his own name. Meantime, the U.S. Consul at Bergen was secretly relaying information to Peary about Sverdrup's (and the Dane, Amdrup's) outfit and preparation schedule — via *unnumbered* correspondence. (If such were later destroyed, no visible gap in the official consular-dispatch record would be created.) By chance, a Bergen note of May 7, 1898 ended up in the National Archives instead of the Memory Hole.

Both expeditions' ships were stopped in an ice choked Kane Basin that summer. The Peary-Sverdrup meeting shortly after this involved a refused cup of coffee which has later been brought forth by most Peary supporters as cause for Sverdrup's later doubting Peary's discovery of the Pole. Sverdrup, unlike some, wrote openly of the encounter:

[Expedition zoologist Edvard] Bay and I were alone at Fort Juliana [east-central Ellesmere Island] on 6 October [a day earlier than Peary dates it]. The weather was unusually clear, and in the afternoon he caught sight of a sledge with two men on it, driving up the fjord. Out came the glasses, and we soon made out two fur-clad men seated on an Eskimo sledge, drawn by eight dogs. It appeared at first as if they meant to drive farther up the fjord, but suddenly they made a turn; they had probably caught sight of us. Who could it be?

My thoughts fixed involuntarily on Robert Peary. Him and no other could we expect to meet in these latitudes. He came driving along by our track, straight towards us, and I went down to the fjord to meet him. When we met, he asked if I was Captain Sverdrup, and we then shook hands and walked together up to the tent, where I introduced Bay to him. I asked him to have some coffee with us, but he refused, saying that his tent was not more than two hours' drive away, and that he was going home to dinner. His expedition had passed Cape Sabine on 13 August, and two days later had been beset off Cape Hawks, where his ship now was, about a mile from land and entirely surrounded by the pack. He had observed that [Kennedy] Channel was full of old polar ice [blocking the American Route to the Arctic Ocean and Pole]. After staying for a few minutes he said good-bye to Bay, who had been grinding coffee all the time, and turning and twisting with every movement of our honoured guest in an effort to hide the ragged condition of a certain portion of his trousers, and the large 're-seating' to which they had been subjected. I took Peary down to the sledge and watched him disappear at an even pace with his Eskimo driver. My heart felt quite warm with patriotism.

Peary's visit was the event of the day in our tent. We talked of nothing else, and rejoiced at having shaken hands with the bold explorer, even though his visit had been so short that we hardly had time to pull off our mittens.

Does this humble account read like that of a man infuriated at a social snub?

Peary referred to the same encounter in a private letter to Jo: "I had a short and not effusive meeting with Sverdrup," which Weems quotes, adding that "Peary was relieved to learn from Sverdrup that the *Fram*, too [like his own ship, the *Windward*], had been unable to push through the Kane Basin ice and had been halted far south of Sverdrup's goal. This had forced the Norwegian to modify his plans — and to withdraw from the competition[?], to the north, with Peary."

Weems seems therefore under the impression that Peary's subsequent strange and tragic actions were not motivated by any special desire to forestall Sverdrup. However, the biographer's ordering of events is awry, as Sverdrup did not abandon his hopes of proceeding north further until forced to do so by the second straight year of impenetrable Kane Basin ice, in August, 1899. So, late in 1898, Peary still expected interference in his domain.

It might be pleasant to suppose that the terrible 1899 mutilation of Peary's feet was the direct cost of an act of noble sacrifice or of curiosity for new geographical knowledge. But, in fact, nothing but the intolerable spectre of Sverdrup's possibly getting latitudinally one-up on him, could have panicked Peary into such an atypically foolhardy risk as that clearly bargained for in his attempt at stealing a march northward via midwinter moonlight sledging of supplies hundreds of miles up to Fort Conger in northern Elllsmere Island, in temperatures as low as −63°F.

We recall that he had run into Sverdrup on Oct. 6 or 7. Peary returned to the *Windward* on the 12th, and the opening stages of the rash northward project were got underway that very month. On Dec. 20, Peary, Henson, expedition surgeon Thomas Dedrick and four natives left the ship with 30 dogs for Fort Conger.

Henson's recollection many years later (utterly ignored in Weems' books, though he has read it) of Peary's reaction to learning of Sverdrup's presence, while fuzzy on detail, rings true on the basics (both on the discreditable reasons for the trip, and on the incredible pain and horror from which Peary was to rebound so manfully). The story, as told by Henson's later close friend and biographer, Bradley Robinson:

> [Peary] paced the floor with nervous agitation.
>
> "Sverdrup may at this minute be planning to beat me to Fort Conger!" he cried, with marked irritation. "I can't let him do it! . . . I'll get to Conger before Sverdrup if it kills me!"
>
> "But . . . [said Henson], this is the dead of winter. It's stormy and damned cold on the trail. Wouldn't it be better to wait until spring?" . . .
>
> "No!" Peary cried vehemently. "I can't possibly afford to lose my one chance of a northern base to a competitor." . . .

42

They could not have chosen more unfavorable weather in which to make the long march to Fort Conger. Several times storms held them up. . . . [Many] miles south of Fort Conger they finished the last of their food. . . .

For hours they stumbled across the ice in the semi-darkness, while the pain of hunger gnawed into them with the same sharp pain of the piercing wind. . . .

They found the barn-sized building [Fort Conger], with its two simple rooms that had once served as living quarters and kitchen for Greely and his men, in complete disarray. . . .

They built a fire in the mammoth range. Then Peary crawled on top of the stove and, seating himself on a huge hot-water heater, placed his feet over the warm plates. . . .

Matt handed a bucket to Ahnidloo [one of the Eskimos] and told him to fill it with snow. Then he inserted the blade of his knife under the top of Peary's sealskin boots. He ripped the boots from both feet and gently removed the rabbitskin undershoes. Both legs were a bloodless white up to the knee, and as Matt ripped off the undershoes two or three toes from each foot clung to the hide and snapped off at the first joint.

"My God, Lieutenant! Why didn't you tell me your feet were frozen?" Matt cried.

"There's no time to pamper sick men on the trail," Peary replied tersely. Then he added thoughtfully, "Besides, a few toes aren't much to give to achieve the Pole."

The ghastly arrival at Conger was in the bleak early "morning of Jan. 7, 1899. Another moon was to pass before Peary, still an invalid, could be returned to the ship, far to the south.

At Conger the restless, tortured explorer was bedridden for over a month:

. . . listening to the howling of the winter winds and the cries of my starving dogs, until in the latter part of February there was sufficient daylight to enable us to attempt to return to the ship. Throughout these inter-

43

minable black days, though I could not at times repress a groan at the thought that my God-given frame was mutilated forever, still I never lost faith, in spite of the encouraging statements of my physician that a man who had lost even a big toe, could never again walk effectively. I *knew* that I should yet do the work which I had set before myself.

On the wall of Fort Conger's humble wooden hut, he inscribed his most-remembered motto (from Seneca): "Find a way or make one."

The return to the ship was aided by dim solar twilight.

Peary:

. . . I remember few more grim and desolate scenes than the environs of Fort Conger as I took them in while being lashed to my sledge, a helpless cripple, on the bitterly cold February morning that I left the fort to return to the *Windward*.

The dead-white slopes of the hills lifting to the blue-black sky, the dead-white expanse of harbor and bay reaching away to the ribbon of pale, steely light past the black dot of Cape Lieber where, in ten days, if the weather held clear, the sun would appear. . . . The unrelieved blackness of the preceding six weeks, during which I lay [at Conger] on my back, accompany the scene as a nightmare.

It is extraordinary to realize that the following year, this same man discovered the northernmost terra firma. And contrast his seemingly hopeless Fort Conger low with his position barely a decade later: riches, comfort, and the world's honor. Certainly on reading of his 1899 ordeal, one cannot help but feel that, regardless of all else, he had earned them.

Sverdrup reentered Peary's life a little after the final amputations (March 13) on about March 22, with the appearance at the *Windward* of Lieut. Victor Baumann, the Norwegian expedition's second in command. Partly in the light of Hobbs' condemning Sverdrup's invasion of Peary's kingdom — because of (among other things) the possibility of

44

"duplication of efforts" — some of Baumann's report of the visit makes interesting reading:

I took the liberty of asking the range of his [Peary's] maps so that we could avoid unnecessary duplication, and confusion. He told me that from 'the heights' he had taken the bearings of the greater part of Bache Peninsula, also northwards in Princess Marie Bay, and to the west of it, but not south of the peninsula, nor inland where he had met Captain Sverdrup. He had not yet worked out his maps. He further told me that it was on a trip *at the end of February* that his toes had been frostbitten, and that he had been obliged to have some of them amputated. When I expressed my regret at his accident, he answered laconically: 'You must take your chances up here, you know.' . . . (Emphasis added)

Evidently Peary wished to hide not just the purposes but the very fact of his northern trip: he never mentioned Fort Conger or anyplace remotely near it, and apparently was so ashamed to admit the indicative fact that he had begun travelling in dark December, that he shifted by two months the date of the fateful trip.

Ironically, Sverdrup, by going west instead of north, discovered almost all the unknown land left to be found in the American Arctic.

In the spring of 1899, Peary was active again as soon as possible. Though still using crutches, he moved more supplies to Fort Conger. In May he brought back some material left by the Greely expedition, for a purpose shortly to be understood.

That summer, with three Eskimos, Peary sledged west, to the top of the central Ellesmere glacier and looked into the unknown beyond. To the northwest, there stretched away into the distance a fjord he named Cannon Bay (for Henry Cannon, President of Chase National Bank and a Peary Arctic Club founder). Beyond this there seemed, perhaps, to be new land, to which, despite uncertainty, he

45

committed the name Jesup Land. Later in the summer he established his base at the Greenland Eskimo colony at Etah.

On April 11, 1900, Peary and Henson and a few natives left Fort Conger, the scene of Peary's lowest ebb, and struck across Robeson channel for the coast of Greenland — on the journey that was to set the one geographical record of Peary's that will never die.

This time he sent natives back at intervals, modestly presaging the multi-stage support party plan used in later expeditions. Rather than cutting over the ice cap, his party kept on the ice-foot along the coast and sped around northwest Greenland at a pace far ahead of Beaumont or Lockwood, reaching on May 8th the cairn of the 1882 Greely-Lockwood farthest — then still the northernmost land ever trod. Taking Lockwood's written record with him and leaving a copy (standard explorers' custom) Peary rushed ahead to determine whether Cape Washington (seen to the northeast by Lockwood and Brainard) was the north point of land he would find.

At Cape Washington on the next day, the ever competitive explorer knew at last:

> Great was my relief to see on rounding this point another great headland, with two magnificent glaciers debauching near it, rising across an inlet beyond. Cape Washington is not the northern point of Greenland, as I had feared. It would have been a disappointment to me after coming so far to find that another's eyes had forestalled mine in looking on the coveted northern point.

It is odd that Peary would speak of the northern tip of *Greenland,* since the "Peary Channel" of his post-1892 maps separated this whole region — now called "Peary Land" — from Greenland. Peary Channel was later found not to exist and is today generally regarded as an innocent error.)

By May 13, he had reached the northernmost land on Earth; he named his estimate of the spot (83° 38′N., 34° W.) Cape Morris Jesup. (Modern explorer Robert Lillestrand has shown that nearby tiny Kaffekluben Island is more likely the exact north point; regardless, Peary discovered both.)

The next two weeks were spent going north (to 83°50'N. latitude, 33°20'W. longitude, compass variation 61°½W. or 61°W.) and returning to Cape Jesup — then east (to 83°N., 23°W., May 20-22). During all this period, repeated records of the sun, clock, and compass (the last purely for science, since it was not required for steering, this close to land) gave full and accurate data for latitude, longitude, and compass-direction throughout the area which was however even more fully covered with the names of wealthy backers.

The year 1901 saw little progress toward the Pole and much sadness. Peary learned in April that his infant daughter, Francine Peary, had died over a year before (August 1899) without his ever having seen her. Then, that summer, news arrived of the death of his mother, to whom he had been extraordinarily close.

Expedition surgeon Thomas Dedrick and Peary rifted. Dedrick resigned but stayed in Greenland and (Weems) "declared [he] would be available to Peary in case of need." Peary traveled from Etah across Smith Sound to Payer Harbor (Ellesmere, near Cape Sabine) in preparation for a 1902 drive for the Pole off north Ellesmere. That fall, as he wondered whether "there is a world . . . different from this black hole," a disease befell his Eskimos at Payer. Hobbs: "With his physician gone Peary was unable to cope with the epidemic, though he did everything possible." Weems explains:

Peary cared for the natives himself, giving no thought to summoning the man he was to refer to as his "crazy doctor," but by November 19th six Eskimos had died. Finally, the disease spent itself, and Peary polished his plans for the polar journey.

All of which seems to verify the truth of later charges that Peary's personally motivated course of action was responsible for a number of deaths. Worse: at one point Dedrick actually crossed Smith Sound to help — but was

47

forthwith kicked off the Sabine area by Peary.

With Henson and a few of the remaining Eskimos that had not deserted, Peary started up the east coast of Ellesmere in early March of 1902. Braving cold as low as –49°F., they reached Conger later that month; from there seven natives were sent back carrying the Greely expedition's instruments, while the rest continued north to Cape Hecla (83°N., 65°W.) — at which point, on April 6, "we swung our sledges sharply to the right . . . due northward" and began the drive for the Pole.

The high speed sledging so characteristic of Peary's work (hitherto over smoothish ice) now ceased abruptly on the chaotic Arctic Ocean pack: patches of deep snow, detours from buckled ice (pressure ridges) as high as a house and from leads (open water). In mid-April a vast lead was encountered. The discovery of this semi-permanent Polynya marking the submarine continental shelf belongs to Peary — who variously dubbed it the "Grand Canal," "Hudson River," "Big Lead," and "Styx." A crossing was accomplished after ice-drift closed the big lead on the 14th. Another week of oft-detoured marches of steadily decreasing distances brought an end on April 21: "My dream of sixteen years is ended . . . I have made a good fight, but I cannot accomplish the impossible."

As always, position was determined (84°17'N. latitude, 67°40'W. longitude), as was compass-direction (99°½W. or 99°W.). Despite the dead reckoning attempt to aim true north, Peary found that he had accidentally traveled 12° to the west of the north — due to drift, detours, etc.

The weary return and recovery of strength at Fort Conger and Payer Harbor brought bitter thoughts:

> . . . four years ago . . ., I looked full of life and hope . . . at this . . . shore mellow in the August sunlight, and dreamed of what I should accomplish. Now a maimed old man, unsuccessful after the most arduous work, away from wife and child, mother dead, one baby dead. Has the game been worth the candle?

And:

. . . as I think of the last four years and what I have been through; as I think of all the little petty details, it all seems so small, so little worth the while that I could cry out in anguish of spirit.

Such uncharacteristic depression and modesty could not last in the man who had sledged more miles than anyone in the history of Arctic exploring. As his energies returned, he came back to his May broodings on his excuse for failure: ". . . that my training, experience, love for the work, and strenuous efforts should be handicapped by a compulsory start from a low latitude . . ."

If only he had the right sort of vessel next time:

. . . a ship with the engines of a battleship. . . . I'll drive and smash my way through the ice [of Robeson Channel] right up to Cape Hecla or Sheridan!

Peary in late 1902:

First, the average air-line distance from start to finish of four sledge journeys which I have made in high arctic latitudes is the same as the distance from the northern shore of Grinnell [Ellesmere] Land to the Pole. Second, the air-line distance from start to finish of my 1900 sledge journey is such that had my starting point been . . . on the northern shore of Grinnell Land, it would have carried me beyond the Pole.

The ship would cost about $100,000. Millionnaires' backing and loyalty could be assured by naming geographical discoveries for them. Remembrances in the official appellations of capes, bays, and glaciers were naturally flattering to hefty capitalists — however, the grandest immortality Peary could bestow was by his discovery and naming not merely of new coasts (of already known lands), but of new land. But Peary had never explored anything of the sort. Yet, we recall that in 1899, atop the Ellesmere ice-cap, he'd thought something was visible to the northwest.

Peary's original 1899 July sketch-map of the area was published that year by the American Geographical Society, showing a Jesup Land beyond Cannon Bay. However, the uncertainty of the sighting is certified by its omission in Peary's official report of the journey, in which the supposed moment (July 20, 1899) and the vista over Cannon Bay are described.

However, from late 1902 on, Peary suddenly became not only sure that Jesup Land was real, he asserted that it was none other than Axel Heiberg Land, the prime discovery of Sverdrup's career, which Sverdrup had attained and mapped in 1900, a year after its actual discovery by Peary.

Peary champion Professor Hobbs as late as 1936 presented a compelling proof of Peary's priority by publishing a map-comparison: Sverdrup's chart of Heiberg Land (virtually identical to modern ones) vs. Peary's final map of Jesup Land, thereby proving their essential sameness of location. Because of Peary's clear priority, Hobbs naturally complained that "Geographers have adopted the name given by the explorer in preference to that given by the discoverer." What Hobbs presumably never noticed is that the Peary map he used in the comparison was *not* the original 1899 one, but rather is based on one (USHO #2142) published by the U.S. Hydrographic office in October, 1903, about *a year* after Sverdrup's sketches of the region first appeared. In the original version of Jesup Land, things appear quite differently. Jesup Land is shown roughly to the northwest of the 4700-foot summit from which it was sighted — seen entirely *to the right* of Cape Lockwood. According to the sketch, the westernmost part of Jesup Land was viewed only 35° West of true North. Referring to Sverdrup's map, or to any modern one, immediately reveals that, from Peary's July 1899 vantage point, every square inch of Heiberg Land is well to the west of this 35° West limit. Therefore, what Peary may have seen was the Blue Mountains region of Grant Land (North Ellesmere Island) — unknown coast of already known land.
Heiberg Land is well to the west of this 35° West limit. Therefore, what Peary may have seen was the Blue Mountains region of Grant Land (North Ellesmere Island) — unknown coast of already known land.

How, then, did Jesup Land ever get mixed up later

50

with Heiberg Land? First, Peary and Sverdrup returned from the Arctic almost simultaneously in the summer of 1902; but Peary, having heard immediately on his return that Sverdrup had discovered much new land in the region of Jesup Land, cagily gave out no authorized map until the following year. Meanwhile, a "preliminary sketch" of Sverdrup's finds appeared in November, 1902, in England, and was reprinted in the December *National Geographic Magazine*. This rough map is of some interest relative to Jesup Land, not in spite of its inaccuracies but because of them. For some reason, Heiberg Land — and little Schei Land — was mistakenly jammed right up against the hypothetical western limit (Garfield Coast) of Grant Land in this sketch, well east and north of its actual place. Peary undoubtedly saw this map — and probably overestimated its trustworthiness only because *National Geographic* had omitted a key footnote in the British publication: "The map . . . is little more than a rough diagram . . . an approximate idea of the . . . position of the newly discovered lands." Peary presumably noted with interest the obvious fact that, according to the 1902 sketch map, his own northwest land-sighting of 1899 would be in the general direction of Schei and Heiberg Lands. It is therefore indicative that Peary's first map (USHO #2142) *after* the publication of this sketch of Sverdrup's discoveries, moves westward, expands, and reshapes Jesup Land — accentuating a channel between it and the Garfield Coast, a channel *already distinctly shown* between Schei Land and that same coast on the 1902 Sverdrup work sketch. By this improved arrangement, it would appear irrefutable that Heiberg and Schei Lands were really Jesup Land — seen and named by Peary well before Sverdrup. This ill-timed map was in turn the basis of the one that Hobbs produced in support of Peary's claim to Jesup Land. And so the Hudson 1607 Spitzbergen slip is repeated: none is so obvious as one's discovery of a geographical feature already shown on another explorer's map — and later found to be nonexistent.

Not all Peary's shifty performance occurred on maps:

his Aug. 28, 1899, handwritten report to the Peary Arctic Club contains no reference whatever to his great July 20 discovery of Jesup Land, stating merely that he "looked down upon the snow-free western side of Ellesmere Land and out into the ice-free fjord [Cannon Bay] extending some fifty miles to the northwest." Four years later, in a 1903 November speech to the Royal Geographical Society, this description was expanded, like the USHO map, to read: ". . . some 50 miles to the northwest, *beyond which appeared yet more distant land.*" (Emphasis added.) When Peary reached Heiberg Land in 1906, he could see for himself that it was nowhere near his 1899 placement of Jesup Land and that Sverdrup's 1903 map was correct. Yet, by the following year Peary was challenging Sverdrup's claim more aggressively than ever, writing publicly that Heiberg Land belonged to him and referring to "that western land which I saw from the heights of the Ellesmere Land ice cap in July, [1899], and named Jesup Land, though Sverdrup has later given it the name of Heiberger [Axel Heiberg] Land." The Peary Arctic Club even went so far as to claim the discovery for itself during the Ninth International Geographical Congress at Geneva in 1908. Peary's 1910 book casually repeats the claim. Of course, no one outside the Peary clique ever took it seriously; but neither was this blatant' attempt to steal Otto Sverdrup's greatest discovery ever condemned in a single United States geographical society journal.

Though the Jesup Land grab did nothing to slow down Peary's continuing enshrinement, the wear of his life style on his domestic situation was proving an impediment to his inner demon. Peary's wife, Jo, had patiently and sympathetically seen him, during all the years spent pursuing the pot of gold at the end of meridians, become a stranger to his family. At least since 1899, Jo had been impressing this upon him. In a letter of early 1901, she tried gamely to encourage him, but she could not hide her true feelings:

. . . Should this reach you *you must not think of coming down* [from Fort Conger]. You must save yourself for your northern work. . . . Sometimes I think you are a physical wreck. If this is so, come home and let Marie and me love you and nurse you. Don't let pride keep you back. Who will *even* remember it ten years from now? . . . Oh, Bert, Bert. I want you so much. Life is slipping away so fast — pretty soon all will be over.

Despite her pleas, the mutilation of his feet, and the repeated failure of his polar plans, he clung to his ambitions. After his return from the Arctic in 1902, Peary underwent surgery on his feet, enabling him to walk better. Jo, seeing him regain his old wanderlust, wrote Peary Arctic Club Secretary Bridgman: "In regard to the Ziegler-Cook expedition, I say let the good work go on but let me keep my old man at home." A month later, Peary's daughter evidently wondered if the Peary Arctic Club was his club or he its man:

My dear, dear Father -

Of course I know the papers are not always right, but I read that the Peary Arctic Club are trying to get your consent to go north again. I think it a dog's shame. . . . I know you will do what pleases mother and me, and that is to stay with us at home.

I have been looking at your pictures, it seems ten years, and I am sick of looking at them. I want to see my father. I don't want people to think me an orphan.

Please think this over.

Your loving

Marie

Perhaps for his family's benefit, Peary acted as if *he* were being persuaded; but the reverse was true. The very next day he was busy privately sending a batch of newspaper clippings to his most faithful fiscal backer Jesup, all of which concluded in effect that Peary "ought to have another try" at the Pole. But an old and weary Jesup responded by writing Bridgman: "Peary evidently still hankers after exploration. . . . I do not know what to do. . . ."

Undaunted, Peary kept after the philanthropist, writing

that, in his regular Navy duties in Washington, "sitting at a desk from 9 to 4 is at first equally or more trying than traveling with a sledge all day." Imparting his priorities around Christmas, 1902, he listed a good ship for the Club's next effort as "practically only expensive item. . . . Require no large pay roll. My Eskimo laborers and dogs cost but a song." Finally Jesup agreed to help him out. And others came through: Peary rejoiced to Bridgman over "another victim for $2,000." Even so, Peary's early 1903-05 fund-raising efforts came nearer failing than is generally known. In early 1903, as old members of the Peary Arctic Club fell away, Peary was barely holding the Club together, intending to try a few more millionnaires "before calling the game off." It took years, but his persistence finally won out again.

Wrote early Peary biographer Fitzhugh Green: "That he and Mrs. Peary were destitute and in debt had become so constant a condition they no longer felt from it an acute unhappiness, but only a sort of dull annoyance unrelieved by any prospect of change."

After his 1906 fiasco, Peary said he could not even pay his men, a burden he passed along to his trusting companion Bob Bartlett, who dipped into his meager sailor's savings. Mrs. Peary even held back salaries from expedition members' helpless dependents. In fact, however, by his own later account, Peary was out of net debt by 1900 and had even begun to buy up land off the coast of Maine not long after his 1902 return.

At about this time Peary began a four-year reign (January 1903 to January 1907) as president of the American Geographical Society, shortly after receiving the first Daly gold medal of the Society, one of four such awarded for his great four-year expedition. Simultaneously, behind the scenes politicking began for an even more prestigious post, a struggle which brought the Greely-Peary feud to white heat.

For a man now nearly forgotten except as an evil misknit in the Great Tapestry of the Hero's life, General Adolphus W. Greely's 91 years of life were filled with such variety and intensity of experience as few persons will ever match. While still a teenager, he fought for the Union in the Civil War, receiving wounds at various times, including two at Antietam (one of them in the face — which perhaps accounts for his sporting a beard the rest of his life). He later saw military duty in hostile Indian country — the Dakota badlands and the Far West.

In contrast to some, Greely never accepted a cent in lecture exploitation of his tragic Arctic experiences.

How Peary came so to despise this gentle man is not completely clear. His bringing back the instruments left at Fort Conger by Greely's expedition may — by the implication that anything of value was left upon the 1883 evacuation from Conger to Sabine (which Greely denied) — have begun the bad feeling, especially as Greely soon realized that, even though he himself wouldn't exploit the related tragedy, Peary would. A private 1902 note from Peary to Bridgman is very explicit about the utility — for an extra "feather in the [Peary Arctic] Club's cap" — of making (in a dignified way) *as much as possible out of*" returning the Greely instruments (emphasis added). What lay behind this ploy is brought out in a simultaneous letter from Jo Peary (also to Bridgman), in which she lampoons a few other Peary pet hates:

> Pardon me for putting my oar in but I can't resist the temptation to suggest a few names for your "provisional list of guests" for the Club dinner to put alongside of A.W.G. [Greely]
> James B. Pond (Biggest man in N.Y.)
> F.W. Stokes, Greatest Arctic Artist
> Thos. S. Dedrick, Only sane man in Peary Expedition.
> In addition I would respectfully suggest that you send A.W.G. no less than *two* invitations (with full amount of postage *pre*paid, not the way you usually send my letters) also [railroad] fare including parlor seats from Washington to N.Y. and return. With kindest regards.
> Very sincerely
Josephine D. Peary
> (Emphases in original)

Next summer Peary was working behind the scenes to prevent Greely from becoming the President of the upcoming

8th International Geographical Congress (and to get its direction out of the National Geographic Society's hands into the American Geographical Society's — the latter society being wealthier and closer to the Peary Arctic Club at the time), suggesting to the powerful Jesup (whom he nominated as I.G.C. President in Greely's place): "I hope you will . . . allow your friends to work (quietly) along these lines. . . ." The upshot was that Peary himself became the 1904 Congress' President instead of Greely, though the site was Washington. (Peary also wrote here that the ever-scheming Greely was now angling for the Presidency of the NGS — actually Greely turned down the post on this and three other occasions.)

In spite of all this harrassment, Greely always lauded Peary's courage and drive, and even accepted his Pole claim as late as 1910.

And even though his greatest fame in his lifetime was as a 19th century Arctic discoverer, Greely, in 1910, praised the work of such as Amundsen, Peary, and Sverdrup. "Few as are the years of the Twentieth Century, they have witnessed Polar discoveries which in extent and interest far surpass those of any earlier complete century." As Bertrand Russell despaired of the oft naive Thomas Paine — who, like Sverdrup and Greely, has had few monuments erected to him: "Some worldly wisdom is required even to secure praise for the lack of it."

In 1904, the genteel Explorers Club of New York was founded, thanks to the efforts of such as Frederick Cook. To help its start, Greely accepted its presidency, but strictly temporarily.

The same year saw the official incorporation of the Peary Arctic Club (April 19, 1904) with the prime order of business the production of Peary's special ship. The vessel was designed by Peary (and Charles Dix of Maine) and its construction went forward from October 1904 to March 1905, when the ship was christened (with a bottle of champagne embedded in a block of ice, swung by Jo Peary) the *Roosevelt,* after the man who had become President during Peary's last expedition.

Roosevelt's machismo style of patriotism made him Peary's sort of President — moreover, he was Republican, like the Peary Arctic Club. The two men were therefore natural friends, and Teddy could be counted on for help in Peary's lobbying for any cause, including himself — even for expediting Jo's receipt of Peary's Navy paychecks. With such high influence behind him, a start in April, 1904 was forthcoming without the difficulties of 1897. The Navy Department's charge: "The attainment of the Pole should be your object. Nothing short will suffice. . . . the President of the United States sympathizes with your cause and approves your enterprise."

Financial support finally poured in by the tens of thousands of dollars, capped on July 6, 1905, by a Peary Arctic Club cruise aboard the *Roosevelt*. Later that month, on the crest of a New York heat wave, the *Roosevelt* steamed down the Hudson River, bound for the Arctic, to the roar of well-wishers' hosannahs and salutes. Peary was not religious, but now he invoked the highest influence available: "I am going now in God's name, and with the help of God I hope to accomplish the end in view." If experience, machinery, bravery, and the blessings of every power under and over the sun could conquer the North Pole, the 1905-1906 expedition was destined for immortality.

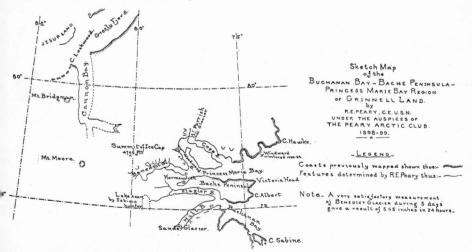

Here, the boundary azimuths (west of north) for Jesup Land are 26° and 35°.

From map based on USHO #2142, October, 1903, showing Peary's 1898-1902 discoveries. Jesup Land now has been moved entirely left of its 1899 far left boundary (azimuth 35° west of north).

4. The Experts

It may puzzle outsiders to observe the silence of professional geographers in the face of the heavyhanded Jesup Land claim jump by the president of their own International Geographical Congress and American Geographic Society. (This approach has a modern heritage — Weems' detailed 1967 Peary biography has not one word on the Jesup Land episode.) However, this was hardly the first time that explorers' misbehavior had been cooperatively protected by such discreditable institutional reluctance to deal effectively with malefactors. The quickly submerged Kane-Morton and Hayes affairs of the Civil War era have already been discussed. That fakery was blossoming in succeeding years became common knowledge among worldly insiders. British Admiral Nares and U.S. Admiral Melville were later to explain how easy it is to sit at home and fake astronomical observations (sextant or theodolite) proving one was at a faraway place one had never actually visited — and Nares openly admitted in 1909 that "such a thing has been done before in arctic exploration."

The Siberian explorer George Kennan, a co-founder (1888) of the National Geographic Society, wrote years later that the reason he had easily seen through a fake 1908 polar claim was that had already been familiar with at least two other invented northern journeys.

Even Jo Peary knew what was up, expressing to her husband in 1907 a disdain for a number of figures at the Explorers Club: "They are all fakes."

If insiders knew the facts, why didn't they cry foul? There are a variety of important reasons.

59

In "soft" sciences such as geography, theories are less testable by experiment, so politics and socializing are more crucial than elsewhere. Personal friendships can demand a stronger loyalty than science or principle, and, it's easy to make light of a genial tall-tale-teller as just a "lovable old faker."

Then there is "professional courtesy" — partly a euphemism for the insecure spectre that if you rat on your fellow pro he could do the same to you some day. Why make unnecessary enemies, not just of exposed explorers, but of their embarrassed backers, often representing powerful institutions, among them men who might be needed for the backing of your own expedition one day? This corruption commonly masquerades as, perversely, *the honor system.* Fitzhugh Green said "There had always been an unwritten code of honor among explorers that discouraged anyone from doubting the traveler's word for a minute." But behind all this sweet verbiage lay sheer hard business sense. As one who knew put it: The societies' latatonic reaction to even the grossest fake was "from reasons of selfish caution and prudence rather than of the true spirit of research and justice which they claim to possess. . . ." Words of a disgruntled crackpot? No, the ultimate judgment of *Peary Arctic Club Secretary* Bridgman and the opinion of *Peary himself.*

In the U.S., where virtually all funds for polar research were of voluntary private origin, a motley but polite exploring milieu of geoscientists, adventurers, and philanthropists had, by about 1900, evolved into pseudo-stable harmony (e.g.: National Geographic Society, Arctic Club, Explorers Club) — especially polite with regard to the taboo topic of possible exploring fraud, which, if openly entertained, would (and did) upset those innocent sources of fiscal munificence that represented the life blood of the entire arrangement. In this uncritical climate, exaggeration was fed while honestly reported failure suffered — in effect making hoaxery an artificially protected industry among explorers, corrupting even the best and strongest men. So, in an otherwise free enterprise situation, cheating became profitable and flourished.

One must keep in mind that the same cozy group of

societies not only promoted expeditions, but also certified their stories of success and bestowed gold medals. And their officers were, in turn, rewarded by explorers' naming discoveries for them — e.g.: Peary's Mount Daly.

Of course, despite an ongoing conspiracy of silence, some members of the inner professional circle (one remove above the philanthropists, one below the explorers in the field) didn't let on simply because they themselves never caught on. Most eminent geographers knew no navigational math. Also this was in some ways an innocent age — indeed, the Barnums of it found such easy pickings that a certain amount of deceit was considered merely good showmanship.

As for the academic world: it was not long out from under the rule of biblical fundamentalism. And an embarrassing number of leading scholars of the day were taken in by dishonest magicians posing as possessors of extra-sensory perception, leading to the formation in the late 19th century of the British and American Societies for Psychical Research.

As for gullibility in the geographical world: about a decade after the great de Rougement fiasco (see below), in the very month (May, 1910) when the RGS gave Peary a special gold medal for discovering the Pole, we find its *Geographical Journal* publishing an account of 85-foot long snakes in Bolivia (without photograph or skin, despite the availability of a camera and the killing of a supposedly-65-foot anaconda by the explorer). No reliable report of a snake over 40 feet long has ever been recorded.

When, a few years later this explorer was lost in Brazel, the RGS Surveying Instructor, Edward Reeves (the major pro-Peary RGS authority after disclosure in 1910 — whose technically incompetent report kept the Society from changing its public posture), believed that he was sending spirit messages to his wife — not hard for Reeves to accept since he says he was psychic himself and was providentially led by God through life.

Curiously, the actual writer of Peary's book *The North Pole* (1910), published profitably in 1914 spirit messages written after her hand had been "seized" by a ghost. Today the current admiring biographer of Admiral Byrd has promoted belief in the genuineness of a well-known stage "psychic." Even so eminent a source as *National Geographic* plugs (1969, 1970) similar crank science if it makes readable copy.

And amazingly, in the 1960's, one finds the international Arctic Institute of North America repeatedly (until warned by this writer of the gross nonsense involved) publishing far-fetched defenses of the clumsiest hoax in polar history. The Italian Military Geographical Institute has been doing likewise. In 1972, the world renowned Scott Polar Research Institute's *Polar Record* describes Guy Potter's hilarious 1970 satire of Peary's North Pole story as a seriously intended defense of it. (No wonder the slightly less obvious original was successful!)

Another side of professional courtesy is related to the herd instinct of a beleagured tribe. The geographical community has long been defensive about its role in the academic world, as well as being insecure about the sort of scientific competency that is taken for granted in real sciences, such as chemistry and physics. (This put engineer Peary at a great advantage with respect to the geographical societies bemedalling him.)

This professional insecurity, often expressed in a fawning on public figures and an over-dependence on the popular press, was even stronger in the 19th and early 20th centuries. Roderick Murchison, co-founder (1830) and four times (up to 1871) President of the ultra-respectable Royal Geographical Society, was more of a prototype of Gilbert Grosvenor of the National Geographic Society than one might suspect, as revealed in the official history of the RGS:

> ... Murchison was the leading exponent of Geography [c.1860]. It may be that his popular methods in the reception of the lion of the hour, and his appreciation of the importance of press notices, were distasteful to some of the great men of science of the middle of the 19th century [Darwin, Wallace, Hooker]. There was some uneasiness even amongst his friends when the editor of *Punch* asked and was granted permission to send a reporter to the meetings.

The American Geographical Society's official history notes: "Leading men on [the N.Y. *Herald Tribune, Sun,* and *Times*] were either founders or early benefactors of the Society."

Of course, occasionally the press could prove a prickly partner. In 1898, the head of the RGS, Secretary and Editor John Scott Keltie (eminently responsible for Peary's 1910 RGS medal), certified an account of 30 years of alleged Australian adventures of a Louis de Rougement, leading to the "explorer's" lecture at the British Association for the Advancement of Science and to a profitable popular magazine serialization. When de Rougement confessed he was really a Swiss by the name of Grin and that his entire story was a fabrication, reporters hounded Keltie so fiercely he was unable to work.

But current RGS Secretary and Director Larry Kirwan explains the reasons why the press was befriended, regardless, by professional societies of a century ago:

> . . . this new development of the nation-wide newspaper coincided with another new phenomenon, the emergence of the privately organized expedition, which now had to rely for the most part, not as formerly on support from governments, but on public and private subscriptions, which depended in turn on the stimulation of public interest. Here the newspapers played a dual role. With their new mass circulation they came to be in a powerful position to stimulate both public interest and support. In addition, they were able to provide large subscriptions to expeditions in return for exclusive articles, if these seemed likely to give their reading public what it wanted, which was adventure and not research.

The danger of too much popularization had repeatedly haunted the AGS. The Society's 1915-1935 director Izzy Bowman, aware of the fiscal need for compromises with popular taste, was:

fully aware of the value of newspaper publicity and his

63

cooperation was appreciated by the great dailies [e.g.: N.Y. *Times*]. . . . He deplored the chaff in newspaper reporting [but] it had to be taken for the sake of the wheat, and he added, "You don't bite the hand that offers food!"

The New York *Times* returned Bowman's cooperation by not reporting plenty of Antarctic misbehavior of the day; for example, when an exploring immortal "navigated" the first flight over the vicinity of the South Pole in 1929, dead drunk, Bowman was able to kill the story, essentially by arguing that its release would disillusion American youth. One recalls that in middle of the last century, the AGS and its councillor Isaac Hayes (whose own curious activities are glossed over in the AGS' official history) had urged polar expeditions because they would raise "our national character."

When a famous scholar-explorer AGS medallist of Bowman's day was convicted in court of plagiarism and exploring fakery, the *Times* effectively buried it. Today, the N.Y. *Times* Science Editor is on the Council of the AGS (and formerly on the Board of the Arctic Institute of North America) and is not eager to make waves with similar stories.

Given such long entrenched customs and circumstances, which genuine scientists observed with a shudder, it is not surprising that nineteenth century geographers became self-conscious and fearful regarding skepticism. (Indeed, the RGS had long thought it almost impossible that their field would ever be taken completely seriously by universities.)

Further subdividing in intra-discipline loyalty and hyper-sensitivity regarding anything reflecting poorly on the field, one of course finds nationalism. After an early 20th century hoax by a recent President of the Explorers Club, a co-founder of the NGS expressed his reflected shame as an American explorer. The President of the Geographical Society of Philadelphia was similarly mortified:

The occurrence [Cook's downfall] is bound to discredit American scientists abroad, and for years to come. Whenever a scientist from this country goes abroad now he is going to experience keenly the sensation that there is a shadow of suspicion on him. You know, there is more or less jealousy of us abroad, and this Dr. Cook incident will give that sentiment an opportunity to crystallize into a more or less definite attitude.

– The manifold forces described — courtesy, naivete, fear, greed, loyalty, popularization, suppression — had by 1900 gotten organized geography into the sort of situation which could only degenerate. The romance and remoteness of high-latitude dashes made them especially subject to an already disgraceful laxity, which increased with each year. Nansen's 1895 farthest North was supported by no shared sextant observations — servations — though its genuineness may now be verified through his figures for compass variation. The fact that Nansen was honest is, however, not the point here. If as a matter of cautious policy, the geographical societies had temporarily withheld formal recognition for the dash, much subsequent woe might have been forestalled. (The *Fram's* drift went nearly as far north anyway and was the major scientific triumph.)

Only five years later, the Italian expedition of the famous alpine explorer Luigi Amadeo (Duke of Abruzzi) struck out over the ice from Franz Josef Land under the command of Capt. Umberto Cagni, in a three-stage dogsled assault on the Pole. As soon as the final party departed from the last supporting-stage, much smooth ice was encountered, by Cagni's account, which quickly brought him to 86°35′N., barely north of Nansen's record, thus saving face for an expedition costing a party of lives and a half-million dollars. On this remarkable final dash, no sextant observations were shared. (And only one longitude determination was made.) The unfakeable compass variation figures are always required, of course, for steering, and Cagni's are fine except for those near his farthest, which are off by over 20°. But this could not be known in that day. (Ironically, Cagni was in 1928 to head the Fascist kangaroo court which disgraced Umberto Nobile, the first man to visit the Pole twice, on both occasions genuinely taking the first magnetic data there.)

Under the explorers' honor system, Cagni's unsupported word was allowed to stand and the Abruzzi expedition was blessed by various geographical society medals, the AGS Cullom gold medal being presented in 1903 by President Peary.

If there had been any doubt that exploring exaggeration could be accomplished with impunity in the new century, Cagni's record and Peary's Jesup Land must have provided assurance in 1903 that fame and/or riches might be gained by successful imposture while little cost was incurred by failure.

The results of this situation would not be long in coming.

New York, October 17, 1902.

Commander Robert E. Peary, U.S.N.
Washington, D.C.,

Dear Sir:-

The Peary Arctic Club acknowledges your preliminary report of the 17th ult. and letter of the 4th inst., and extends to you its cordial welcome upon your return to country and home. It honors you for patience, courage and fortitude, undaunted by formidable obstacles; thanks you for the wise and effective use of the means placed at your disposal, and congratulates you upon your achievements memorable in the annals of science and discovery.

Assuring you of our appreciation and regard, we subscribe ourselves ~

Peary Land — the north tip of Greenland, with Peary Arctic Club contributors' signatures at capes named for themselves.

5. Faster, Farther, and Crocker

On the *Roosevelt* as it went north in 1905 were men who would figure prominently, even tragically, in the final 1908-1909 expedition. Ship's captain was the strapping, lovably profane Bob Bartlett, a veteran of Peary's earlier work. The major scientist was Ivy Leaguer Ross Marvin (soon to join the faculty of the Cornell College of Engineering), who was surprised to find that Peary was not bossy. All were so sure of success, that discussion turned to tackling the South Pole next. Two of the boilers conked out, but the ship had double music power (pianola & phonograph) which led to jesting of using such to "rend icebergs later on." One way or another, the *Roosevelt* battered and clattered its way up the American Route, "turning, twisting, straining with all her force, smashing her full weight against the heavy floes. . . . the crash, the upward heave, the grating snarl of the ice as the steel-shod stem split it. . . . or trod it under, or sent it right and left in whirling fragments were glorious."

During the August Greenland stopover, first-timers were initiated to Arctic delicacies such as baked walrus heart and Arctic hare. The discovery of Danish preparations for a station north of Cape York (which might interfere with Peary), led to a written complaint (never published) by Peary to the U.S. Secretary of State. The arrival at Cape Sheridan on Sept. 5 was a genuine and memorable success, the ship berthing a few miles north of the *Alert's* 1875 record latitude by a ship under its own power: right on the shore of the Polar Sea itself.

From Feb. 28 to March 6, Peary's multi-stage sledge

assault left N. Ellesmere (at 83°N., 67°W.) and wove its way through the same obstacles as in 1902, hoping vainly for the smooth ice Cagni had reported finding way out from land, fortuitously lurching well to the left (west) while plunging north to the big lead. There Peary made (March 30) the customary determinations: latitude 84°38′N., longitude c.74°W., and compass-variation 107°½W. The position showed there had been an average westward aiming error of over 15°.

After a few more marches with Henson in the lead, a week long storm pinned down the advance party of Henson, Peary, and six natives, during which time they drifted eastward at about 10 miles a day, thereby disrupting communication with the supply parties and so destroying the relay scheme, along with any hope for the Pole. As the gale died, Peary quickly found position astronomically (85°12′N.) and then bolted north in a desperate dash for at least a farthest North. Bartlett, Marvin, and other witnesses who knew navigation (and could thus check the latitudes astronomically) were now separated from the party.

A Hayesian explorer will end up reporting what he expects to find. Suddenly the ice becomes Cagniesque, there is "no occasion for snowshoes or pickaxes," and Peary makes unprecedented speeds over the Arctic Ocean pack.

The expedition had heretofore taken about 40 days to go roughly 140 miles: barely three miles a day. The first two un-witnessed marches make *30* miles a day. Dates start getting a little vague in Peary's account about this time, but by April 21, he has gone 114 miles north of Storm Camp, to a new farthest: 87°06′N. Peary:

> As can perhaps be imagined, I was more than anxious to keep on, but as I looked at the drawn faces of my comrades, at the skeleton figures of my few remaining dogs, at my nearly empty sledges, and remembered the drifting ice over which we had come and the unknown quantity of the big lead between us and the nearest land, I felt that I had cut the margin as narrow as could reasonably be

expected. . . . I told my men we should turn back from here.

But if the latitude represented a record, so did the longitude — because there *wasn't* any, the only instance in exploring history where a farthest North lacked longitude and compass variation figures — two more firsts. The farthest was later (February, 1907) mapped at 45° W., and then 50° W. (April), where it has since stayed, making the aiming error of the final dash over 15° to the east. No longitude for the farthest was ever written down anywhere by Peary. The private reason was that only a single, imperfect sextant observation was made on April 21, and the record latitude was figured on the assumption that it was made at local noon. Without knowledge of longitude (requiring a second observation at another time of day), the premise assumption (and thus the latitude) is worthless.

The return to land was one of the most frightening experiences in polar annals (some of Peary's recollections will be quoted later).

Unfortunately, those interested in figures instead of drama are now left with less than ever in Peary's book *Nearest the Pole*. After his farthest North on April 21, he does not supply a single date (for forty pages — over a month) until his June 2 start from the *Roosevelt*, upon a whole new coastal journey westward. (In 1909, the Explorers Club rejected Dr. Cook's 1906 expedition's claim partly because his book's omission of dates for a *week* "makes intelligent criticism impossible. . . .") A magazine version gave May 12 as the date of Peary's 1906 return to land, but even this lone figure was dropped from his book. (The original log of the *Roosevelt* shows that Peary reached the ship on May 26.)

Perhaps all this non-dating was due not to any obscurantism but simply to losing track of dates during the rush back to land? Nonetheless, a diary was kept (Bartlett saw it), and it survived the expedition; Peary refers to it occasionally in his book. Therefore, one might expect to examine it today for some explanation of the vagueness evident in the book. No such luck. By coincidence, this particular diary has disappeared.

Has any contemporary document managed to survive? One finally was recovered in 1953 from a cairn atop Cape Columbia, built there by Peary on June 8, 1906, during a trip west, less than a month after the return from his Farthest North trek. As it is customary for explorers to deposit written records of their accomplishments in such monuments, Peary left a note referring to his recent Farthest North — the one which he presented to the world later in the year without revealing his longitude. At this point, as one can see from the original record, he wouldn't even volunteer a latitude! The only comparable records, those of May 17 and 20, 1900, claim merely a Western Hemisphere farthest North, but both give the exact latitude attained. Never again.

Peary's 1906 stab for the Pole had failed miserably. He had started about as early as the weather would permit (his 1909 starting date was virtually the same) and marched so hard on crippled feet that his jaw ached *just from clenching his teeth against the pain.* Yet he had managed to sledge only halfway to the Pole, barely escaping with his life when spring caught him still out on the ice. Heroic adventure though it surely was, this would hardly satisfy his backers as a tangible achievement. Claiming a new farthest North, however, would provide a glamorous superlative, and the experience gained in achieving it might be — and was — sold as the key to success next time. Still, by itself, it was an insufficient return on such an enormous investment.

Peary's furlough from the Navy expired in April, 1907, which meant he could spend only a single season for travel in this expedition. Desperate for a hard yield in the little time left him, and despite his swollen legs and the dangerous lateness of the season, he set out, only a week after his return, upon a westward trip to explore a 100-mile unexplored gap in the coast of west Grant Land (N. Ellesmere) extending to the north tip of Axel Heiberg Land. If he could reach it, this would be a guaranteed unknown territory, ready and waiting to be littered with the names of the wealthy members of the

70

Peary Arctic Club. That Peary's attitude toward his arduous western trip was not one of pure explorer curiosity is clear enough from his own written anticipation of doing his "duty" by it. Not that the thrill of exploration was gone, but the desire for fame was, as always, dominant. In mid-June, after 200 miles of hard, swift travel, he arrived at the limit of the previously explored coast of Grant Land and "was now looking into the unknown." June 16 ". . . what I saw before me in all its splendid, sunlit savageness was *mine, mine* by the right of discovery, to be credited to me, and associated with my name, generations after I have ceased to be." But the more immediately important names, those of generous Club members, were now to be placed on the map: Bourne (Cape), Kleybolte (Island — really a small peninsula), Colgate (Cape), Phillips (Bay), Thomas Hubbard (Cape). Good enough? Though he'd found new coast, it was that of known (Grant) land. On June 24, perhaps recalling Otto Sverdrup's 1902 acclaim for finding new land west of Ellesmere — and his own near miss of it in 1899 — Peary climbed the 2000-foot peak of Cape Colgate and carefully searched the horizon with binoculars. At first he thought he saw land to the northwest; but further observation soon revealed its dubiousness. He looked again, on the 28th, from atop the 1600-foot summit above Cape Hubbard with the same disappointing results, then built cairns and left records at both places as well as at nearby areas. All July was spent backtracking 300 miles, much of it through summer slush, to the *Roosevelt*. On July 4, the weather was so awful that Peary could not fly the flag. Physically, it was the most trying of all his journeys. On the last march to the ship, "I . . . set my teeth and struck a good pace . . . the pain reached to my knees." Bartlett recalled his arrival: "His footgear was so saturated with water that it had long ceased to be of any use. He had on his feet pemmican tins and the inside ones were even reduced to the size of a Canadian nickel. Can you imagine a man with all his toes gone doing this? But he did."

The *Roosevelt* was in bad shape by this time. A terse note in the ship's log while Peary was nearing his remotest point to the north: "Crew trying to repair rudder. Whoever made it for a voyage like this should give up the trade of ruddermaking." Those responsible far to the south were at the moment presumably more occupied with the bills not yet paid them by the Peary Arctic Club and with earthquake and fire news from San Francisco — the army relief of which was performed under Peary's old admirer, General Greely.

Bringing the partly crushed *Roosevelt* from the shores of the Arctic Ocean all the way to New York on the remaining steam boilers and propeller blades was one of the most remarkable naval feats ever, later written up as early black comedy by Bartlett: using as fuel frozen and dynamited coal, then green wood, then odiferous blubber, they fought their way back to civilization on five successive rudders — even in spite of the late start — terrifying Eskimos, girls, and cows all the way.

Had his public and backers rewarded suffering as generously as they did new land, Peary would not have been tempted to add to his remarkable adventure. Perhaps rankling over his own timidity in not having expanded more consistently upon his Jesup Land claim, he was in no mood to lose a chance to gain credit for another such discovery. At the time, an expert at the U.S. Coast and Geodetic Survey suspected anyway that land existed somewhere northwest of Cape Hubbard; whatever was later found there might well be credited to Peary if he were not vague this time. These factors, in addition to the pressures arising out of the productivity vacuum of the 1905-1906 expedition, finally led him to present in 1907 the chimeral visions of "land" on June 24 and 28, 1906, as the definite, unambiguous discovery of Crocker Land (named for George Crocker, director of the Southern Pacific Railway, Peary Arctic Club member, and heavy 1906 contributor — $50,000). From Cape Colgate he recorded in his 1907 account, "And northwest it was with a thrill that my glasses revealed the faint white summits of a distant land which my Eskimos claimed to have seen as we came along from the last camp." Four days later, from Cape Thomas Hubbard, he could make out, possibly even better, the same;

. . . snow-clad summits of the distant land in the northwest, above the ice horizon. My heart leaped the intervening miles of ice as I looked longingly at this land, and in fancy I trod its shores, and climbed its summits, even though I knew that that pleasure could be only for another in another season.

The "another" was to be Peary protege Donald MacMillan. In the spring of 1914, with explorer and first Peary biographer, Fitzhugh Green, and two Eskimos, he struck out onto the ice, going 150 miles northwest from Cape Hubbard. En route they too saw landlike mirages, but the Eskimo Pee-a-wah-to, a veteran of Peary's 1906 farthest North, rightly judged them to be mist. When 30 miles inland (according to Peary's 1907 map of Crocker Land), they concluded "we were in pursuit of a will-o'-the-wisp, ever receding, ever changing, ever beckoning." The 1914 return to land was a close thing, the ice breaking up from the new moon as the party fought back toward Heiberg. Green and Pee-a-wah-to were then sent south from Cape Hubbard to explore the small uncharted gap between it and Rens Fjord. Green returned alone, having murdered the Eskimo, thus leaving a widow and five semi-orphans. But he atoned for the woman's loss by moving in with her later.

It is remarkable that the pseudo-discovery of Crocker Land was ever taken seriously at all, for Peary never stated anything definite about it other than its sheer existence and a very rough direction — nothing concrete in writing regarding distance. Typically, the society which expensively sponsored the later search for Crocker Land simply assumed without checking that Peary's mapping of it was based on scientific data (triangulation from transit azimuths taken at the sightings). No such measurements ever existed.

None of Peary's published references to Crocker Land quote from his 1906 field notes (which were never examined by the Societies before they disappeared). It is curious that both of Peary's discoveries of new land (Jesup Land and Crocker Land — neither of which is now taken seriously) occurred on the only two exploring sallies of his career when he was not accompanied by a civilized witness (not even Henson, exceptionally) who might be questioned, say, by the press after the expedition's return.

Right on the heels of his 1906 return, Peary resigned after four years as American Geographical Society President, for undisclosed reasons. His sole 1906 gold medal (after two in 1897 and four in 1902-4) came from the incurious National Geographic Society. Anyone today who wishes to review his 1906 records will discover that the relevant journals (Farthest and Crocker Land) are now missing from the Peary Papers. The U.S. Hydrographic Office and the Bureau of Navigation records at the National Archives contain no original sketches submitted by Peary of his supposed 1906 discoveries.

Has the laxity of 1906 left modern Polar historians with no records at all in relation to Crocker Land? Not quite.

For example, Peary's first 1906 telegram (Nov. 2) survives. It mentions the "farthest" and the reaching of Sverdrup's Heiberg Land, plus a good many other details. But the newly discovered Crocker Land — *the second most important achievement of the expedition,* according to Peary's later book — is nowhere even hinted at. His November 23rd telegram to the Navy mentions his expedition as having eliminated "the probability of the existence of any land [north of Canada], through 10 degrees of longitude, between parallels 81 and 83 [north latitude]"; also "secured an interesting series of soundings." Still — no new land. The same day an interview in Sydney, Nova Scotia, regarding possible future work, resulted in the following report: "Commander Peary said . . . [there previously] was a gap of 100 miles in the survey of [west] Grant Land. . . . Peary has closed this up. Probably the *only* section of unknown coast remaining in the Arctic is the northeast coast of Greenland. . . ." (Emphasis added.)

At a Peary Arctic Club dinner of millionnaires on Dec. 12, Peary met George Crocker again, and shortly thereafter Crocker Land made its debut in print — in Peary's *Harper's* article of February, 1907. Did Peary discover Crocker Land in the summer of 1906, as claimed? Or did he only much later finally discover that he had discovered it? The last hope of knowing rests upon an examination of the three obscure handwritten cairn records left by Peary near the site of "discovery" on June 28, June 30, and July 5, 1906. All have been recovered by later explorers. Curiously, Peary's subsequent publications quote none of the three nor the telegrams. The first cairn record provides just the June 28 date and Peary's name, and is thus informative only by its reticence. The July 5 record notes having reached the already known Heiberg Land, but, like the November 2 telegram, fails to mention his newly discovered Crocker Land. This then, narrows things down to the crucial June 30 record, even the bare existence of which, in contrast to those of June 28 and July 5, is not mentioned in his book. That the June 30 cairn was examined at all was due to the curiosity (or confusion) of Green in 1914. Within the cairn's stones, he found a record which actually refers to the view out over the Polar Ocean on June 28 from the summit of Cape Hubbard, the vista of *the very moment* when Peary later reported he had seen Crocker Land for the second time, and his "heart leaped the intervening miles of ice as I looked longingly . . ." Since his only other previous cairn record was the brief name and date note of June 28, this detailed June 30 record represents Peary's very first opportunity to jot down for posterity the original azimuthal data of Crocker Land. Or, at least to note the description and general direction of his discovery, insurance against the possibility of death on the hazardous return trip cheating him of his claim. It would silence any subsequent doubters who demanded documentary proof of his priority of discovery.

One reads, and comes to the crucial paragraph: "The 27th and 28th [June] fine clear days giving *good view of northern horizon.* from the summit of the cape." (Emphasis added.)

And . . .?

And *nothing.* The next sentence is of a gale on the 29th and 30th. The rest of the note is given over to deerkill counts, party description, and departure plans. Of the discovery of the second "main result" of the expedition, the only new land of Peary's career and possibly part of the northernmost island or continent on Earth — *not one word.*

75

On his return from the 1906 Polar try, Peary wrote in his diary; "To think after all the preparation, the experience, the effort, the strain, the chances taken, and the wearing of myself and party to the last inch, what a little journey it is on the map and how far short of my hopes it fell. To think that I have failed once more. . . ." It would be unfeeling not to try to empathize and to imagine the weight of the injustice he felt the fates had dealt him. Twenty years of hard work, incredible suffering, mental and physical sacrifice — yet enduring fame and fortune had eluded him. He tried to be realistic and philosophical:

I . . . told myself that I was only one in a long line of arctic explorers, dating back through the centuries, all the way from Henry Hudson to the Duke of Abruzzi, and including Franklin, Kane, and Melville — a long list of valiant men who had striven and failed. I told myself that I had only succeeded, at the price of the best years of my life, in adding a few links to the chain that led from the parallels of civilization towards the Polar center, but that, after all, at the end the only word I had to write was failure.

Scientifically, the 1905-1906 expedition was disappointingly barren. For example, the entire collection of humidity data was scrapped due to use of wrong equipment. The Smithsonian *Reports* exceptionally ignored the trip and no serious society's medal was forthcoming — compared with the earlier gold bonanzas. The Peary institution was going popular, but the financial rewards were skimpy; Bob Bartlett recollected why:

He had published his book, *Nearest the Pole,* in the winter '06-'07. He had been counting on the royalties from this volume to help his bills. But, like his attempt at the Pole, the book was a failure. Somehow people weren't interested in reading about hardships that didn't get the explorer to his goal. I realize now that the world prefers to read about success.

This same realization doubtless occurred to Peary.

Though technically out of debt, what gave Peary a just sense of grievance in 1906-1908 was the fact that he had now put over two decades of his life and a half a million dollars of his own, his family's, and his friends' and backers' money into his ventures. Whether he hoped to retire after his farthest North claim or was pondering yet another attempt on the Pole is immaterial, since his modest financial position seems to have forced the choice. He was caught up in a nightmarish gambling cycle. All that each expedition's achievements seemed to do was help him scrape up the stakes for that next crap game. Like a veteran high-roller deep in hock, he could only recoup his invested thousands and redeem the lost years by giving the dice yet another roll. For his last chance, in 1909, he would shoot it all.

Left, record left by Peary in cairn on foreshore of Cape Hubbard June 30, 1906 and brought out by MacMillan in 1914. Right, record left at Cape Colgate, July 5, 1906. Recovered in 1954 by Geoffrey Hattersley-Smith.

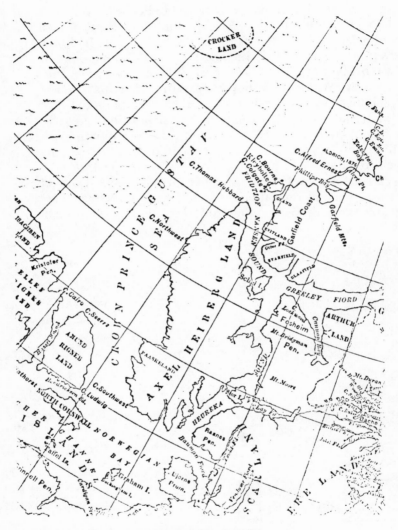

Map from Peary's *Nearest the Pole* (April, 1907)

6.   Buffalo Angel

On September 16, 1903, in the rough Alaskan terrain surrounding Mt. McKinley, Robert Dunn and Frederick Cook, returning co-leaders of an unsuccessful attempt to scale North America's tallest peak, held an unwittingly symbo-prophetic conversation, never previously noted throughout the long Cook-Peary literature:

"Don't you think" I [Dunn] asked the Professor [Dunn's name for Cook], that the leader who rouses per-sonal devotion and enthusiasm in his men, though he may be sometimes unfair and his temper quick, will reach the Pole before the easy-going, forbearing, color-less sort?" "Dunn, your sort of leader would have to be an angel, too," said the Professor. "Well, then only an angel will reach the Pole," said I.

Frederick Cook's niche in history is permanent. Antholo-gies of hoaxery regard his North Pole fraud as one of the most classically perfect in history, the ultimate harmonious combination of fleecer and lambs. Because of this, few are now aware that, before his spectacular 1909 downfall, he was a highly respected veteran polar explorer. After his creditable early work with Peary (1892), he was a genuine first survivor of the Antarctic winter (with the young Roald Amundsen of Norway) on the 1897-1899 "Belgica" expedition — of which he was the nearest thing to a hero, and which probably made him the first explorer to have wintered in both polar regions. Leader of expeditions, surgeon and

79

anthropologist, contributor to the 1904 International Geographical Congress, Cook's credentials seemed impeccable in 1906 when the Explorers Club elected him to succeed Greely, its first president.

Cook's 1903 attempt to scale Mt. McKinley failed but was honestly reported and Dunn was able to correct a map error in the nearby Wrangell Mountains. Cook's next attempt started from Seattle on May 16, 1906, for Tyonok, Alaska. It had been made possible when a sportsman — Henry Disston, a Philadelphia millionaire's son — promised to finance the expedition in return for Cook's organizing a hunt for him in Alaska.

The project was in fiscal trouble anyway, when, as the defeated expedition arrived back in Tyonok on August 3, Cook received the news that Disston had changed his mind about joining the group and would not send further funds — having only so far covered about a third of the trip's expenses. This turned to rubber a number of checks Cook had already written, and simultaneously turned a once noble gentleman to a life of crime.

Cook took a single companion, Ed Barrille, and sped back toward Mt. McKinley, stating (since the season was very late) that he was merely intending to reconnoiter for a later attempt. The others wondered why he quietly packed an American flag into his rucksack.

He was soon back in Tyonok wiring success to his friend Herbert Bridgman (of the Brooklyn *Standard-Union* and Peary Arctic Club). His published account, unsupported by a diary, is conspicuous by the lack of dates during the climb, the absence of any chart indicating his route, or of a photo showing the unique scene from this 20,000-foot-high summit — but including photos the vistas of which have *all* since been identified as having been taken at sites over 15 miles from Mt. McKinley and at altitudes of less than 6,000 feet. He claimed to have taken "a round of [transit] angles" from the summit — but this data has never been found. His photo of the "summit" accidentally shows (lower right hand corner) Mt. Grosvenor — at an angle not possible from Mt. McKinley.

Some expedition members, for example, Herschel Parker of Columbia University (a co-contributor to the expedition) and Belmore Browne (who had immediately understood the truth from a private chat with Barrille), while knowing the claim was fake, cooperated with Cook's subsequent public exploitation of it. Peary later fumed regarding Parker:

> We have the spectacle of the man who accompanied Cook and who claimed to have had just as much financial and other interest in the expeditions as Cook, saying in private and behind Cook's back that Cook never got to the top of Mt. McKinley, and yet sitting at the same public dinner table with Cook and listening to him recounting his ascent of Mt. McKinley (as I saw him do on two occasions) and never raise his voice in protest.

Nor did Peary raise his own voice — so long as the Doctor kept clear of "his" route and goal. Thus Cook got away with his McKinley caper, and lectured on it by invitation before the Explorers Club, the National Geographic Society, and the Association of American Geographers. However, the mountain did not have the time honored glamor of the North Pole, so the financial rewards were modest and did not (by a margin of a few thousand dollars) defray his own investment. Cook later confessed his situation — the similarity to Peary's emotions is obvious:

> I had no money. My work in exploration had netted me nothing and all my professional income was soon spent. Unless you have felt the goading, devilish grind of poverty hindering you, pursuing you, you cannot know the mental fury into which I was lashed.

Pre-1906 laxity had led directly to the 1906 Cook and Peary claims. This success now in turn set the stage for the confluent grand climax.

Though both explorers' 1906 stories were empty of evidence and full of crucial lacunae, neither's journals were examined by any of the believing institutions, and on December 15, 1906, both men were guests of honor at the

81

annual banquet of the National Geographic Society. Peary watched as Cook, whom even Mrs. Peary knew for a fraud, was introduced and praised by telephone inventor Alexander Graham Bell, second president of the National Geographic Society (and son-in-law of the first president, G.G. Hubbard). He was completely accepted by an audience of hundreds of the most respected and powerful persons in Washington. Cook then looked on while Peary was presented the Society's first Gardiner Greene Hubbard Gold Medal by President Theodore Roosevelt, for the strangest farthest North claim in exploring annals. Behind the scenes at the dinner, Cook learned directly that Peary had no case. The Doctor's determination to fake an attainment of the North Pole probably originated on the spot.

The exploring world's seemingly lemminglike rush toward catastrophe was now playing its last prelude — its only remaining chance for judicious and provident reform before the final act of 1909. The inadequacy of Peary's scientific results was known to professionals. Due to Barrille, private rumors spread rapidly regarding Cook's McKinley prank. But *nothing* effective was done *before the public,* whereas this was exactly the arena to which both men were now almost exclusively turning in fiscal desperation, in order to cash in on their previously earned professional respect. And they were, of course, not alone. For example, the cartographer of Ernest Shackleton's popularized privately sponsored Antarctic expedition (1907-1909), which actually discovered the South Magnetic Pole and Beardmore Glacier, later "went crazy" and confessed that he had faked solar observations to slightly enhance the record latitude reached. (This fact goes unmentioned in any Shackleton biography.) The RGS therefore called in the expedition's records, which then were permanently "mislaid."

How long such an orgy of invention would have persisted is hard to say, though such corruption, once acquiesced in, knows no check and eventually grows with malignant abandon until spectacularly consumed by its own greed.

The culmination in this case was poetic justice in that

Cook and Peary each grabbed simultaneously for the grand prize, the North Pole. One claimant was thus absolutely forced to lodge a public charge of fraud against the other. And so, the ironic upshot of money sensitive institutional silence on such a possible scandal as fraud was nothing but the most hideous money-curdling hoax in exploring history.

In brief, the situation in the geographical community had degenerated by the end of 1906 into an R.S.V.P. invitation to fraud. Pleased to respond, Cook got out of sight to the North just as soon after the winter festivities as he could. He was last seen by literate man in February, 1908, heading west across Ellesmere Land with Eskimos, dogs, sledges, and supplies, more than 500 miles from the Pole.

Cook reappeared in Greenland the following year, having left no recoverable dated record at any place visited in the interim, and steamed from there for Denmark, claiming to have penetrated the Arctic Ocean pack in the spring of 1908 and reached the North Pole on April 21. When asked in July in Greenland for details to assist a possible interview with his Eskimos, Cook refused on the grounds that his exploit wouldn't interest anyone: "I supposed that the newspapers would announce my return and that there would be a three-days' breath of attention, and that would be all." Actually he wired the New York *Herald* a demand of $1.50 per word for a 2000 word story. Having established this rough rate of exchange, he immediately sold the *Herald* an already prepared 25,000 word story at a dollar per word for serialization in twelve installments (every other day in the *Herald* from Sept. 15 to Oct. 7).

Cook's 1909 triumphal return and pre-arranged five-week lecture tour was primarily intended as a cleanup on his reputation, the engaging Doctor banking on the public's proclivity to gauge substance from image and to read a man's face more carefully than his facts. His alleged disposition of original data with hunter Harry Whitney, his seemingly forthright expectation that this and his two Eskimo companions at the Pole would eventually verify his journey to doubters, his reporting of and even photographing the wholly mythical Bradley Land — all these maneuvers he knew would cause him embarrassment sooner or later, but his lecture fees would be safe in a bank in Brooklyn by then.

Cook's sweet and modest manner endeared him to almost all who were acquainted with him. The vase of his former self showed, the toad within did not. The powerful English journalist William Stead wrote of Cook (from interviewing him, at the very peak of the delusion): ". . . in business affairs . . . almost as innocent as a child . . . — a naive, inexperienced child, who sorely needed some one to look after him and take care of him, and tell him what he ought to do in his own interest. . . . he is not, I should say, an imaginative man. . . ."

A few knew first-hand that Cook's fine character, like that of too many successful public figures then and now, was largely surface, and private correspondence warned Peary (who initially just couldn't believe Cook's tale would be taken seriously by anyone) what he was up against: "Cook would not turn a hair if caught with the goods" and: "an adventurer of the rarest and most artistic sort."

Failure to appreciate Cook's short-term, extemporaneous approach to the flimflam has been the most common shortcoming of his commentators, who make his behavior seem more complicated than it really was. One of the first to express this misjudgment was Cook's friend, American explorer Anthony Fiala, who reasoned; "No man would be foolish enough to make such a claim unless he had proofs to back it. . . ." Washington scientists Otto Tittmann, Francis Perkins, and Henry Gannett took the same initial view, Tittmann adding; ". . . what he [Cook] says will have to be accepted until the contrary is proved." The geographical community was simply unprepared for Cook's sudden and daring fiscal coup. Geologist-explorer William H. Hobbs, who doubted from the first, later recalled:

In very large measure the endorsement of Cook at Copenhagen by the well-known explorers Knud Rasmussen and Otto Sverdrup, accounts for his immediate acclaim there. . . . Cook was . . . feted in Copenhagen and the minutest details covered the front pages of newspapers throughout the world. The day after his arrival, he was received by the King of Denmark at a state dinner, and there was tendered to him a dinner by the municipality of Copenhagen at which there were four hundred covers. During this almost insane orgy of hasty approval, pertinent questions were repeatedly asked by the officials of the University of Copenhagen and by those of the Royal Danish Geographical Society, both of which institutions had other honors under consideration for the explorer. But to all the requests that he submit as evidence his observations of the sun's position taken at the Pole, together with the journal of his dog-sledge journey, Cook replied that all these precious documents had been left behind in the keeping of a wandering sportsman [Harry Whitney] in Greenland.

This stall and various other alibis were so earnestly told that few could be so hard as actually to doubt the angelic Doctor. Danish explorer-writer Peter Freuchen, who witnessed the "orgy of approval," observed:

The trusting Danes never suspect anyone. It did not occur to them that a man could go north, come back and tell anything but the truth. And to support his story, the astronomy professor at the university [of Copenhagen] talked with Dr. Cook and reported that Cook knew so little about astronomy that it would be impossible for him to concoct false observations. It never occurred to any of them that there might have been no observations at all.

Indeed, in November, Cook — who knew nothing of navigation — finally hired the expertise of a Norwegian navigator, August Loose, who worked out a set of faked data in New York. But Cook welched at the last minute, so Loose told all to the pro-Peary *New York Times*. Loose's lengthy affidavit verified in oft-amusing detail the impressions of Cook's 1903

85

and 1906 Mount McKinley companions, namely, that Cook was an incompetent as regards the use of scientific instruments. Loose wryly wrote:

> It took me only about three minutes on my first acquaintance with Dr. Cook to get the idea into my head that he had never found the north pole. I found that he was entirely ignorant on many vital points of the method of taking observations. It amazed me that a man who needed so much enlightenment would have the nerve to come out and say he had discovered the north pole.

In response to the inevitable criticism that the testimony of a confessed conspirator is not trustworthy, Loose publicly challenged Cook to prove that he could work a sextant at all, something no one had yet thought of, not having realized the brazen extent of his bluff. The Doctor chose to stay in hiding.

Ultimately Cook, unable himself to fix up any data (solar altitudes and times), sent merely positional results (latitude-longitude places) of alleged navigational calculations to his University of Copenhagen judges, who swiftly rejected them. Later Cook claimed he'd had the data all along, but just hadn't thought it worthwhile to bother submitting them! What he ultimately published was indeed of questionable worth. To quote this writer's recent analysis, published by the University of Oslo:

> There are some remarkable feats implied by Cook's astronomical data [but setting foot on the North Pole isn't one of them]. Cook's alleged solar altitudes. . . . demand that he must have hovered for [over 24 hours straight] four miles sunward of the Pole, while the Earth spun just beneath his feet.
>
> The indication that Cook was riding a flying saucer is not to be taken lightly — e.g., his only doublelimb solar altitudes (April 8 and 14) make the Sun's apparent diameter $\frac{1}{4}°$ (not $\frac{1}{2}°$, as it appears from the Earth), thus placing him about two astronomical units from the Sun, presumably on the planet Vesta!

86

(No one who had ever used a sextant and artificial horizon *once* — *any*where — could have made the error responsible for this.)

In addition, Cook had said he'd kept *all* his data, a story he stuck to when Whitney returned without the box of instruments Cook had left with him in Greenland. (Cook claimed that duplicates of the data were inside the lost box.) Cook's later book said that the loss had made his data *in*complete. This set up his explanation of why, though his story specified longitudes en route to the Pole, he never published a single piece of data supporting them.

It should be rather obvious that efficient practical navigation toward the point called the North Pole requires knowledge of position: latitude (north-south) tells how far (colatitude) one has to go to reach 90°N. latitude (North Pole) — and especially longitude (east-west) for aiming, since (in practice, for polar travel) every bit of longitude uncertainty causes an equal number of degrees of unsurety in one's aim toward the Pole. These positions are customarily determined from sextant (or theodolite) observations of the sun's altitude (angle above the horizon). In simplified terms: latitude is most easily found by *noon* observation of the sun. Longitude may then be computed from a *non*-noon solar observation — a more difficult calculation.

Out of sight of landmarks on the chaotic pack ice of the Arctic Ocean, steering daily marches between astronomical position fixes is performed by aiming the sledges in the direction indicated on a compass carried along for the purpose. However, the compass does not in general point precisely north, its direction being specific to any given geographical position. (Indeed, in the north Ellesmere area, the north end of the compass needle points nearer *south* than north.) So the compass' *variation* from true north — i.e., the direction of the needle — *must* be known for steering by compass. For example, if the compass variation is 120°W. of north, then aiming 120°E. of the north compass needle's direction will take one due north. A simple observation (comparing the bearings of the compass and the sun) with a theodolite (or prismatic compass) enabled an explorer to determine the compass variation for any position.

All of this was, of course, standard knowledge and practice among 19th and early 20th century polar explorers. Before the shadowy claims of September, 1909, *every* extended attempt on the Pole (including all of Peary's own previous ones) involved the en route recording of *longitude* and *compass variation,* since it was a part of one's practical navigation. The variation (being previously unknowable at any remote geographical point before physical investigation by the explorer) was scientifically useful information, not to mention irrefutable proof of one's attainment of a place (crucial on the Arctic Ocean, where no permanent record will stay put on the ice).

The December, 1909, decision against Cook was based in large part on such considerations. For the past 60 years, virtually none of the Doctor's legion of apologists has shown any awareness of the truth of the verdict, naively following Cook's own misuse of the temperate language of the official report's conclusion that Cook had "no proof. . . ." Typically, Cook explained; "They did not say mind, that I had not found the Pole; they merely said my [proof] was not absolutely positive. . . ." The 1909 report had in fact stated; "There are lacking in the documents turned over to us, to an outrageously inadmissible degree, such guiding information as might show the probability of the said astronomical observations [sextant sights of the sun's altitude] having been really performed at all. . . ." After seeing Cook's notebooks in 1910, the Committee added its explicit opinion on the material, observing that it looked as if "important parts of it are manufactured." None of the eminent members of the Committee believed in any innocent explanation of Cook's 1909 presentation. What was particularly incredible to the Committee's foremost navigation expert was the Cook records' entire lack of compass variation data for steering.

Looking back on the autumn of 1909 and counting all the odds against him and the many warnings he and others emanated throughout the charade, one can only wonder: how did Cook get away with it for so long? Consider:

a) Quite ignorant of navigational mathematics, he for three months procrastinated on presenting his non-existent observational data and so all the while successfully claimed credit for one of the greatest navigational feats in history. (The lie was simply *so* enormous that apparently no one ever thought to challenge Cook just to compute one sample elementary observation reduction. Even Peary, his severest detractor, couldn't believe that Cook was fantasizing to the extent he really was.)

b) Doubts of the 1906 McKinley climb had been explorers' gossip for some time, and Peary had, in 1908, apprised various institutions of Cook's possible current intentions.

c) Enough intelligent critics voiced reasonable doubts just in the first week or so after Cook's 1909 return that any fool should have been at least cautious. For instance, Philip Gibbs, the very first English-speaking reporter to interview Cook, suspected fraud right away, and his sardonic remarks on Cook's convenient lack of competent witnesses and his high sustained speeds were widely printed. British Admiral Nares publicly wondered at Cook's sudden and uncorroborated good fortune in finding so much smooth ice on the largely hummocky pack. On Sept. 8, Peary reported that Cook's two Eskimo companions (who supposedly went over 500 miles of sea-ice to the Pole with Cook) told his men that Cook did not go far north. (Sverdrup, supposing like Fiala that a hoaxer would think long-term, rejected Peary's report: "Cook could not have been such a fool. No one would keep Eskimos on the land and pretend they had left it. The Eskimos would know better.") In mid-October, explorer George Kennan published proof of the impossibility of hauling sufficient supplies to sustain working men and dogs on an 84 day journey away from land without return trail depots.

A major reason Cook prevailed for so many weeks was that his critics were relatively few, an exceptionally daring handful who were not intimidated by certain tribal customs, lay and professional. Freuchen recalled his own experience:

89

I did not hesitate to state my [doubts] publicly. I gave several lectures, and I wrote an article presenting all the evidence against Dr. Cook. But my editor refused to print it. "We cannot wine and dine a man one day and call him a fraud the next," he declared.

So I took my article to another paper and was received with open arms by the editor, who did not use it.

Telling the public it was being buffaloed certainly got no gratitude from the intended beneficiaries of the effort. Gibbs was publicly caricatured, cursed, and even challenged to a duel. Doubting Admiral Melville (U.S.) was accosted and insulted continually in the streets. Kennan's mail was almost pure invective. Cook's followers simply ascribed all criticism to the machinations of a "Peary trust" or to base motives. Admiral de Richelieu to Cook, Sept. 10: "Green-eyed Envy and Jealousy Is Doing Its Work, But We Believe In You Absolutely." Peary was hated (and his own claim rejected without a hearing) by many simply for telling them what he knew to be the truth of Cook's journey: "I . . . am blackguarded by my own people because I attempt to warn them and keep them from making damn fools of themselves. . . ." Under such circumstances one can understand even bold Teddy Roosevelt's admission that (if in office) he would have welcomed and congratulated Cook on his return "even though I knew all along that he was a faker." And the usual professional courtesy helped out: though explorers Scott, Shackleton, and Nansen concluded privately within a fortnight that Cook's claim was baseless, all three were silent and Nansen verbalized the feelings of most pros by later criticizing Peary for *not* being quiet! So the public heard only the boosters, and an embarrassingly large number of explorers accepted and lauded Cook's story temporarily.

Of course, its fraudulence has now long been quietly admitted among professionals. Some eventually talked with Cook's two Eskimos, who were glad to recount the actual trip and even describe the Doctor in the process of faking his photos. But because of Cook's personal attributes, his inexhaustible supply of excuses, his apparent underdoggedness

90

and genuine doggedness, and institutional reluctance to denounce his Pole fantasy officially and publicly, belief in it lingers to this day. Currently it is having an especially virulent outbreak in North America. Within the past few years, about a dozen reputable periodicals and publishing houses have printed articles or books, most recently, *The Big Nail* (1970) and *The Great American Loser* (1973), defending the ill-treated Doctor. Extraordinary is these writers' imperviousness to Cook's manifold giveaway blunders and to the fact that all three of his 1906-1908 witnesses stated that they and Cook went nowhere near the trip's claimed goals.

But some may wonder, in spite of all, how can we be *sure* of the fraudulence of Cook's 1909 claim? Of course, a scientist should not accept a claim on an inverted basis — the burden of proof ought to be on Cook, who in fact never imparted anything true regarding the North Pole that could not have been known or easily guessed beforehand. (Speaking of Hayesian guesses: Cook stated that at the North Pole, the compass points toward the north magnetic pole. This is wrong by over 30°.)

Where Cook really went in 1908 has been characterized as a "mystery that will never be solved" — but actually the answer can be deduced beyond reasonable doubt. Instead of the North Pole, Cook discovered Meighen Island. Only he didn't dare admit it.

Officially, Meighen Island was first sighted June 12, 1916, by Harold Noice of Canadian explorer Vilhjalmur Stefansson's party, which claimed it for the Dominion of Canada.

But in 1909, Cook's actual 1908 route was described to Peary's men — Henson (capable in the Greenland Eskimo tongue) and others — and mapped by Cook's two Eskimos, and eventually published in various American newspapers on October 13, 1909. It depicts the 1908 party's visit to a "small low island" right where Stefansson found Meighen Island eight years later, though Cook denied any such encounter. Compared with a modern aero-photo based map, the Eskimos' diagram shows for Meighen Island a resemblance of size, shape, and position that cannot be remotely ascribed to chance, especially considering the scarcity of unknown land in the Arctic at the time. Therefore, Cook and his two Eskimos certainly visited Meighen Island and even camped there one night. Regardless of Cook's reasons for later shying, away from the island in his story, it must be recognized by the obvious test of predictivity that Meighen Island proves that the Eskimos, not Cook, told the truth. No single point of evidence has ever demonstrated with such untechnical force the falsity of Cook's Polar story and the truth of the Eskimos' map, the latter showing that claimant Cook was never in his life closer than 500 miles of the North Pole!

Even today, though there is no credible evidence that Cook had any ability as a sledger over rough ice, the heads of the Explorers Club and of the Royal Geographical Society actually take Cook's alleged 1000-mile Arctic Ocean journey at least partly seriously — the latter speaking without a smile of Cook's clipping along at speeds up to 26 miles a day. The fact is that Cook's *entire* journey north of land was less than half of 26 miles, according to his two Eskimo companions, who also noticed that the Doctor took care never to get out of sight of land. Given Cook's abilities as a navigator, to do otherwise would have been suicide.

Considering the claims he made, it is not hard to understand why Cook's main legacy to the Eskimos was a one-syllable word for "whiteman-liar."

The subsequent adventures of this "naive inexperienced child" involved promotion of questionable oil stock; Cook explained, "Exploring for oil is more profitable than for the North Pole." Though by 1922 he had members of New York's Four Hundred on his board of directors, Cook shortly landed in Leavenworth for using the mails to defraud. Predictably, he became the most popular man in prison. After his release he involved himself in various good works. Tenacious to the end, he had several damage suits pending against detractors when he died in 1940.

He was buried in Buffalo. But the movement to resurrect his reputation may never die. Thackeray's unregenerate con-woman anti-heroine, Becky Sharp, though as unambiguously exposed as Cook, ended similarly: "A very strong party of excellent people consider her to be a most injured woman. . . . She busies herself in works of piety."

Periodic Cook revivals are to be expected regardless of proof against him. Each time (due to such interest) that the body of evidence is closely examined, it is obvious to competent scientists that Cook was a clumsy faker, and so the push for recognition fades. But memories fade, too, and in a few decades, the paranoid saga of the poor wronged polar hero returns anew upon a public entirely ignorant of facts once commonly known. It is really quite embarrassing to see learned scholars taking at all seriously a man every cub reporter of 1910 rightly regarded as merely a national joke.

It is also pitiful that the Cook movement is composed of such decent, if overinnocent, folk — a criminal who tried to steal the *life's* work of at least two men did not merit such friends. (They have never understood why the Peary Arctic Club was so upset!) Cook's daughter has now spent thousands of dollars and a lifetime of disappointments in a vain effort to erase the blot he put on their family.

In 1909, Greely privately predicted, "If Cook lies, a terrible retribution awaits him and his children."

Published by Peary, October 13, 1909, this is a copy of Sverdrup's 1903 map on which Cook's two Eskimos drew their 1908 route. ▶

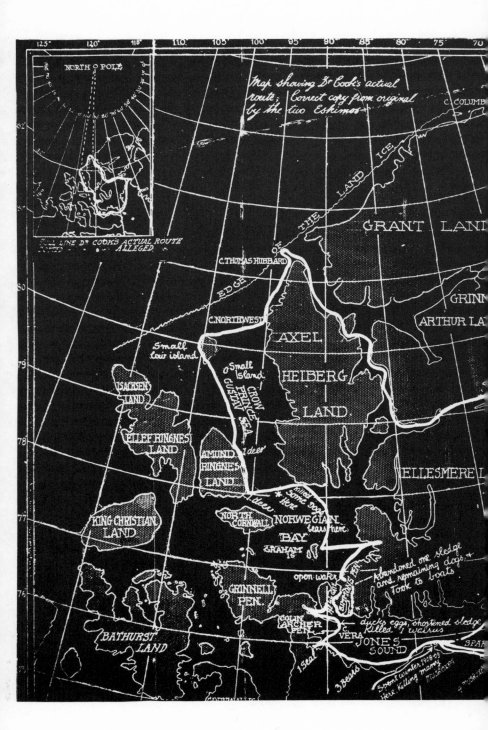

7.   Last Arrow in the Quiver

In early 1909, Peary was almost 53 years old. He knew that this was to be his last expedition, win or lose, "my final chance. . .the last arrow in my quiver." The appeal of the Peary Arctic Club for funds referred to Peary's "final attempt . . .to reach the North Pole." Anything less was unthinkable, unacceptable. Another farthest North now would seem but a stale repeat of 1906, a reiteration of the failures that had already shrunk his backers' fiscal support so drastically that for a while it seemed he might never get another chance. The public too was interested only in a tale of the complete conquest of the Pole; and popular interest — as reflected in book sales and lecture fees — would determine whether, at the end of his career, Peary would be wealthy and famous or broke and forgotten.

A month before his fiftieth birthday in 1906, in an igloo far out on the Polar pack, he was already ". . . planning what I would do when I got back . . . [but] unless I win *here,* all these things fall through. Success is what will give them existence." Though exploration intrigued him, he wanted to go to that unique spot, the North Pole, less for the achievement itself than for its by-products of wealth, fame, and admiration.

No matter how well Peary had planned for success, the chance of failure had to be considered — and of course was — especially in light of the collapse of virtually the same plan in 1906. (Even Peary himself later admitted that the mechanics of his 1909 attempt stood a one-third chance of failure.) Nonetheless, before his last trip, he confided to the Secretary of the

Navy — perhaps revealingly — "I have a strong feeling that if I go North again, I shall accomplish the objects of the expedition. . . ."

Peary's final sendoff was the most auspicious of his career. The very day the Great White Fleet embarked from San Francisco, President Roosevelt at Oyster Bay was bellowing his characteristic blessing upon the ship named for him. Bartlett: "The first thing T.R. said when he came aboard [the *Roosevelt*] was *'Bully!'* in a loud voice."

Staying in Bartlett's cabin at this time was hunter Harry Whitney, later to figure prominently in the Cook affair. After its inspection by the whole Roosevelt family, the vessel steamed North.

The usual stop was made at Etah, Greenland, and last contact with civilization was lost in mid-August. Peary, a man who had come to risk his life for a living, penned his final possibly-last letter to Jo; ". . . I . . . dream of you and my children and my home till I come again. . . ."

Aboard with Peary and Henson were a collection of Eskimo workers and dog drivers and over a dozen score dogs. (Also rats — not in evidence in 1905-1906.) The all-American crew was under Captain Bob Bartlett, and an Anglo-Saxon expedition force consisting of — in addition to Bartlett and Marvin — Bowdoin grad and prep school math instructor Donald MacMillan, young Yaley jock George Borup, and John Goodsell, a doctor from Pennsylvania, and nearly a score of native women for sewing and other services.

The *Roosevelt's* ice-fight up to the Arctic Ocean was so nerve fraying that family man Peary atypically on Aug. 29 forgot his son's birthday (though his book was to report otherwise). After an Eskimo was stopped from striking matches on open dynamite (used for blasting ice) and after the ship was "kicked about by the floes as if she had been a football." Cape Sheridan was at last attained on Sept. 5 (within a quarter hour of the 1905 arrival time), and even temporarily exceeded for a new steamship latitude record, 82° 30'N.

Peary's recent lapse was atoned for on the 12th, his daughter's 15th birthday, as men and ship were dressed for the holiday occasion. Marvin, Borup, and perhaps MacMillan presumably joined in with extra gusto, as their hero-worship of Peary extended to mild crushes on Marie.

However, Borup's interests had been diversifying since arrival in the North. Marvin's diary relates:

> Borup was telling [Commander Peary] how strong one of the little [native] girls was. . . . and [Peary] interrupted him to ask if he was going the rounds with all the women trying their strength. The laugh was on Borup, especially to those of us who have been up here before.

In general, though, awe of Peary made lively conversation easier in his absence.

On October 12, the sun disappeared not to be seen again until next March. Despite the dim and dark months that followed, the isolated little band at the edge of the Polar sea had safe quarters snug in the *Roosevelt*. Bartlett made things a bit too warm in November, when he started a fire in his room, was smoked out, and ended up with a wet room after dousing it.

Part of Marvin's November 22 diary entry is slightly eerie to anyone familiar with the 1909 trip: "I am trying to do a little writing now and Kudlooktoo stands here watching me." Just 139 days remained before one of these two men was to murder the other.

The pre-spring months were spent fattening the dogs on walrus meat and transporting supplies to Camp Crane (named in honor of Zenas Crane, a $10,000 contributor) at Cape Aldrich (83°07'N. lat., 70°W. long.), about 90 miles away, on the northernmost part of Ellesmere Island and the planned takeoff point for the 1909 plunge onto the Arctic Ocean. (Nearby Cape Columbia had a more patriotic label, so Peary always referred to that as his starting camp, a convention followed here as well henceforth.)

This was to be no ordinary hike. Though half the expedition's United States members were amateurs, the prospect of plunging hundreds of miles across the treacherous ice that hid the unknown deeps of the Arctic Ocean was enough to petrify even an old pro like Bartlett, who knew better than the first-timers what was coming. He confided to Henson that he had little expectation of ever returning alive.

Sledges left the *Roosevelt* for Cape Columbia on February 15 Peary left the ship on Washington's birthday, and on the 25th came upon the relay operations still in progress along the route to Camp Crane. MacMillan:

> The great white hills must have wondered what it was all about to see twenty-six men and one hundred and fifty dogs passing and repassing. We shook hands with the Commander and were surprised to hear him say, "Borup, your face is frozen," and, turning to me, "Mac-Millan, your nose is gone." It was there, but as hard as wood. We had no idea it was cold enough for that. In reply to our question, "How cold is it?" he answered, in a matter-of-fact way, "About fifty-seven below."

After supper on February 27, the night before the fatal embarkation, Borup recalled, "the Commander called us all into his igloo and gave us a little talk. . . . He told us he wasn't a believer in hot air, but in action. Said the next six weeks were going to be undiluted hell, the only variation in the monotony being that occasionally it would get worse." Then to cheer up the group he reminded them of the relatively worse travails of the ill-equipped 1900 Italian expedition, one party of which had disappeared forever on the return.

Later, Borup, Marvin, and MacMillan visited Bartlett's igloo and talked and sang college songs and pledged to see Peary to the Pole at any cost. MacMillan wrote: "We wanted him to win, as he deserved to. . . . We were to give him our best, perhaps our hands, our feet, or even our lives as one did. Peary never knew how loyal we were." They shook hands and parted, wondering, noted Borup; "When shall we four meet again?"

On February 28th-March 1st, in the dim Arctic twilight, Henson, Bartlett, Borup, Marvin, MacMillan, Goodsell, Peary, 17 Eskimos, and 140 dogs ahead of 19 sledges shoved off in stages from the ice foot of Cape Columbia onto the frozen surface of the Arctic Ocean and drove roughly North, towards a geometric point 413 miles away.

The plan of travel was a slightly modified version of that which had failed about half-way to the Pole in 1906. As formerly, the 1909 attack was by dog-sledge, with supporting parties to carry supplies and break a trail northward. However, Peary had learned: "The theory of establishing permanent depots for food and relief on the way to the North Pole was entirely shattered by [the 1906] trip. That is all right as long as the ice is firm, but on *moving ice* it is impracticable. . . ." [Emphasis added.] It is well to remember this and similar references when analyzing Peary's ultimate 1909 navigational tale, a tale requiring that the Arctic Ocean's ice stand as still as Joshua's sun, for 36 days straight.

The 1909 strategy called for each supporting party to turn back from the main group, one by one, until a single party, with the pick of freshest men and dogs, was left to go all the way to the Pole. The multi-stage plan was impressive on paper, as it had been in 1906, when its early stages collapsed from overextension. But even without major mishaps, its practical value is questionable. The limits of the supporting party scheme were to be fatally dramatized later in Antarctica, as Scott's massive, many staged 1911-12 expedition to the South Pole apparently failed substantially to better the prior travel schedule of Shackelton's essentially lone four man party.

Another change in Peary's intention, published in May, 1908, stated that an

> essential modification [of the 1906 plan] will be a more rigid massing of my sledge divisions en route, in order to prevent the possibility of a portion of the party being separated from the rest by the movement of the ice, with insufficient supplies for a protracted advance, as happened on the last expedition.

Bob Bartlett on the practical trials of keeping it all together:

> Eskimos get discouraged, sledges break down, fuel

tins leak, dogs die, leads break the trail, and there are the thousand and one minor delays and difficulties which complicate the whole problem.

But despite all, no permanent separations occurred as in 1906. Also from Peary's 1908 hopes:

There is no doubt in my mind that this "big lead" [a wide east-west lane of open water at about 84°-85° north latitude], encountered in both my upward and return marches in my last expedition, is an essentially permanent feature of this part of the Arctic Ocean. I have little doubt of my ability to make this "lead," instead of the north coast of Grant Land, my point of departure with fully loaded sledges. If this is done it will shorten the route to the Pole by nearly one hundred miles and distinctly simplify the proposition.

(In fact, this shortening was only to be about 50 miles.) Peary's plan to use the southern side of the big lead as his 1909 takeoff point was based on his strong 1906 impression that beyond this lane *the motion of the ice was so unpredictably shifty* "that it was impossible to keep up communication" between widely separated parties.

The navigational alteration cited in the 1908 outline is also highly relevant to the key of the 1909 mystery:

. . . leaving the land, my course will be more *west of north* than before, in order to counteract or allow for the easterly set [transverse motion, toward the east] of the ice between the north coast of Grant Land and the Pole, discovered on my last expedition. (emphasis added)

Peary blamed his 1906 failure greatly on not having known of the easterly drift until he was too far advanced on the trip to make much use of the knowledge:

. . . had I known before leaving the land what actual conditions were to the northward, as I know now, I could have so modified my route and my disposition of the sledges that I believe we could have reached the Pole even in spite of the open season.

He was fully prepared, then, to take advantage of his 1906 experience. But on the morning of March 1, 1909, the day his party was to start onto the ice, Peary looked out of his Cape Columbia igloo and saw his plans literally blown to hell:

The wind was from the east — a direction from which I had never known it to blow in all my years of experience in that region. This unusual circumstance, a really remarkable thing, was of course attributed by my Eskimos to the interference of their arch enemy, Tornarsuk — in plain English, the devil — with my plans.

Peary caught up to the lead party, only ten miles out, the same day. For the next two days, the wind continued to blow from east to west (right to left) "with unabated violence." On March 2nd, the first lead of water was encountered. The north side of the broken trail was found on the 3rd, about a mile and a half west of the south side; but Borup's group, returning to land that day for vital supplies, completely missed Peary's outward-bound party because of their relative transverse (east-west or left-right) displacement. On March 4, the wind was completely reversed. The big lead (or what Peary thought was it) was found a little south of 84° north latitude, about 45 miles from land, and a week's delay ensued. Bartlett: "Open water held us up until I thought we'd go crazy, but through it all Peary never lost his head, his temper or his nerve. Peary and I said little to each other. Silence was better." Peary wrote that during this time there was no relative transverse motion of the two sides of the lead (which says nothing whatever about their common drift), while MacMillan wrote in the same period that "this enforced delay, the sight of the big lead, and the very apparent *rapid motion* of the ice, played havoc with the nerves of the Eskimos." (emphasis added)

The party finally crossed over, aiming straight north. Peary left a note advising Marvin, then unaccountably trailing, of this, giving an estimated compass direction for such a course. The next day, a lone, sleepless march by the daring native Seegloo knitted together the forward and rear contin-

101

gents, and the new supplies partly atoned for the lost *week* at the big lead. On March 15 Goodsell, a few Eskimos and a frostbitten MacMillan turned south with orders to lay a food cache about 35 miles *west* of Cape Columbia. (Previously only eastward caches had been considered.)

"We plodded," recalled Bartlett, ". . . north day after day with the ice twisting and changing, now rough, now smooth." On the 18th, Bartlett nearly tore his jugular vein while accidentally falling on his pickaxe. The next day, according to Borup's account; "He attacked a large mass of ice which blocked the trail. The pick glanced from the ice and cut through the outside of his kamik, slightly damaging his big toe. An inch more and the pick would have gone through his foot."

On March 20, at about 85°23'N. lat., Borup turned back, carrying orders to place a cache *over 80 miles west* of Cape Columbia. Plainly, Peary no longer had confidence in his original 1908 directional plan. Since this has a critical bearing on Peary's entire claim, it would be of interest to know just what course Peary set beyond 84° north latitude. Strangely enough, nothing of the matter appears throughout Peary's lengthy writings and 1911 Congressional testimony on the trip, even when elucidation was specifically called for.

As the expedition moved along, the trail was hewn and course set largely by Bartlett and/or Henson. A few soundings were taken by Marvin, pieces of wires being lost in the process. Bartlett recalled the frustrations:

On the 22nd I made a good march of fifteen miles. It was hard going at first through rough ice. The Eskimos complained a lot but they got relief by breaking the sledges and delaying our march. I kept my temper, however, as we were all working hard and keyed up and not getting much rest. I realized what a stake we were striving for and that the Eskimos could not be expected to understand it all. I could walk easily three miles an hour on snow-shoes and many times I found myself almost 20 miles ahead of them. Then I would return and find them repairing a sledge. This meant a rest for them.

The next-to-last supporting party was that of Marvin, who, on March 22, determined from a noon solar altitude observation, a latitude of 85°48′N. On March 25, he similarly got 86°38′N.; next day, he headed back for land. Before reaching it, however, one of his Eskimo companions murdered him (a fact hushed up until 1926) for reasons never explained to the satisfaction of MacMillan, among others.

Bartlett, Peary, Henson, and six Eskimos continued north. On March 28 and 29, open water made travel impossible, and the parties' igloos — only 100 yards apart — *suffered such drastic transverse drift* from the motion of "our treacherous antagonist — the ice" — that Peary feared a serious separation of the two parties. Here, at a position Peary specified as 87°15′N., 70°W., Bartlett took a sounding, getting 1260 fathoms without touching bottom. It is interesting to note that the best estimate of the depth at this point, according to the most recent Arctic bathymetric maps is not deeper but shallower than this figure.

On March 31, Peary initiated one of his most critical moves: he told Bartlett he would have to turn south the next day. As events at this juncture have been sweetened up in many accounts, it may be enlightening to try to report them as they occurred. Peary wrote in his 1910 book merely that, toward the end of Bartlett's last march, the Captain

> was very sober and anxious to go farther; but the program was for him to go back from here in command of the fourth supporting party, and we did not have supplies enough for an increase in the main party. The food which he and his two Eskimos and dog teams would have consumed between this point and the Pole, on the upward and return journeys, might mean that we would all starve before we could reach the land again.

The fact is that Peary's and Bartlett's parties parted on April 1 carrying virtually *the same* amount of food per man (enough for about 40 days).

This seems to have been accidentally provident, since both reached land about the same time. But there was, one presumes, no way of knowing on April 1 that Peary's return would be so quick. Accepting Peary's version: someone was to be sent back, and the only question was, who? Peary tried later to explain that if he had sent Henson south instead of Bartlett, the former might not have made it:

> . . . while Henson was more useful to me than any other member of my expedition when it came to traveling with my last party over the Polar ice, he would not have been so competent as the least experienced of my white companions in getting himself and his party back to the land. If Henson had been sent back with one of the supporting parties from a distance far out on the ice, and if he had struck conditions similar to those which we had to face on the return journey in 1906, he and his party would never have reached the land. While faithful to me, and when *with me* more effective in covering distance with a sledge than any of the others, he had not as a racial inheritance the daring and initiative of my Anglo-Saxon friends. I owed it to him not to subject him to dangers and responsibilities with which he was temperamentally unequal to cope.

Certain rather dated aspects of the foregoing may divert one from its other curiosities. After all, if Henson had pioneered the early marches in 1906 and some of the northward marches in 1909, then he could do all right on his own. His only trouble lay in not knowing precise astronomical navigation, which is what Peary's reference to the '06 dangers means; but, since Bartlett was given neither instruments nor astronomical tables for the return, what difference would that make? As to relative endurance for the final kick northward: Bartlett was a decade younger than the aging Henson. For the final 1909 group, one more strong fellow like Bartlett — a good dogman, anyhow — could have only helped the group.

A New York *Herald* account of a September, 1909, interview with Bartlett reported him "arguing, begging, almost quarrelling . . ." with Peary on April 1. Maintaining that he "didn't know that [he] was not going to the Pole until the last moment," Bartlett declared:

I really didn't think I would have to go back. . . . Then the Commander said I must go back — that he had decided to take Matt Henson.

. . . It was a bitter disappointment. I got up early the next morning while the rest were asleep and started north alone. I don't know, perhaps I cried a little. I guess perhaps I was just a little crazy then. I thought that perhaps I could walk on the rest of the way alone. It seemed so near.

Here I had come thousands of miles, and it was only a little more than a hundred more to the Pole.

The Commander figured on five marches more, and it seemed as if I could make it alone even if I didn't have any dogs or food or anything. I felt so strong I went along for five miles or so, and then I came to my senses and knew I must go back.

They were up at the camp and getting ready to start. Never mind whether there were any words or not. I told the Commander if I was going to be any hindrance and perhaps make a failure out of it, I would turn around and go back. He said I must go; so I had to do it. But my mind had been set on it for so long I had rather die than give it up then. When I started on the back trail I couldn't believe it was really true at first, and I kind of went on in a daze.

Peary's published account of Bartlett's actions at this point provides some interesting comparisons: "After about four hours' sleep, I turned everyone out at five in the morning. . . . After breakfast Bartlett started to walk five or six miles to the north in order to make sure of reaching the 88th parallel." Odd. If the jaunt was cleared with Peary, why didn't Bartlett take a light sledge with dogs to save time? Peary later recounted the Bartlett affair before a Congressional hearing:

Bartlett never had any idea that he was going to the Pole with me, so far as I know. He never had any reason for any such idea. At Columbia I told Bartlett that, God willing, I hoped he would assist me in getting to the Pole beyond the farthest of Abruzzi, and Bartlett knew I

105

meant it. It was on what he counted. On the last march Bartlett, as he and I were walking along to make the last part of that march, said: "Commander, I would like to go all the way with you, if it can be so arranged." It struck me as a most natural thing for him to have said. I said: "Bartlett, there is no man in the world I would like to have with me more than you, but we have to carry out the program. I would rather you would turn back from the next camp, as proposed," or words to that effect. If you doubt the exact words, Bartlett can probably repeat them to you.

In 1935 Peary believer Edward A. Reeves reported, however reservedly, quite a different version to London listeners. Shocked British gentlemen heard Bartlett's profanity as he "told me . . . that he had no special cause to love Peary for leaving him behind and not letting him go on the last lap with him." Aboard the *Roosevelt,* in September, 1909, Bartlett admitted to a visitor that "Peary had promised him before the expedition started that he would be his companion on the last lap to the Pole, if they got anywhere near." Peary's program and Henson's qualities are the reasons most often cited for Bartlett's return. However, presumably in desperation, Peary tried to divert the Congressmen with yet other plausible excuses:

I have always made my final spurt work up there, with the one exception (when Lee was with me [and Henson, in 1895] across the Greenland ice cap) with one man and the Eskimos. The reason for this has been stated in the book, that the man I took with me was more effective for the combined demands of extended work than any white man I have ever had with me, but perhaps, what you want in a way is this:
The pole was something to which I had devoted my life; it was a thing on which I had concentrated everything, on which I had expended some of myself, for which I had gone through such hell and suffering as I hope no man in this room may ever experience, and in which I had put money, time, and everything else, and I

106

did not feel that under those circumstances I was called upon to divide with a man who, no matter how able and deserving he might be, was a young man and had only put a few years in that kind of work and who had, frankly as I believed, not the right that I had to it. I think that conveys my idea.

It does indeed — and Peary put this more succinctly when asked why he had not taken a white witness along: "Because after a lifetime of effort I dearly wanted the honor for myself. . . . [of being] the only white man who has ever reached the North Pole. . . ."

When pondering our latest 1909 coincidence, that Peary turned back exactly as many supporting parties as he had educated witnesses, one realizes the obvious. More such men should have been brought along in the first place. The heavy reliance, for witnesses, on illiterate savages in itself places the 1906 and 1909 claims of Peary (and Cook's 1908 one) in a uniquely peculiar category.

It might be supposed that the Eskimos were preferred for the expedition because of their strength. Actually, both Borup and MacMillan could beat the strongest native, Ootah — who eventually went to "the Pole" — at the Eskimos' own strength test sports. Besides, the Eskimos were, in Borup's words, ". . . scared to death of the sea ice, with the possibility of going through young ice or of their getting blown to they don't know where. They were not interested in his [Peary's] getting the Pole." Bartlett reports constant slacking by the natives. Even the famous Ootah was "a quitter and a troublemaker," said MacMillan. The Eskimos' sole advantage, an important one to be sure, lay in their experience at dog-driving; a skill that can, however, be quickly acquired to a remarkable degree, as novices Borup and MacMillan were to prove.

Whatever Peary's excuse, at 3 P.M. on April 1, Bartlett headed back as ordered, with two Eskimos, one sled, 18 or 19 dogs, and "just enough [food] for 40 days," leaving Peary with enough for 40 or 50 days. Peary, Henson, four Eskimos, five sleds, and 40 dogs were ready to set out on April 2 across the ice northward with, as they hoped, only 133 miles to go, to

107

the North Pole. The estimate of remaining *forward* distance was Bartlett's, who, like Marvin, had taken a solar altitude at Cape Columbia noon before turning back. (The Captain's quick arithmetic gave latitude 87°47′ — or colatitude 2°13′ = 133′ = 133 nautical miles.) The month of accumulated *transverse* wander (off the Columbia meridian) — which would tell how far left or right Peary must swerve to aim towards the Pole — was *still* unknown and exercised a curious lack of fascination on the usually provident Peary. But, on April 1, the mysteries were just commencing. Bartlett was now out of sight. As Peary critic Captain Thomas Hall put it; "All Fool's day, 1909, marked the beginning of an epoch in arctic history."

Robert A. Bartlett in the summer of 1908

8.   April Fool

From April 2 to April 5, Peary's party drove northward
over ice, Henson recollected as being little different from that
encountered earlier (beyond the big lead). Peary said otherwise: "We encountered no difficult [pressure ridges] in our
later marches to the Pole that I recall now." It is amazing how
suddenly things got better after April 1. The very first march
(April 2); "going was the best we had since leaving land."
Bartlett, who had walked five to seven miles of this ice the
previous day, later tried to support Peary's report by saying
that it was "like Pennsylvania Avenue." However, his April 1
certificate, written just after the walk, says flatly, "The going
fair."

On April 3, Peary admitted that pickaxing through
pressure ridges "delayed us a little." But midnight, April 3-4:
"The weather and the going were even better than the day
before. The surface of the ice, except as interrupted by in-
frequent pressure ridges, was as level as the glacial fringe . . .
and harder." April 4: "the going was the same . . . we came
upon a lead running north and south, and . . . we traveled on
it for two hours, the dogs galloping along and reeling off the
miles in a way that delighted my heart." April 5: "The going
was even better than before."

Those supposedly easy days left a different impression on
Henson. "We marched and marched," he recalled, "falling
down in our tracks repeatedly, until it was impossible to go
on." Like Peary on another occasion during the final dash, he
had had the misfortune to fall into the icy water. Henson's

day-by-day account portrays more of the same hard struggling over the ice that characterized earlier parts of the journey. After recording an estimated 20 miles in 18 hours' sledging on April 2, Henson logged:

> April 3 was another glorious day. . . . The ice was so rough and jagged that we had to use our *pickaxes constantly* to cut a trail. A great many leads were encountered but we had no difficulty in crossing them. . .
> On April 4 and 5, the monotony of the trail was unbroken by any incident of importance. There was *the same laborious struggle over pressure-ridges,* the same detour to the *east or west* to avoid crossing a lead or the same skilful manipulation of the sledges in going directly across the *running* water. (Emphasis added.)

Henson, in his first written account, nowhere even hints that the going improved just after Bartlett's return, recording that "conditions were much better" only on April 6, when he felt that they covered thirty miles. Peary directly argued the matter of speed in his book *The North Pole:*

> Many laymen have wondered why we were able to travel faster after the sending back of each of the supporting parties, especially after the last one. To any man experienced in the handling of troops this will need no explanation. The larger the party and the greater the number of sledges, the greater is the chance of breakages or delay for one reason or another. A large party cannot be forced as rapidly as a small party.
> Take a regiment, for instance. The regiment could not make as good an average daily march for a number of forced marches as could a picked company of that regiment. The picked company could not make as good an average march for a number of forced marches as could a picked file of men from that particular company; and this file could not make the same average for a certain number of forced marches that the fastest traveler in the whole regiment could make.
> So that, with my party reduced to five picked men,

every man, dog, and sledge under my individual eye, myself in the lead, and all recognizing that the moment had now come to let ourselves out for all there was in us, we naturally bettered our previous speed.

Peary's arguments on party size and delay from broken sledges work more against than for him, especially so since his proclaimed mode of operation was for the expedition to travel in small separate parties (three men in each after March 20). For the 67 miles from Marvin's return up to April Fool Camp, Bartlett's three-man group had led and traveled *at its own pace* with far fewer sledges than Peary's six-man, five-sledge party took after April 1. Moreover, according to Peary's own plan, Bartlett's sledges were intentionally lightened to ease the burden of trailbreaking. In Peary's own words, ". . . the advance party with its light sledges. . . was the pacemaker of the expedition." But Bartlett's April 1 certificate mentioned that *all* five of the final party sledges were fully loaded. It would therefore stand to reason that Bartlett's light little group should have covered that 67 miles at a faster pace than Peary's bulkier party could later proceed, especially as about ten percent of the former distance was over the only stretch of level going on the entire poleward march. (Indeed, 57 miles of it were pretty smooth.) Appreciably longer time per day on the trail now was out of the question, since already the ordinary day's march was 14 or 15 hours. In fact, the April 2-6 march times were rather shorter, about ten to twelve hours.

Peary speaks of picked men and how "Every man and dog of us was as lean and flat-bellied as a board, and as hard." His theory had been "to work the supporting parties to the limit, in order to keep the main party fresh. . . ." Which, he assumed, should enable him to better the pace of a tired Bartlett. Good theory perhaps; but Peary was in fact a 53-year-old cripple, most of his toes having been amputated, and for all his vigorous talk of now taking his proper place in the lead and "Whatever pace I set, the others would make good . . .", he was, in fact, virtually a dead weight on the expedition by this time. According to Henson, "He [Peary] because of his

111

crippled feet, [rode] on the sledges the greater part of the journey [north] as he did upon the return . . . He was heavy for the dogs to haul. . . . We knew he could walk but little in rough ice."

By April 6, the six-man party, sledging a heavy load (including Peary) had gone five marches in less than five days. Compared with the pace set by the smaller Bartlett group — five marches in six days to cover 67 miles — it figures that Peary's party could hardly have exceeded 75 miles at the very outside, which would have put him, at best, no farther north than 89°, sixty miles and about four days short of the Pole, even neglecting transverse wander. Lest it seem that 15 miles per day is rather slow, remember that Bartlett's pacemaking team barely made 12. To appreciate the cause of this apparent slowness, read of the difficulties encountered, as described by Peary himself:

> . . . pressure ridges may be anywhere from a few feet to a few rods in height; they may be anywhere from a few rods to a quarter of a mile in width; the individual masses of ice of which they are composed may vary, respectively, from the size of a billiard ball to the size of a small house.
>
> Going over these pressure ridges one must pick his trail as best he can, often hacking his way with pickaxes, encouraging the dogs by whip and voice to follow the leader, lifting the five-hundred-pound loaded sledges over hummocks and up acclivities whose difficulties sometimes seem likely to tear the muscles from one's shoulder blades.
>
> Between the pressure ridges are the old floes, more or less level. . . . These fields of ice are anywhere from less than twenty to more than one hundred feet in thickness, and they are of all shapes and sizes. As a result of the constant movement of the ice during the brief summer, when great fields are driven hither and thither under the impulse of the wind and the tides — impinging against one another, splitting in two from the violence of contact with large fields, crushing up the thinner ice between

112

them, having their edges shattered and piled up into pressure ridges — the surface of the Polar sea during the winter may be one of almost unimaginable unevenness and roughness.

At least nine-tenths of the surface of the Polar sea between Cape Columbia and the Pole is made up of these floes.

Read, too, of the conditions Nansen had found a decade earlier at his farthest North (86°N., 97°E.) in one of the deepest parts of the Arctic and as far from land as Peary got. (Some have argued that rough ice is a major problem only near land — whereas, in fact, it is pretty uniform, on the average, beyond the big lead.) Nansen:

We hardly made four miles yesterday. Lanes, ridges, and endless rough ice, it looks like an endless moraine of ice-blocks; and this continual lifting of the sledges over every irregularity is enough to tire out giants.

Clearly, travel in these regions is not exactly a holiday jaunt, as Congressmen were asked to believe at the Peary hearings. Many of Peary's own photos are evidence to that, and so are his words: ". . . oftentimes . . . the heavily loaded sledges [must be] pushed, pulled, hoisted, and lowered over hummocks and steep acclivities, even unloaded, and the equipment carried over on one's back." Aerial photographs taken at the Pole by National Geographic President Gilbert H. Grosvenor in 1953 show an average of five major ridges every mile.

Whatever the explanation, Peary waited until well beyond the halfway mark before locating himself transversely, for the first time in 1909, on the memorable days of April 6-7. It is a fantastic irony — though no coincidence, as will be seen — that this time, which history has recorded as the days of Peary's conquest, was, in fact, that of his greatest disappointment.

A glance at the expedition's marching schedule within Peary's narrative reveals that its basic unit beyond 84½°N. latitude was five marches. Goodsell and MacMillan returned from Camp #7, Borup from #12, Marvin from #17, Bartlett from #22. Observations had been made from the last two, so Camp #27 (Camp Jesup) was the next camp for observations, five marches after Camp #22. April 1 + 5 = 6: Thus was history actually determined!

If Peary really intended to reach the Pole in those five marches as he must later claim — it seems strange that the last sentence of Bartlett's April 1 certificate should read "At the same average as our last eight marches Commander Peary should reach the Pole in eight days." Odd that Peary would not have corrected that. Ah, but not really. One must look again at the narrative: Peary just happened to decide on doing five extra long marches to the Pole *right* after Bartlett's departure. Well, that clears up that. Back to reality: obviously, Peary had intended to go the five-march run, the established unit, and then take observations for forward *and* transverse position — well short of the Pole.

Peary's later, published account of his April 1 plan reads: ". . . five marches of at least twenty-five miles each. . . [ending with] an immediate latitude observation." Since the distance per march mentioned would put him virtually at the Pole, this part of the plan has to be an invented afterthought: no one would seriously plan to postpone navigational observations until *at* the very place he was using them to find! Not only is this self-evident, but it is corroborated by Peary's own diary of April 1: "Eight marches [Bartlett's figure, too, recall] same average as our last eight, or eight equal to the three from 85°48, or six like yesterday's will do the trick." So he naturally had planned his next observations to be some marches short of the Pole — which, aside from transverse wander effects, is obviously just about the way it turned out.

Incidentally, Peary's plan of making five rushed marches right to the Pole just in time for a noon observation is without any navigational merit. (As one nears the Pole, noon — i.e., the local time of the mean sun's transit — becomes increasingly indistinct.) Worse, the alleged rearrangement of the sleeping schedule for April 2-6 for this purpose would necessitate travel *into* the sun and thereby invite snowblindness and

114

poor steering. Moreover, all of Henson's writings refer to the April 6 arrival as being in the *evening* (10:30 P.M.) rather than morning. Peary marks the time of arrival as 10 A.M., a differential of more than 12 hours. (The lapse was essential to Peary's account of his extensive activities at the Pole.)

Camp Jesup was prepared there and, of course, observations were contemplated before sleep. However, Henson recalls: "The sun being obscured by the mist, it was impossible to make observations and tell whether or not we had actually reached the Pole, so the only thing we could do was to crawl into our igloos and go to sleep." At this point Peary, without telling Henson, prepared to leave camp and go out of sight to make observations. Henson, learning of this from the Eskimos, reported that on the morning of April 7,

... Commander Peary set out with ... two Eskimos and one sledge with a tin of pemmican and instruments, leaving me repairing a sledge and in charge of the camp. *In about an hour* the Commander returned. I can make observations but of course I did not meddle at this time.

The Eskimos and I had plenty of work to do in repairing the sledges, which had suffered from our rapid marches over untried roads.

The Commander waited with impatience for the hour of noon to arrive, and then began to make his observations. These were made at *three* different points, and while he was at work on his calculations, we were detailed to reconnoitre in different directions for the purpose of ascertaining if any land could be seen.

The results of the first observations showed that we had figured out the distance very accurately, for when the Flag was hoisted over the geographical centre of the earth, it was located *just behind our igloos.* Observations taken later in the day showed that the Flag should be placed about a hundred and fifty yards to the westward of the first position — on account of the continual eastward movement of the ice. [Emphasis added.]

By comparison, Peary's account would seem to describe

115

events on another planet altogether. The mists Henson referred to on April 6 do *not* prevent an observation Peary allegedly took a little after noon. Peary's action-packed hour with the two Eskimos permits a jaunt to a point he estimated to be ten miles beyond camp, a midnight observation there, *and* a trip back. After an observation (the first one *yet* for transverse position) at 6 A.M. on the 7th, Peary supposedly took a second side trip, going eight miles to the right, perpendicular to the original incoming path. This is all methodically neat: observation for forward distance to the Pole, and a forth and back thrust; then 6 A.M. (transverse) observation for distance to Pole, followed by transverse jog. Thus the trip out of sight was innocent after all. Of course, the first observation and the second jaunt never happened, according to Henson's account. And the first dash naturally makes no sense before the critical transverse observation. (If he was out in left field, there was no use going *further* out.)

Peary, by his version, returns from trip number two in time to make the April 7 noon observation Henson describes. Peary ordered preparations for these last at 10 or 10:30 A.M., only about four hours after the morning observations and his *16-mile* round trip. Such speed — so quick Henson never even saw Peary move at all.

It is difficult innocently to explain why Peary's April 7 noon sextant work required *three* different sites, off by himself. There is no possible navigational value to such a procedure, when using, as Peary did, a mercury artificial horizon. This report, along with that of Henson's being ordered to move the Pole flag a distance not possibly determinable by observation suggests the picture of a leader trying to avoid his companion's over the shoulder gaze.

The observations Henson remembers after noon of the 7th are never mentioned by Peary. And Peary's account places the Pole about four or five miles away, not "just behind our igloos." Though clear on Marvin's and Bartlett's solar observations' positional results, none of Henson's writings *ever* give Peary's alleged Camp Jesup figures.

Henson recorded times that seem to place the first trans-

116

verse observation as the one taken out of sight beyond camp. Whenever it was taken, it probably indicated to Peary that he was at least a week away from the Pole, which would have to be approached now at a sharp angle (see Fig.   ) with respect to the previous trail, and the return would either be equally circuitous or partly over an unbroken route.

Peary's provisions had been, five days previously, "ample for forty days," perhaps "fifty days if it came to a pinch." Whether or not this was comforting (or is trustworthy) is ambiguous, inasmuch as Peary mentioned the shortage of rations as a factor in his decision to send Bartlett back on April 1. Likewise, Marvin told Borup at 85°23′N. that he (Marvin) "wasn't hoping for . . . [the good luck to go all the way to the Pole], as there wasn't food enough." Peary's pre-Camp Jesup pondering of the possible necessity of a light sledge dash starting April 6 also intimates a close situation. Peary's uninterrupted return made it appear later that such fears were needless, but he had, on April 6-7, no way of judging the future except by the past — and *that* was enough to scare anybody.

In 1906, Peary had very nearly starved to death on his return, over a far shorter distance, while waiting for the big lead to freeze over (to allow crossing). His accounts of this harrowing episode are filled with morbid terror: though referring to the lead as the Hudson River when he encountered it going north, on the desperate return he came to think of its broad, dark expanse as the Styx. Drifting eastward helplessly for *five* days,

> . . . we lay in this dismal camp, watching the distant southern ice beyond which lay the world, all that was near and dear, and perhaps life itself, while on our side was only the wide-stretching ice and possibly a lingering death. . . .
>
> Each day the number of my dogs dwindled and sledges were broken up to cook those of the animals that we ate. . . . One day leads formed entirely around the ice on which we were, making it an island of two or three miles in diameter.

117

A first attempt at crossing on half-formed ice ended in retreat and near-disaster. It was now into early May and warm weather would soon open more and more leads that would make further progress impossible. May 6 marked his 50th birthday. On May 7 the worst tides of the year were at their peak. Finally, in preference to sitting and waiting for death, the desperate party was forced to risk crossing ice far too young to be trustworthy:

> Frankly, I do not care for more similar experiences. . . from every man as he slid a snowshoe forward, undulations went out in every direction through the thin film incrusting the black water. . . . It was the first and only time in all my Arctic work that I felt doubtful as to the outcome. . . .
>
> I was the heaviest one in the party — 160 pounds, net . . . fortunately I had six-foot snowshoes. Yet for a considerable part of the distance I doubted if I should ever reach the firm ice.

The Styx re-opened just after the men had inched across. For all they knew, it might not have closed again until next winter.

The big lead had delayed the 1909 expeditioners a full week, even in winter, when they were outward bound. Just north of 87°N. a six-mile-wide lead had barely frozen before their arrival, and all the way to 88°N. was thin. What would this young ice be like going back? Peary later was to write:

> Every day we gained on the return lessened the chances of the trail being destroyed by high winds shifting the ice. There was one region just about the 87th parallel, a region about fifty-seven miles wide, which gave me a great deal of concern until we had passed it. Twelve hours of strong wind blowing from any quarter excepting the North would have turned that region into *an open sea.* [Emphasis added.]

What better way to gain days than to start homeward early? Who could count on the return good luck eventually in fact encountered at the 87°-88°N. thin ice? Peary certainly didn't as can be seen from his April 11 account:

Despite the expectation of trouble with which we began this march, we were agreeably disappointed. On the upward journey, all this region had been covered with young ice, and we thought it reasonable to expect open water here, or at the best that the trail would have been obliterated; but there had not been enough movement of the ice to break the trail. So far there had been no lateral - east and west - [transverse] movement of the ice. This was the great, fortunate, natural feature of the home trip, and the principal reason why we had so little trouble. We stopped for lunch at the "lead" igloos, and as we finished our meal the ice opened behind us. We had crossed just in time. Here we noticed some fox tracks that had just been made. The animal was probably disturbed by our approach. These are the most northerly animal tracks ever seen.

Peary's diary entry of April 5 shows his "constant and increasing dread" of wide leads stopping progress north. One can just imagine his feelings at the thought of being stopped on the return! And, of course, a delay from a lead at, for example, 88°-87°, while returning, could start a lethally cumulative chain reaction of such delays, since delay itself would cause the party to face warmer weather, and thus *more* leads and ensuing delay. The last possible moment for retreat would not be known beforehand, but the critical, unstable nature of the time element was obvious. In this respect, the situation is much like that of the fan who wants to leave a close ball game before the last out in order to beat the traffic, except that life or death hung in the balance.

The sudden temporary rise in temperature on April 6 from about −25°F. to −11°F. must have worried Peary as he took such behavior in the thermometer to indicate open water nearby. Though eleven below zero seems cold enough to temate zone man, it was virtually the highest reading observed thus far on the trip and had a special significance to the Polar man. Explorer-physicist Green's biography of Peary described the southward return in 1909; "With each day the temperature average would rise imperceptibly higher as the run rose [in declination]. And there was a point around minus twelve where sea-ice would not freeze solid enough to bear the marchers. That could mean but one thing — the thing so barely escaped in 1906 — starvation."

With spring's warm weather coming on, Peary wondered what the Styx would be like going back, especially in late April as the full moon approached with its tides, opening leads which, so far on into spring, might never refreeze?

It will be remembered, doubtless, that the greatest dangers of the expedition of 1905-06 were encountered not upon the upward journey, *but in the course of our return* from our farthest North over the Polar ice, for it was then that we encountered the implacable "big lead" whose perils so nearly encompassed the destruction of the entire party. And it will be further remembered that even after the big lead was safety crossed and we had barely managed to stagger ashore upon the inhospitable edge of northernmost Greenland we escaped starvation only by the narrowest possible margin.

Memories of this narrow escape were, therefore, in the minds of every member of our little party. . .and I dare say that every one of us wondered whether a similar experience were in store for us. We had found the Pole. Should we return to tell the story? Before we hit the trail I had a brief talk with the men of the party and made them understand that it was essential that we should reach the land *before the next spring tides*. [Emphasis added.]

There is the key to the temptation for turning back short of the goal. To prevent the risk of again finding himself adrift in a lethally lead-filled ice field, Peary had to get back in about three weeks. The full moon he dreaded was due early in May, about the time of near disaster in 1906. So, if reaching the Pole would require another week, he would have but two weeks to return, over a 400-mile trail not yet completed in five weeks of travel. Every single step taken farther out on the ice actually committed Peary to two steps, for extra miles north meant extra miles on the return. The common argument that, at Bartlett's turnaround, Peary was virtually at his goal should be read not only in this light, but also with an awareness that from the April 1 Camp to the Pole and back to land was about 550 miles — *twice* Bartlett's return distance.

It is noteworthy that, though much of Peary's book *The North Pole* was an incorporation of his magazine articles, the following highly revealing passage on thoughts during the return was, despite its dramatic appeal, largely tamed in the book. The original version:

> . . .we were approaching a region just above the 87th parallel, which gave me serious uneasiness. I knew, from what I had seen going up [northward, end of March] that the ice there was so light in character that a few hours of strong wind from the west, east, or south would send the ice all abroad and leave a stretch of open water perhaps fifty miles wide, with only scattered cakes of ice. Much of the ice there was so young that it would have crushed under the influence of the wind, for it had been all open water not long previous to our going north [over it]. This may sound like a simple geographical statement; but when one considers that that region, about twice as wide as the widest part of Long Island Sound, lay between a party of human beings, with scanty supplies and no boat, and the land - it will be understood that the question as to the condition of that stretch of ice was one to cause some anxiety.

If it was a memorable experience being stopped (1906) by a few miles of open water at 84° North latitude (big lead), then just try to imagine waiting on the bad side of 50 miles of it — at 87°-88° North latitude — almost 300 miles from land! Peary wisely believed that "one should never feel encouraged at anything nor ever expect anything in these regions except the worst." If the trail to land were lost, as in 1906, the return could hardly be much faster than the trip out. It was to happen, by good fortune, that the return was under much

121

better conditions than could be anticipated (marches taking 40% less time than northward trail breaking), and Peary even gives the impression that the going was rather easy. However, Henson, who did not ride, speaks of "... a horrid nightmare ... We crossed lead after lead ... balancing on cake after cake of ice. ..."

As if dangers from the climate were not enough, the unpredictable Eskimos (also haunted by '06 memories, as Peary had learned before the trip from their wives), worn by weeks of virtual slave labor on unaccustomed rations, had been complaining of the cold:

> ...and at every camp fixed their fur clothing about their faces, waists, knees, and wrists. They also complained of their noses, which I had never known them to do before.

This was a deadly serious matter (worse, perhaps, than Peary knew), indicating, in men accustomed to far colder weather, an incipient health breakdown. Accepting the eventual official account of Marvin's murder at the hands of his Eskimo companions, it seems likely that the Eskimos' stability was partly upset by wear and rationing of food and water. Henson's description of the four Eskimos on their return to land gives one some idea: "lean, gaunt faces, seamed and wrinkled, the faces of old men. ..." Half of them were — as subsequent events were to show — quite capable of murder. At Camp Jesup even the trusting Henson began acting possessive about his rifle, the only one in the party.

Under extreme conditions, an intelligent explorer will always turn back, no matter how close he may be to his goal. Shackleton's 1908-09 dash apparently took him roughly seven-eighths of the way to the South Pole, within 100 miles — but he turned back and survived; and Scott's death in 1912, eleven miles short of a saving depot, after a journey of about 1400 miles, proved his predecessor's wisdom. Had Scott turned back just five miles short of the Pole, he might have lived. Peary, like Shackleton (who never lost a man) and the early Amundsen, had the knack of bringing his men and himself back alive. "The more dramatic the expedition, the less efficient the leader," was a familiar Peary motto. Though assuring the reader of an innate confidence of returning, Peary admits knowing "that there was a *possibility* that we might end our lives up there, and that our conquest of the unknown spaces and silences of the Polar void might remain forever unknown to the world we had left behind." The thought of winning the Pole at the cost of not returning for the renown the conquest would bring him must have been galling, especially beside a mental picture of Cook's winning the fame without the effort.

Peary in 1906 had already refused to commit suicide for the North Pole, for reasons (excepting, perhaps, food and dogs) very similar to those of April 7, 1909. We recall his account of April 21, 1906:

> . . .as I looked at the drawn faces of my comrades, . . . and remembered the drifting ice over which we had come and the unknown quantity of the big lead between us and the nearest land, I felt that I had cut the margin as narrow as could reasonably be expected. I told my men we should turn back from here.

A genuine 1909 diary might have read, as did that of April 21, 1902 (the Western Hemisphere farthest North):

> The game is off. My dream of. . .years is ended. . . . I have made the best fight, I knew. I believe it has been a good one. But I cannot accomplish the impossible.

No reasonable person could fault Peary for turning back in 1909 in the face of the odds and in an increasingly exposed and excruciatingly precarious situation. But Peary knew that he was not returning to a reasonable public: American readers by now wanted nothing less than the Pole, and he needed their acclaim and their funds to escape an old age in the obscure semi-poverty of an also-ran. Such were the terrible factors that Peary faced as he pondered his future for an hour or so, out beyond Camp Jesup and the sight of Henson. "I had many sensations that made sleep impossible for hours, despite my utter fatigue — the sensations of a lifetime. . . ."

After getting the party started back, Peary became, in Henson's words, "practically a dead weight," and rode on the sledges. The return, being largely over the upward trail and with lighter loads, was swifter by a factor of five/thirds, and land was reached early on April 23. The happy swiftness of the return must surely have set him wondering (as even in 1906) whether "I might have done more and yet got back . . ." The thought must have haunted him to the day he died.

Left, Matthew Henson, and right, Ross Marvin, both photos taken in the summer of 1908.

9. Miraculum in Vacuo

Peary to the Secretary of the Navy (April 6, 1907):

The point of view of the Peary Arctic Club is that Arctic exploration at the present time should combine in intimate coordination the attainment of the Pole as a matter of national prestige and the securing of *all scientific information* and material possible from the regions surrounding the Pole. (Emphasis added)

A self-sustained trip to and from the North Pole by dog-sledge without return depots is, as we have seen, more than just a formidable feat. No one before or after 1909 has ever come anywhere near its accomplishment. Peary himself in 1902 called it "the impossible."

When a person claims to have performed such a unique journey, miraculously unique navigationally, is it reasonable to believe and officially accept the assertion only until it is *dis*proved, as explorers' self-serving etiquette decrees? Obviously, it is not only proper science but simple common sense to do precisely the opposite: to demand not just proof, but, for "the impossible," unusually compelling and complete proof. Let us see what in fact the situation has been regarding the Peary 1909 claim.

Down through the years, believers in Peary have wallowed in apologia trying to explain away their hero's failure to supply convincing evidence of his career's crowning achievement. When someone goes to a place no one else has previously been and returns with the expectation of being rewarded for his achievement, he at least ought to have taken along competent witnesses. A more enduring certification would be the description of a specific characteristic of the spot that was previously unknowable.

Since the North Pole is unoccupied by land and there is only Arctic sea ice to describe, it seemed inevitable to many observers that the world would just have to accept a claimant's word that he got there. Peary himself was aware of this dangerous popular misconception, and, with Cook on the loose in the Arctic, suddenly it began bothering him. Hearing inside word of Cook's fake climb of Mount McKinley, Peary in 1908 requested of the Explorers Club that "in the event of Dr. Cook's returning and claiming to have found the North Pole, proper proofs would be demanded of him. . . ." Peary could hardly expect Cook alone to be the object of doubt. With a dispute likely, both men should have sought hard evidence more assiduously than most explorers. Instead, both ended up returning with less proof than any other adventurer of the time would have dared to try getting away with.

Peary knew the odds were substantial that his final expedition would fail. But this would be more difficult for the world to learn, the less the evidence available for evaluation. Therefore it is interesting that even before starting onto the ice, Peary had made decisions which destroyed two out of the three possible main proofs (thus potential *dis*proofs) of his Polar claim by taking inadequate sounding equipment and taking to the Pole no companion who knew navigation. (He could hardly have left behind his sextant, theodolite and compass, since without them he would have been lost. So, if failure forced a hoax, the lack of magnetic data would just have to be blustered through.)

Most of the explorers of the early twentieth century, particularly South Pole attainers Roald Amundsen and Robert Falcon Scott, lodged claims supported by competent, first-hand witnesses to the genuineness of astronomical observations made with sextant and/or theodolite. These explorers took along companions who not only could navigate but who could share in the gathering and evaluating of raw data, thus verifying their reality.

126

Peary's 1909 expedition included a group of five educated men, any of whom would have been a competent witness to the Pole. Instead, beyond 88°N., Peary took four Eskimos and Matthew Henson, none of whom knew navigational mathematics.

True, Peary was just following the precedent of his three earlier farthest points out on the Arctic Ocean, but in those cases he had no choice — certainly not five of them. Regardless of precedent, he could easily have foreseen a special need for corroboration in 1909 and so altered his plans to allow at least one of the formally educated members of his expedition to accompany him on the last leg. He chose not to take such a witness, sending back his doomed scientist Marvin at about the halfway point and the last supporting group, Bartlett's, at least 135 miles from the Pole. Upon hearing of Peary's first brief cables claiming discovery of the North Pole, Herbert L. Bridgman, Secretary of the Peary Arctic Club, thought it probable that either MacMillan or Borup, or both, had gone all the way to the Pole.

Peary's decision not to take a thoroughly qualified witness to the Pole was purely premeditated. He said: "When each man has fed me and my men up to a certain point, within striking distance of the Pole, their work is done. . . . but Henson is not to return." (From the Explorers Club skeptical report on the Mount McKinley hoax: Dr. Cook "sidetracked all members of the expedition until there remained only himself and his guide Barrille. . . .") Though essentially "no member of the party knew how far he was to go," Peary had adhered to a definite program of who was to return when, though obviously "it seemed hardly worthwhile to make it known" until the expedition was far out on the ice. Whatever his reasons, Peary took no one on the final dash who knew navigation. Furthermore, he carried just one sextant and one theodolite, both on his own special sledge, which meant that no unsupervised astronomical observations could be performed by anyone en route to the Pole or on the return. Such a curious practice obviously placed other parties of the expedition in serious danger of becoming lost on the return if bad weather broke the trail and caused substantial drift — as had actually happened to a party on Peary's previous expedition — and if anything had befallen Peary, his five final-dash companions would have perished, he said, on the ice. More important, however, than Peary's not taking navigators with him, was his treatment of the civilized man he did take. Henson, though not a formally trained scientist, could make sextant observations (and had been tutored in math by Marvin over the 1908-1909 winter). He was not asked to do so nor even allowed to sign, initial, or so much as *look* at Peary's data sheets. Nor were any of the results pinpointing geographical position, data later alleged to have been calculated out at Camp Jesup, ever given him, though Henson had readily obtained *all* previous positions and noted them in his diary. The ignoring of Henson at this crucial juncture—really a direct evasion, as will be seen from a newly recovered Henson account of events, is doubly strange considering Peary's concern in soliciting sextant observations and detailed, handwritten certificates of latitude by Marvin and Bartlett before they turned back. MacMillan and Borup also supplied similar certificates of estimated latitudes. Thus *all* turnback camps' positions were independently verified — except Camp Jesup.

Aside from astronomical observations, what data not previously knowable, thus requiring no witnesses, could be obtained at the North Pole that would identify a specific physical characteristic of the place, which could be verified by future explorers? As pointed out, there is no land, so likely a probability that Cook guessed it first, and the icy surface looks pretty much the same over the entire central Arctic Ocean. The South Pole occupies a uniform plateau similarly featureless, so what could first-attainer Amundsen bring back? Some have supposed, mistakenly, that his claim depended upon Scott's subsequent finding of the Norwegian Polar camps, but this is not so. Besides sharing astronomical observations, Amundsen and his men determined a continuous topographical section of the Antarctic Continent from the Bay of Whales to the South Pole over a new route and recorded the variation of the compass at every opportunity. The Norwegians also placed previously unseen mountains, which Peary could not do; but they had no current to note, so Peary could have made a valuable record of something they could not. He didn't. Analogously, Peary, even with no witnesses, could have determined a bathymetric (underwater topographical) section of the Arctic Ocean north of Cape Columbia right to the Pole. He could have brought back information about the terrestrial magnetic field in the Arctic. He was supplied with the necessary instruments to do so; indeed, there was little other scientific justification for his jaunt than to obtain such data. Peary had explicitly promised the Navy Department in 1907, when requesting leave for his last expedition, the "securing of all scientific information and material possible from the regions surrounding the Pole." But, beyond 85½° North latitude, he reported no specific figures for depth or magnetism, or anything else of hard scientific value.

As for the importance of making soundings, Peary himself had proposed in 1906-07 that the next expedition attain not only the Pole but one of the "remaining principal desiderata in the central Arctic Sea, namely, a line of deep-sea soundings from the north shore of Grant Land to the Pole." Supplied with 4,000 fathoms of sounding lines (contra his report to the RGS), he was certainly aware of the fact that the northernmost depth yet measured in the Arctic Ocean was more than 2,000 fathoms, and some other Nansen soundings were even deeper. But, in leaving ashore his 2,000 fathom line — which was eventually given a last-minute use on a short dash by another party off North Greenland (deepest sounding: 91 fathoms!) — Peary made it impossible from the start to determine the depth of the ocean at the Pole, even had not 500 fathoms of wire been lost en route.

Also on hand was a clamping device to be hung from the end of the wire, to capture at each sounding a sample of the ocean floor. With this apparatus, Peary could literally have brought back a "piece" of the North Pole.

What happened? First, he proceeded with only his two short reels onto an ocean known to be a good deal deeper (than their combined length) in many regions. He arrived in the vicinity of what he asserted to be the Pole with only a makeshift 1500 fathom wire, which broke there at the conclusion of the sole sounding taken after Bartlett's departure. In fact, not one of the soundings attempted during the last two-thirds of the poleward trek reached bottom. The major feature of the Arctic basin is an underwater mountain range that rises to within 1000 fathoms of the surface and extends from the New Siberian Islands to Ellesmere Island, right across Peary's reported path. But he never knew it was there. As a result, what might have been called the Peary Ridge is instead known today as the Lomonosov Ridge.

In addition to the poor showing in plumbing the depths, one finds an absolutely inexplicable lack of magnetic data from the Polar trip. A record of the direction (variation) of the compass would not only have been of scientific value and an ideal proof of Peary's achievement; it was necessary to his *practical navigation* and, in addition, would have provided important information to later explorers steering in the region. Use of the magnetic compass in the area of the 1909 trip is not as simple as one might think. Up there, compass-north (the direction the "north" end of the compass needle points) is slightly south of true west, so the compass is worthless without knowledge of its variation from north. Needless to say, *every* major Polar adventurer of the day did not fail in such circumstances to check and record the direction of the compass. There were two exceptions — Cook in 1908 and Peary in 1909.

If the traditional apology for Peary's refusal to take along educated witnesses to his achievement is that he was just following his own precedent and plan, what can be the excuse for his failure to record magnetic data? On all three of his previous Polar Sea adventures, Peary had made precise determinations of the vital compass variation; i.e., the variation of the compass from true north, the direction to the North Pole.

Why nothing in 1909? That Peary had not suddenly that year forgotten the value of magnetic data for steering is a matter of record (Peary letter to MacMillan, April 28, 1909, regarding the latter's upcoming sea-ice journey north of Peary Land). Even back in 1905, Peary had promised:

> The attainment of the Pole means opening up the way for observations of refinement. . .in the realms of. . . [e.g.] *magnetism*. . . . [Emphasis added)

From a short list of queries written in his 1909 notebook by Borup, which he evidently intended to put to Cook in order to show that the Doctor knew nothing at all about the North Pole he was claiming to have attained;

> "At the Pole what is the variation of the compass"[?]

Aside from magnetic data's scientific value, the determination of compass variation from true north was obviously necessary to Peary's maintaining a northward course *by* compass, then the standard steering method on ice — *Peary explicitly stated this was his own method.*

For example, an extant note of March 11, 1909, to Marvin's rear-guard party ordered Marvin to proceed "E.S.E." — i.e., 112½° east of the needle (compass north) at 84° North latitude. This is the same as saying that the compass variation on that date was 112½° West of true north at 84° North latitude, 70° West longitude. (This figure, not based on observation, is mistaken by over 5°. This is the last existing digit on Peary's steering, still 360 miles from the Pole.) In short, Peary's practical course *for aiming north* not only *required* compass variation but was (if east is substituted for west) absolutely *equivalent* to it. And how does one get to the North Pole without knowing which way is north?

It is amazing that, though the necessary equipment and time were at hand, though Peary fully realized the necessity of knowing compass variation to steer a true northward course, and though he needed to arm himself with hard facts for the anticipated tussle with Cook, he (for the first time in his career) brought back no magnetic observations whatever to support his claim. Navigationally, it is syllogistically simple: the expedition's steering north was determined exclusively by compass, and throughout the trip Peary never determined the variation of the compass from north.

131

But surely Peary must have brought back *some* precise data supposedly from Camp Jesup. Quite true — he presented 13 alleged sextant observations of the sun's altitude. Nothing else. However, in their stark isolation, these figures only raise the worst of all questions regarding Peary's journey.

Since these are the *only* specific data presented by Peary as being from the North Pole, it is of interest that solar altitudes are also the *only* such data observable at the Pole that could just as well have been faked without making the trip at all, a fact agreed to by every knowledgeable scientist, even Cook and Peary. Since Peary was never able to explain how he aimed at the Pole to get himself there, his possession of such figures is as suspicious as, for example, a politician's sudden accumulation of wealth he cannot account for.

The fact is that Peary had no hard technical yield from the trip. The dash was thus not only scientifically pointless, it was unprovable. And he knew it. Later, when repeatedly challenged to submit his North Pole claim to the University of Copenhagen Committee which rejected Cook, Peary refused to do so. Undoubtedly he had seen the mirthful reaction of the Committee's best qualified expert, Danish Navigationsdirektor (also Arctic expedition leader and navigation textbook author), Commodore Jens A.D. Jensen, to Cook's presentation. Jensen's sarcasms had been gleefully quoted by the pro-Peary *New York Times* in December, 1909. Now that Peary's own story is known, the faithful may be less amused at them:

> There is nothing in Dr. Cook's records to show that he made azimuth observations [to determine compass variation]. In the arctic regions, where variations of the compass are most important [being large and changing rapidly from place to place] — the compass is of little use unless its variations are [checked by fresh determinations] at short intervals [of distance].

> When one realizes that Dr. Cook [nonetheless] set his suppositions as to his wanderings are possible.

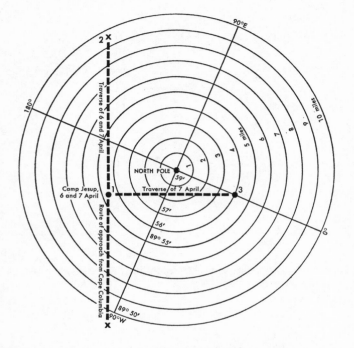

Adapted by the U.S. Naval Institute *Proceeedings* from the 1911 Mitchell-Duvall chart. Peary's alleged itinerary and observations near the Pole:

Arrival at Point 1 (from Cape Columbia) April 6 about 10 a.m.; observation about noon at Point 1.

Point 1 to Point 2, between 6 p.m. and midnight; observation midnight at Point 2.

Point 2 to Point 1, between midnight and 6 a.m. (April 7); observation 6 a.m. at Point 1.

Point 1 to Point 3 and back, between 6 a.m. and noon; observation noon at Point 1.

Departure from Point 1 (for land) April 7 about 4 p.m.

Distance from 1 to 2 equals 10 miles. Distance from 1 to 3 equals 8 miles.

March 25th, 1909.

This is to certify that I turn back from this point with the 3 rd supporting party, Commander Peary advancing with nine men in the party, seven sledges with the standard loads, and 60 dogs, men and dogs all in first class condition. The Captain with the 4th and last supporting party expects to turn back at the end of five more marches. Determined our latitude by observation on

March 22nd and again today, March 25th. A copy of the observations and computations is herewith enclosed. Results of observations were as follows.

Lat at Noon March 22nd
85° 48' North

Lat at Noon March 25th
86° 38' North

Distance made good in three marches 50 minutes of latitude, an average of 16 2/3 nautical miles per march.

The weather is fine, going good and improving each day.

signed,
Ross G Marvin
College of Civil Engineering
Cornell University

Facsimiles of Marvin's certificate of March 25, 1909. Below, facsimiles of Bartlett's certificate of April 1, 1909.

```
obs At      13   9   00
IS         +     4   00
            13  13   00
Refrak? P   -    3 . 55
            13   9   05
Semid      + 16 . 02
            13  25 . 07
Ther Cor + 10   -   33
         2 ( 13  24   34
Sact     6   42   17
            90
            83  17 . 43
             4  29 . 06
Lat in      87  46   49 u
at Noon
April 1.09

Adif   57 . 91
      289 . 55
        4 . 50
Ap ded   4 . 24 . 16 . 1
         4 . 50
Sun ded  4 . 29   06
```

Robert A. Bartlett, Master, S.S. "Roosevelt"

Arctic Ocean, April 1.09

I have today personally determined obs latitude to be by sextant observations:-

Lat in 87.46.49 N

I return from here in command of the 4th. Supporting Party.

I leave Commander Peary with 5 men, 5 sledges with full loads, and 40 picked dogs.

The men & dogs are in good condition, the going fair, the weather good.

At the same average as our

last eight marches Commander Peary should reach the Pole in eight days

Robert A. Bartlett,
Master, S.S. "Roosevelt".

10.   Quiver in the Arrow

The North Pole, a geometric point marked at the earth's surface by no fixed feature, lies on a deep ocean covered by moving ice. Traveling on this surface from Ellesmere Island to the Pole (413 beeline miles) cannot be a direct jaunt as might be depicted on a map, for the way is repeatedly interrupted (often east-west) by leads and by long, high walls of ice (pressure ridges). In addition, the course is constantly being altered, as the ice on which one travels is moved by the effects of wind and ocean currents. The resultant ice motion or drift cannot be felt any more than can the daily rotation of the earth. Thus, away from landmarks, drift is not determinable except by astronomical means (in practice: sextant or theodolite observations). At various times in 1906, Peary's Eskimos, Peary himself, and a supporting party were each grossly misled by appearances, their visual estimates of the direction of drift making their dead-reckoning judgments of position worthless and rendering direct travel, without astronomical aid, impossible. In the first month of that journey, Peary was under the distinct impression of an eastward drift and his reports of wind are all of gusts from west to east. Yet his first astronomical determination of position (about 100 miles out from land) showed him off his meridian by over 30 *west*ward miles, an error in aim of more than 15 degrees to the left as compared with the half a degree he claimed in 1909.

A good deal of any trip over such a natural obstacle course would resemble broken field running in football. Expedition member George Borup's book has a photo, showing the difficulty early in the trip, which he captioned: "We guessed and groped, north, ever north, with many a twist and turn." These twists were estimated by the 1909 expedition as averaging about *40 degrees* off course, though modern explorers have encountered a mean detour nearer 55 degrees. Henson observed, "The course from land to the Pole was not direct and due north, for we followed the lines of least resistance, and frequently found ourselves going due east or west, in order to detour around pressure ridges, floebergs, and leads." With so much zigzagging, not only is greater mileage required than would be as the snow-owl flies, but it is virtually impossible to make a trail by dead reckoning in precisely the right direction, the goal being, after all, just a far away, quite invisible little spot.

Other Pole bound explorers had run into great difficulty in their attempts to keep going straight toward the goal. The map at the back of Peary's *The North Pole* shows Nansen's (1895), Cagni's (1900), and some of Peary's own earlier attempts (1902, 1906). Each is so weavy and circuitous that, were one not aware of the difficulties of Polar sea travel, it would seem a sure bet that the explorers' dogs were fueled on alcohol. Except for the 1909 path. Alone among those shown, it goes virtually straight to the mark and right back again. Cook's invented 1908 route is the only comparable one.

Amazing! How was it done? One can search in vain for the explanation, in *The North pole* or elsewhere. The truth of the matter is, it could not have been done so simply; even Peary's own account mentions disorienting detours, long delays (while the drift goes right on) and the eye-straining difficulty of aiming sledges by compass. Peary could not seriously mean for anyone to believe he traveled in the beeline shown, yet his written report to the U.S. Coast and Geodetic Survey on October 28, 1909, supposes that all the 1909 soundings "were made on the meridian of Cape Columbia." The unsuspecting Survey did not learn until later the incredible fact that, throughout the entire northward trip, he claimed he never took, needed, or even *contemplated* a *single* non-noon astronomical observation to determine how far transversely to the left or right he might have strayed from the

136

Cape Columbia meridian, his alleged beeline. It is this peculiar feature of Peary's account (utterly unique in the annals of Polar travel) that places the burden of locating en route the correct direction to the Pole entirely on the compass, which was also regarded with unprecedented casualness: no checks of compass variation, over a route where the variation changes by 13° — vs. a claimed compass-steered aim of 0°.6 accuracy.

Aiming north all the way to the Pole just by compass in 1909 would be for Peary to ignore the clear lessons of 1906 and early March of 1909, which is unthinkably improbable, given Peary's temperament and intelligence. His *own* description, in his magazine series, of this dead-reckoning method of navigation remarks on the well-known limitations of it: "Dead reckoning was simply the compass course for direction, and for distance the mean estimate of Bartlett, Marvin, and myself as to the length of the day's march. . . . Dead reckoning alone, unchecked by astronomical observations, should not be depended upon for too great a number of marches. . . ." (Like the 27 in 1909?)

Why was distance checked (up to 87¾°N. latitude, at least) but direction never? This so bothered Henson — innocent as he was of the technical details of navigation — that, at Camp Jesup, before observations, he said to Peary: ". . . I have a feeling we have just about covered [the distance required. Thus, if] we have traveled in the right direction we are now at the Pole. If we have not traveled in the right direction then it is your own fault."

Though Peary's previously (1908) published plan for the Polar trip mentioned the intention of aiming west of north to counteract a supposedly prevailing easterly drift of the ice, Peary in 1909 seemed oblivious to such subtleties. He just blundered straight north (as in 1906), aiming to travel along the meridian of Cape Columbia (c. 70°W. long.); and, after leaving land, by his account, he never once thought to check his transverse deviation off his meridian until he'd gone *over* the Pole.

There was a multitude of possible important causes of aiming error, for example: the fact that, because of errors in the map of North Ellesmere, he unknowingly started about five miles to the left of the meridian he thought he was on. In addition, there was the unpredictable rate and direction of drift from wind and current. A few miles of drift a day is not unusual in the central Arctic; in a month, this could easily add up to 50 or 100 miles.

The current is leftward near land, slightly rightward (but mostly *against* an expedition from Ellesmere) farther out. As for the winds' directions, on this trip the stronger appeared more often blowing from the right than from the left, a trend verified by Henson in all his accounts.

Sources of random steering error: the incessant lead-caused detours, the inevitable human error of course setting in such optically difficult regions — only "fairly accurate" according to participant Macmillan whose casual and apparently minor rounding off of the compass course at the big lead from 112°½ to 112° is virtually equal to all Peary's alleged aiming error from all causes for the whole trip! Also, the transverse instability associated with the diverging of the terrestrial magnetic field in Peary's general direction, and the unsteadiness of the compass needle (merely "fairly constant," admitted Peary) from local attractions and magnetic storms would doubtless produce a large random uncertainty. Indeed, considering that the 1909 steering to Camp Jesup was done entirely by an unchecked compass, it is interesting to read the latest *Bowditch Navigator* (SecNavy) on polar navigation in an area of weak horizontal terrestrial magnetic field strength (along Peary's route this is about 0.03 oersteds — roughly 1/10th the strength common in equatorial regions of the earth):

It is good practice to keep the magnetic compass under almost constant scrutiny, as it is somewhat erratic in dependability and its errors may change rapidly. Frequent compass checks by celestial observation or any other method available are wise precautions. A log of compass comparisons and observations is useful in predicting future reliability.

As may be seen from a chart of compass reliability in the

138

Navigator, Peary's 1909 route started from an area the Navy labels ERRATIC and proceeded toward the North Pole, where the compass (which allegedly steered the whole trip with 0°.6 accuracy) is declared USELESS.

Also to be remarked are systematic aiming factors or personal tendencies (even dog teams have them) such as those attributed by Peary to Henson in 1906, which, if uncorrected and continued, would by themselves have amounted to a 150-mile error to the left of the Pole. Granted, it is faintly possible that all these effects might cancel each other out, but why would Peary just blindly assume this as he approached the Pole? Even as a schoolboy, he guessed in a primitive way the importance of allowing for drift, as witness this chronicle of a triumph written to his mother:

> In throwing the baseball I had two of the best throwers in college, Frank Payson and Knight, against me, and no one had any idea that I should do anything. As it happened my turn came last, and after they had thrown and only reached 306 feet, I was pretty confident that I shouldn't come out last. While I took my place to throw, some of the boys laughed at me a little and told me I better not throw as I couldn't do anything better than that, not having had any practice. I didn't say anything but picked up the ball and threw it the first time. . . . The wind took the ball and carried it to one side so it only went about 290 feet. The second time it did the same thing only it went farther, but the third time I made full allowance for the wind and the ball struck 316 feet distant, this time being ten feet ahead.

However, en route to Camp Jesup, Peary made observations only at Columbian noon (70°W. longitude, local time) in order to measure, by the sun's lowness, his forward progress over the curve of the earth. A transverse position determination at a given camp would have required an extra observation earlier or later in the day; but this would have been a "waste of time," he later told Congress. Peary's (and Bartlett's) aim and luck must have been mighty good, because, despite all the problems of straight travel, which had always deflected his own and others' paths so drastically, Peary "missed" the Pole in 1909 by barely four miles, after a 36-day trip of more than 400 miles — an error of only six-tenths of a degree to the left!

Poor, clumsy Roald Amundsen. He may have been the greatest Polar explorer of all, but he and his South Polar party, 80 percent of whom were navigators, though they traveled over an unobstructed non-drifting plateau with an undistracted eye ever on the compass, and covered only 95 miles — less than one-fourth of Peary's trip — from the last point of determination of true South, still they ended up about six miles to the right of the South Pole, over five times worse angular aim than Peary.

In contemporary terms, to try hitting the Pole without determining transverse position en route makes about as much sense (even less in fact) as to expect a rocket aimed from Cape Kennedy to hit the moon without any in-flight guidance system.

Of course, it is possible Peary could have done it; he had maybe one chance in a hundred. What is utterly impossible is that a cautious Arctic veteran such as Peary would have depended on blind luck in a life-and-death matter. And it must be kept in mind that the first two-thirds of the trip was not aimed by Peary but primarily by Bartlett, who was previously untried at steering a course over sea ice, and whose scientific precision Peary had long distrusted. Bartlett's cumulative transverse wander — from February 28 to March 31 — was never checked before April 7. The only map Peary ever drew of the 1909 trip shows the expedition, when only 50 miles out from land, already at least 20 miles to the left of where he ultimately told the Coast and Geodetic Survey to chart his soundings. This uncertainty was never compensated for, all the rest of the way to the Pole, which he supposedly missed by only four miles. Thus, in angular terms, Peary had an *alleged* accuracy of barely half a degree off his beeline for the entire trip as opposed to a *demonstrated* unsureness of more than 20 degrees in the first leg.

It is known that Peary was cautious enough to cover more than 300 miles of the coastline east and west of his starting point with food caches; indeed, as late as March 15-20, he ordered supplies for an additional 80 miles — all this just in case he returned to land far from the 70°W. meridian. A man this concerned about wandering off his intended beeline — and by such vast distances — but who later avoids explaining the methods he employed to stick so close to it, is clearly not being frank.

As Peary was never shy about his own accomplishments, and as this supposed 0.°6 steering feat constitutes the most superhuman aiming achievement in the entire history of Polar exploration, it is most remarkable that he never once draws attention to it in any of his writings.

Peary's supporter, Henry Gannett, tried in 1910 to persuade the inquiring Congressmen that determining true north — thus the direction to the Pole — could be easily performed by noting the direction of the sun at noon, since that is south. (In practice, in order to steer at other times of the day and on cloudy days, the compass is checked for its variation at every clear noon against the sun in the south, and/or midnight, in the north — thus the compass *with checked variation* assumes the role of a handy north-south meridian.) But actually, on the average, during Peary's trip the sun was (due to the equation of time) nearly 2° (8^m of time) to the left of its mean position; and his chronometer was about 10^m (2°½) fast. Thus, if aiming via the sun's azimuth, he would average over 4° steering error to the left, which would land him about 30 miles left of the Pole — an illustration, incidentally, of how surprisingly sensitive aiming is, even to seemingly trivial factors.

The chronometer-noon compass check is all right otherwise, *if* an explorer stays on the longitude meridian his chronometer is set (or corrected; for; but it provides no compensation whatever (rather, a trifle to the contrary) if he wanders off this meridian due to drift, the personal equation, or any other of the myriad above-detailed causes. By this hypothetical Peary-Gannett navigation, even with an unrufflable compass, a perfect chronometer, and a mean sun, one could only be sure of aiming virtually *parallel* to the intended path. There was in practice no way other than by astronomical determination from *two* solar altitude observations (sextant) at the same spot — which Peary says he didn't waste time with en route — to determine how far left or right his expedition had wandered and/or drifted off 70° W. (Columbia) longitude on the rugged, blinding, ever-shifting ice of the Polar Sea. The bare (Columbia-time) noon altitudes of the sun would unfortunately yield nothing but a measure of how far *forward* the expedition had travelled — without a hint of transverse error.

What sort of unnecessary trouble could such a method cause? Well, after, say, 360-plus miles of travel forward — judging by the previous experience of himself and others — Peary could not have been sure that his transverse position was closer than 50 miles to his ideal beeline. (In fact, even this close would be unexpectedly good luck. In 1906, Peary and Henson both were off by like amounts on jaunts of only 100 miles.)

Suppose, then, hypothetically, that Peary is 50 miles off to the left and 50 miles short of the Pole. A non-noon sextant shot here will enable him to realize this and thus to re-aim (about 45° rightward) his path toward the Pole — a direct run of about 70 miles. If he does not make such an adjustment until his single noon observations tell him he has gone forward far enough, he will end up about 50 miles to the left of the Pole, and will then need to make about a 90° right turn to go another 50 miles. The net result is an added 30 miles, representing about two days of travel, with its cost in strength, food, and deadly risk. Moreover, since the Peary System rightly called for a return in the outward track, when possible, in order to use the pre-pickaxed trail and the igloos already built, either the same ridiculous right-angle dog-leg would have to be retraced or some extra camps would have to be constructed on the return over a newly broken trail, greatly slowing progress. Another day or so lost, either way. An extra non-noon solar observation might be a bit of a bother (Bartlett said it would take "only a few moments"), but it could hardly be as much of a waste of time as three or four days tough travel! Nonetheless, if one takes Peary's account seriously, he really prefers to take the 30-mile (or possibly far worse) risk rather than take that extra solar observation.

This is so silly that it might be assumed that no explorer

142

could be so dumb (true) and thus that the writer has distorted Peary's tale in some way (false). Any such doubter should either check the source citations or note that the above analysis was published by the U.S. Naval Institute in June, 1970, without the slightest change, by unanimous vote of the USNI Board of Control, after a thorough review by the country's leading navigational institutions.

A further indicator of the obviousness of Peary's aiming folly is the embarrassing fact that his biographers Green and Hobbs both speak with naive admiration of the careful navigational methods that they assumed Peary *must* have used for checking dead reckoning estimates on the shifting pack; likewise, believing explorers Henry Bryant, Vilhjalmur Stefansson, and Richard Byrd all remark innocently on Peary's skillful conquest of the special navigational difficulties caused by the *moving* ice. Clearly, none of these men ever read the Peary Hearings, the most important available source on the question at issue. And thus none knew the stark truth: though Peary "filled pages with mathematic calculations of pounds of supplies required relative to miles. . .travelled. . . . [etc., for] maximum effectiveness with minimum weight. . .", he (like Cook) never presented a single observed datum — not a *digit* — relative to an efficient route (i.e., steering!) toward the North Pole.

Peary's unique aiming ability is equalled only by his intuition for gauging distance. In his written stories of the final dash, he at least used a solar observation to determine how far forward he had traveled parallel to the 70° meridian. Peary's *N.Y. Times* story and *Hampton's Magazine* article, as well as his book and his allegedly genuine diary, are all in agreement on his having made an April 5 noon observation, giving, on the assumption that he was still on the 70° meridian, a latitude of 89°25′ North latitude. However, Henson's 1910 published accounts consistently contradicted this. When, finally, in the January, 1911, hearings, Congressman Robert Macon asked Peary how many observations were taken between the point at which he left Bartlett and the Pole itself, Peary at first evaded the matter by expanding on the April 6-7 observations at the Pole. But Macon brought him back to the point with the direct clarifier:

> Mr. Macon. Then you took no observations, longitude or otherwise, for a distance of one hundred and thirty-three miles after you left Bartlett at 87°47′?
> Captain Peary. No, sir.

So, there really wasn't an observation at 89°25′, after all. Leaving aside momentarily the interesting question of why this nonexistent observation previously had appeared in all of Peary's accounts and diary, how, one might well wonder, *did* Peary know how far he had traveled? How could he go 130 miles without any check to make sure he didn't overshoot by a few percent and so waste ten or so miles of hauling? Could he just tell these things? Henson says Peary rode most of the journey and that "Riding one cannot so well judge of distance traversed." Besides this handicap, there were the confusing detours and the drifting ice, on which Peary blamed a 14-mile distance misjudgment at about 88° North latitude, after a run of only 67 miles — over 20% off. But how about that clutch performance on the next run, right *to* the Pole: Barely a mile short in more than 130, an error of about one percent, about 20 times better accuracy than before. As if this weren't enough, Peary later (though his diary said different) told it to the Congressmen as if he *meant* to be short, and thus was off by, at *most*, a mile. When pressed by Macon, Peary finally defended his intuition for distance by mentioning that he had performed similarly remarkable feats by counting *paces* when traveling over the Greenland ice-cap years before. Such an analog cannot have been presented innocently. Peary knew very well that travel over the smooth Greenland inner ice was without detour or rough places, so that distance was measured automatically by a wheel sledgemeter (or "odometer"), useless on the rough Arctic Ocean ice, as is obvious — and as his own book states.

Peary's whole claim on precise distance estimation is preposterous, as his own figures show. Peary's original September, 1909 (*New York Times*) version gave for his best estimate of the magic marches of April 2-6, respectively (in miles): 25,

144

20, 20, 25 "or more," and 40. But the last figure perhaps seemed overdone, so his March, 1910, pamphlet "How Peary Reached the North Pole . . ." gave instead: 25 miles, 20, 20, 25, and 30. Finally, for Congress in 1911 he offered, like Cook, that he had formerly been the victim of misprints, and that his original diary contained the correct mileages: 30 miles, 20, 25, 25, 30. The desired total of 130 miles (= 89°57′ minus 87°47′) appears originally and ultimately; therefore, Peary — again, like Cook, in another context — was blessed in his first version by obligingly canceling misprints.

This from an explorer who supposedly could gauge 130 miles virtually on the nose. Incidentally, Henson, who later claimed he, too, could tell his distance to the mile, called the first march (April 2) 20 miles. Peary's diary for the same day notes, "Have no doubt we covered thirty miles, but will be conservative and call it twenty-five. My Eskimos say thirty-five miles. . . ." The range of uncertainty (20 to 35) covers nearly a factor of two. Plainly, such guesstimates would have to be checked — to guard against overshooting the Pole — by solar sights. Peary's abortive attempt to invent such for April 5 is the ultimate witness to his own assent on this point.

In a nutshell, then, the navigational story finally amounts to this: Peary sped over the ice for 27 marches without knowing which way was north, pacing the distance of the last 130 miles from a sitting position. On April 6-7, opining he was at his goal, he chanced solar observations that showed him to be only a mile and a half short and four miles to the left, the straightest, best-gauged dead reckoning feat of all time — a veritable 413-mile Pole-in-one!

145

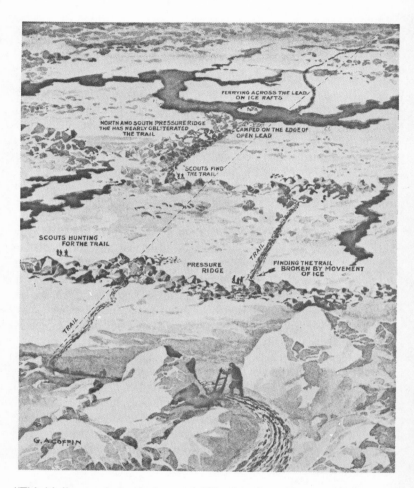

Labels within image:
FERRYING ACROSS THE LEAD ON ICE RAFTS

NORTH AND SOUTH PRESSURE RIDGE THAT HAS NEARLY OBLITERATED THE TRAIL

CAMPED ON THE EDGE OF OPEN LEAD

SCOUTS FIND THE TRAIL

SCOUTS HUNTING FOR THE TRAIL

TRAIL

PRESSURE RIDGE

FINDING THE TRAIL BROKEN BY MOVEMENT OF ICE

TRAIL

G. A. COFFIN

"This bird's-eye view covering over 100 miles of the Polar Sea shows how moving ice tears a trail to pieces and how open leads of water obstruct progress. The dotted line marks the trail of the advance party. At the first pressure ridge the ice has been carried to the right of the line of march, and at the second to the left and almost obliterated by another pressure ridge. As this drawing shows, the trail may be constantly shifted, imperiling at any moment the advance of the expedition." — from Peary's series in *Hampton's* magazine (July, 1910).

146

11.   Find a Way or Fake One

Hopefully, the booster mentality's inevitable replace what you destroy demand will ultimately be sated by presentation (in our last chapter) with a finer hero than Peary. But, for now, it must be content with a more believable replacement for Peary's 1909 story, regarding which marvelous tale the writer has heretofore exercised almost exclusively a critical approach, sticking to demonstrable fact, datum, and statement. Now at this point, temporarily, he will enter the realm of speculation — in order to arrive at an explanation of the known facts of the 1909 trip which is at once consistent and non-paranoid, a goal never previously approached in the extensive Cook-Peary literature.

A true philosopher of science is content to regard a claim devoid of verifiable evidential support as metaphysical fluff which is not true (and not false) because it is untestable. Had the responsible societies taken such an attitude in 1909, there would have been no medals for the Peary claim and thus no entrenched diehard attitude by these groups today. Given their ongoing political priorities, however, one is going to have to show them in detail just how they were gulled.

The first step is to face the overwhelming likelihood of fraud.

It is unfortunate not to be able to explain all away as an innocent mistake. Such a diplomatic course has been tried in the past, but the Peary clique will not accept a graceful out, and this is proper as the claim *is* either valid or a lie. The former is hardly likely regarding a story with supporting evidence as firm as quicksilver and which is full of crucial inconsistencies, convenient lacunae, and outright howlers — and whose unique marvels occur in inverse proportion to the number of competent witnesses to them. Thus we are left with the latter option. Certainly Peary's motive is obvious enough. And the previous Jesup and Crocker Land episodes indicate an already developing capacity for exploring exaggeration, even prior to the desperation especially attendant to a man's very last chance.

No matter how conclusive a net of evidence — unless the proof is 100% — some are not going to face the unpleasant truth and will cry "unproved" to their graves. But once one sees analogies uncloaked in the patriotic and glamorous aura in which exploring has too often wrapped itself, one sees how obvious the truth would be, in everyday life.

For example, a suspected thief who claims he wasn't at the scene of a robbery because he was alone at a movie at the time had better remember something about the movie. If he can't, he has proved himself guilty. Likewise, Peary, whose inadequate alibi for not being far from the Cape Columbia meridian was that he had his eye on his compass, had better remember something about that compass. It is not enough to say that it cannot be proved that the variation-less explorer was lying; neither can it be proved that the thief did not go to sleep at the theater. But no jury would be so naive as to believe it.

As the writer (a specialist in planetary motion) is hardly an unreserved admirer of Conan Doyle's hero (a pre-Copernican boor, whose arch-enemy was a celestial mechanist), he may perhaps be indulged a little further Holmesian analysis of the mystery before us. Surely there must be some key, some coherent explanation behind so many strange aspects to Peary's claim. Holmes: "The more bizarre a thing is the less mysterious it proves to be." (*Red-Headed League*). And: "The more *outre* and grotesque an incident is the more carefully it deserves to be examined, and the very point which appears to complicate a case is, when duly considered and sci-

148

entifically handled, the one which is most likely to elucidate it." (*Hound of the Baskervilles*, Chapter 15)

Why, for instance, should Peary try to claim he could travel straight north by compass, ignoring drift and other variables, without even knowing which way his compass pointed? And why would he claim high speeds at certain times, though his pace for most of the trip is reasonably modest? Given the above established background regarding the events of early April, 1909, these questions may now be answered, while bringing into focus the essentially simple mechanics of the imposture.

Suppose we start by assuming that Peary's statement is true; i.e., that he indeed made no determination of his transverse position (necessary for steering) until April 6-7 at Camp Jesup (supposedly at the point steered for!). A little pondering brings the realization that what this tale is telling us is that Camp Jesup was *actually* the point at which Peary first decided to cease just plunging outward from Ellesmere and to start steering accurately to zero-in on the North Polar point that was his goal. And *this* only makes sense *if Camp Jesup was many miles short of the Pole.* And so it was.

Now, all of the pieces begin to fall into place.

Adhering to his observations-every-five-marches schedule, Peary took the first solar altitude after April 1 on April 6-7. Here the trip's first complete (noon and non-noon) set of sextant data was recorded, thus enabling him to compute complete position (forward and transverse, or latitude and longitude, figures which no one knows to this day) — and thus the direction (at last setting up the capability to steer accurately) and hopelessly great distance to the Pole — probable order-of-magnitude of 100 miles. (An estimate based on probable distance traveled beyond April Fool Camp in five marches, not to mention transverse wander. Also, Peary would not in reality, forgetting his incredible story, go much closer without taking zeroing-in data.)

There was now no point in taking compass-variation for Poleward steering, since there wasn't going to be any. Though the variation still could aid navigation back to land (especially if the upward trail were lost, and/or in cloudy weather), Peary wasn't about to record compass data, or even set up his theodolite for such, in front of witnesses, since the variation at Camp Jesup could not be expected to be the same as that at the North Pole, where compass-direction would someday become known.

The wise April 6-7 decision to speed back for land naturally made Camp Jesup the "Pole Camp," perforce, in his eventual story. This, unfortunately, also would put the actual April 6-7 zeroing-in observations, performed in order to find his way *to* the Pole, right at the camp (Jesup) he'd had to tell Henson was virtually *at* the Pole! But, Henson and those four Eskimos might remember that there were no observations anywhere else after April 1. A ghastly dilemma. But a contrary witness was more to be feared (back in the U.S.) than the commonsense of societies. So what was Peary to do in his tale *but* find his way right to the Pole by course-setting from the hip, and distance-gauging literally by the seat of the pants? — marvels which need not be stated explicitly unless squeezed out by cross-examination, a social indignity no geographical institution would dare inflict on him, if precedent meant anything.

Thus, the origin and explanation of Peary's hitherto mysterious North Pole story.

At only one key point, apparently realizing the absurdity of claiming he could gauge distance so perfectly, did he waver in his resolve on this story, when he added the April 5th "noon" observation at 89°25' North latitude, in contradiction to his April 1 plan to wait five marches before his first observation. He explained this away by saying he feared it would be cloudy the next day. Subsequently, Peary denied this April 5th observation altogether, as had every account Henson had published. Peary's own mathematicians, Mitchell and Duvall, who reduced all the March 22, March 25, April 1, April 6, and April 7 data for their 1913 presentation at the Rome 10th International Geographical Congress, later explicitly stated that *all* of the astronomical observations taken by Peary and his assistants on the Polar journey are given in the Rome paper."

Thus Peary is caught in an ineradicable contradiction — the likes of which would have caused Cook to be flayed — at a juncture in Peary's story that multiplies a thousandfold the suspiciousness of his already incredible claim to a super-intuitive finding of the Pole.

One of the difficulties of hypothesizing in historical analysis, as against the same pursuit in the exact sciences, is that what is past history cannot be reduced to repeatable experiment; thus an historical theory is usually fitted — with as many *ad hoc* adjustments as necessary — to a fixed set of past facts. In experimental science, a theory can be pitted against competitors by comparing predictive abilities in a laboratory contest, so that mere cleverness at weaving an elaborate theory around a set of facts is no protection against new data. But, when dealing with past history, how can there be prediction? Fortunately for the historian, theory can now be supported by a crucial document contemporary with Peary's claim: A copy of Henson's *Boston-American* article, discovered after being unnoticed for more than 50 years, thoroughly recounts his memories of events at Camp Jesup — and thereby unintentionally gives away Peary's whole pretension. A few references to it will illustrate why the above theory of what Peary must have done at Camp Jesup is remarkably well verified by Henson's account of what Peary actually *did:*

Theory: On April 6-7, Peary could not expect that he had gone far enough to be at the Pole.

Henson: On discovering himself to be at the Pole, Peary was "surprised", having underestimated the rate of travel ("having fooled himself in the matter of distance . . .") since April 2, and thus arrived at the Pole on April 6 only "by an oversight."

Theory: Peary's April 6-7 solar observations told him not that his life's goal was attained, but rather that it was impossibly out of reach.

Henson: ". . .O-tah. . .with E-tig-wah [the two Eskimos who accompanied Peary out of sight for the first observations]. . .witnessed the disappointment of

151

Commander Peary when, a few miles from the camp [Jesup], his observations [were reduced]. . . . [After about one hour] the Commander returned [to Camp Jesup]. His face was long and serious."

Theory: Peary had to watch out for Henson's presence while at "the Pole." (Henson liked to record the results of observations in his diary.) Also, Peary's later silence on the *Roosevelt* about his achievement was not truly due to the factors suggested by his various excuses but, rather, stemmed from the desire to be non-committal while he arranged the hoax's details, before arriving at a final story.

Henson: After the out-of-sight observations, ". . .the Commander returned. His face was long and serious. He would not speak to me. . . .

"'Well, Mr. Peary,' I spoke up, cheerfully enough, 'we are now at the Pole, are we not?'

"'I do not suppose that we can swear that we are exactly at the Pole,' was his evasive answer.

"'Well, I have kept track of the distance and we have made exceptional time,' I replied, 'and I have a feeling that we have just about covered the hundred and thirty-two miles. . . .'

"Commander Peary made no reply. . . . From the time we knew we were at the Pole Commander Peary scarcely spoke to me. . . .It nearly broke my heart on the return journey from the Pole that he would arise in the morning and slip away on the homeward trail without rapping on the ice for me, as was the established custom. . . .On board the ship he addressed me a very few times. When he left the ship [for good] he did not speak."

In the light of the foregoing, reports that would normally read innocently may now appear significant. For example, Henson's later account of the joyful moments after completion of one of the April 7 observations, as he went forward, perhaps to ask what the results were:

With the resolute squaring of his [Peary's] jaws, I was

152

sure that he was satisfied. . . . Feeling that the time had come, I ungloved my right hand and went forward to congratulate him on the success of our eighteen years of effort, but a gust of wind blew something into his eye, or else the burning pain caused by his prolonged look at the reflection of the limb of the sun forced him to turn aside; and with both hands covering his eyes, he gave us orders not to let him sleep for more than four hours, for six hours later he purposed to take another sight about four miles beyond. . . .

It is remarkable how easily so much evidence was misinterpreted at the time. Henson, after learning of the intended secret jaunt, was convinced Peary was trying to beat him to the Pole. This naturally made Henson prone to hope and convince himself — certainly his weary bones told him he'd gone at least 130 miles! — that Camp Jesup was smack on the Pole. This conviction Peary opportunistically exploited via subsequent flag-raising ceremonies right at camp. His thought-filled silences were then seen as just a jealous pet over having to share the honor of attainment of the Pole. (Many Cookites later interpreted the Peary silence by their own theory; that Peary had not claimed the Pole until hearing that Cook had done so.)

The more he thought about it, the more Peary realized that an account without observations for transverse position en route, despite its inherent improbability, had the advantage of keeping one's deceptions to a minimum. Faking non-noon observations some distance from the Pole would formally seem to require spherical trig and extensive calculations. It could be done, of course, but why chance a possibly revealing error?

By contrast, even the brazen Cook did not have the nerve to try getting away with claiming not to have needed observations for longitude, and accepted professional mathematical help in order to fix up some data; but then, the mathematician turned informer. The attempted faking of observations for transverse position was probably Cook's most important single public blunder. Peary, on the other hand, played it safe and settled for just the genuine Marvin and Bartlett noon observations en route, plus a few manufactured North Pole observations.

A few simple points may be listed briefly here relative to the important fact (never appreciated by the societies judging Cook and Peary) that consistent solar altitude data is worthless per se as proof of navigation or geographical position.
1. If one is capable of navigating by the sun, then one is capable of inventing solar altitudes, as the math is the same type either way.
2. Computationally, it is easier to fake data than to use real data on a genuine trip, quite aside from the labor saved by not making the journey.
3. The Poles are the easiest places on earth for which to manufacture such data.

So, once one has decided upon the place one wishes to be, in an exploring fantasy, a little arithmetic is the magic carpet to the spot. As for the 1909 spot, the writer suspects that he has found Peary's rationale for his story's positioning of Camp Jesup which was: to claim 1% dead-reckoning accuracy. Peary's tale took him the last 100+ miles without checking his forward progress and all 400+ miles without a transverse check. One percent of 100+ is 1+; of 400+, 4+. Thus Camp Jesup was put 1+ miles short, and 4+ miles to the left, of the North Pole.

Other details would also require attention.

Whereas calculations presented on "loose sheets of paper" might somehow get by Peary's judges without comment, no diary purely of that sort could be counted on to be believable. Presuming that retroactive changes for the April 2-5 entries would be required, the original diary would have to be altered or a revised one written up in its place. This occurred to the Congressional subcommittee members who, after a ten-month wait, were finally permitted to examine Peary's diary. It was asked how the diary had been written. "With the bare hand, usually," Peary replied. Congressman Roberts passed the book around among the members, re-

154

marking: "It shows no finger marks or rough usage; a very cleanly kept book." (Peary said his long experience had taught him to protect his diary from the elements by use of a waterproof bag.)

Five years later, Congressman Henry Helgesen stated explicitly what the skeptical Roberts was evidently implying:

. . .it is a well-known fact that, on a long Arctic journey, ablutions [soap, etc.], even of the face and hands, are too luxurious for the travelers. Pemmican is the staple article of food. Its great value lies in its greasy qualities. One's hands necessarily come in contact with this greasy food frequently. How was it possible for Peary to handle this greasy food, and, without washing his hands, write in his diary daily; and at the end of two months have that same diary show "no finger marks or rough usage; a very cleanly kept book"?

Bartlett's memoirs, published in 1928, contained an incidental description of Peary's 1906 journal as, "his little greasy diary. . . ." But maybe Peary's habits had changed by 1909. Still, when it was suspected that Cook might be about to submit a fake diary to his Danish judges, explorer Anthony Fiala reminded everyone that it wasn't so easy to make up a false journal:

I don't believe any one could come up with a substitute for those old blubber-stained, snow-marked notebooks familiar to every Arctic explorer. This is where the weak part of an attempt to deceive will be found.

The startling (and long-suppressed) discoveries of writer Henshaw Ward, on the history of Peary's field records will be reserved for an Appendix.

Whatever the condition of Peary's diary, his lack of the navigationally required but unfakeable compass-variation data was insoluble. If he revealed the actual Camp Jesup compass course and/or guessed the variation for regions beyond where he turned back, later explorers' findings would reveal all. Far safer to obscure the whole matter by waffling,

155

i.e., on the sun being "too low" for using a theodolite.

But surely, the no bottom 1500 fathom "Pole" sounding seemed safe. It was not a precise depth — which would be impossible to guess beforehand — merely a limit, either true or false. Not one of the depths recorded by Nansen in the *Fram* beyond the continental shelf surrounding the Arctic Ocean was shallower, and the latest hypothetical map (Nansen's, 1907), which Peary had access to, had water deeper than 1640 fathoms at the North Pole. Peary's actual 1909 soundings, together with Nansen's, made deep water at the Pole appear a near certainty. Moreover, the fact that the Camp Jesup sounding was made so quickly and ended with a break not far from the reel would provide sufficient excuse even if later explorers did, against all expectation, find shallow water at the real Pole. The possibility did not upset Peary when asked about it before the Congressional subcommittee. "If. . .somebody else should go there [to the Pole] and get only 100 fathoms, that would not look well," he replied. Would it destroy his claim? Peary certainly never said so. His reading might have been explained away, if it had ever become necessary, by attributing it to a trick of a swift current in shallow water or some other difficulty. Other Peary fantasies — especially Crocker Land — have been shrugged off similarly, so why not this too? In any case, Peary really had to report the sounding, come what may, since Henson took part in it.

There was, however, one remaining kind of physical evidence of conditions at Camp Jesup that might incriminate Peary: photographs. The fact that the length of a given object's shadow depends on the sun's angular altitude, means that scrutiny of photos might establish their inconsistency with claimed sextant values. Admiral Colby Chester's letter of April 4, 1910, has therefore always been a favorite of Peary advocates:

It is a well-established fact that the altitude of the sun can be determined approximately by measuring the length of its shadow thrown over a raised object on the earth's surface, as shown in pictures. I have examined a number of photographs made by Commander Peary while en route to the Pole, and by this measure of the sun's altitude established the latitude of the place at which they were taken, and in every case the result accorded with his record and observation.

This is very comforting — if Chester saw *all* Peary's photos. Especially crucial were the Camp Jesup ones, since slight discrepancies elsewhere could usually be obscured by inexactitude about the local time. But at the Pole there is no local time, so a photo there is especially indicative. Thus it is interesting how particularly unhelpful Peary's published North Pole photos are on this matter, being uniformly shaded, fuzzy, or with shadows on irregular surfaces or extending beyond the picture's edge, etc. Chester perhaps found likewise, since he speaks only of his using photos "en route to the Pole" for his analysis. Would Peary select only safe pictures for publication? How could we ever know? Fortunately, Peary wasn't the only civilized person at Camp Jesup with a camera. Henson had one. And he used it to take more than *100* pictures at this camp. Surely his collection should provide a basis for testing Peary's claim. Should, but doesn't. In the most dramatic revelation of the Henson newspaper article is this innocent report:

Besides those I am now exhibiting I exposed 110 films about the Pole which, upon his request, I loaned to Commander Peary. . . [who] borrowed [them] saying he would use some and then return them to me. He has never done [so]. . . .

Henson wrote Peary three letters plus a telegram during this period, but received no reply and no pictures in return, thus forcing Henson to use one or two fuzzy, end-of-roll would-be rejects for his lectures. Peary's theft thus effectively destroyed photographic evidence which could have literally exposed his Camp Jesup ruse.

Another curious aspect of Peary's tale is the unprecedented sustained sledge speed implied. The reports are striking: his arrival at land (April 22) only 4+ days after Bartlett, the covering of 300 miles in just eight days (April 2-9) with a finishing kick back to April Fool Camp of nearly 50 miles per day, his reluctance to admit that he rode as dead weight during most of this zippy trip. Further, we have used (and will continue to do so, for simplicity of comparisons) beeline idealizations for mileages. But, in fact, when sledging over the Arctic Ocean, detours add 75% distance to the net displacement achieved — i.e., 50 miles a day made good requires moving sledges nearer 90 (or about 100 statute miles) over the worst possible traveling surface. (Though the validity of the comparison is questionable, it might be mentioned in passing that, in a 1910 Navy test, Peary could only endure walking 25 miles a day over flat American roads.)

Walking, riding, running, or flying on wings of fancy, Peary certainly came up with some terrific bursts of speed on occasion in his 1909 story. But why? After all, if he had really traveled only 75 miles beyond the April 1 camp, his rather reasonable average speed would not have been unbelievably inflated (roughly 15 percent) had he incorporated about 60 more imaginary miles into the whole. But if this inflation were spread evenly, it would have required 15 percent cheating every march, thus necessitating a conspiracy with Bartlett and/or Henson. This would have also been the case if Peary had added extra days to his account. Instead, Peary again deceived at as few places as possible. Whether for simplicity or because there were at least five witnesses (one with a diary) with him all the way, he did not change the date or number of a single camp. Thus all difficulties exist only between April 1 and 9. Peary's dates at the camp whose position was fixed by Bartlett. From the April 1 camp to Camp Jesup was actually 75 miles at most; but to reach the Pole, this distance had to be stretched — roughly doubled — in Peary's account, to about 130 miles. Therefore his speed after April 1 also had to be about doubled, which is what leads to the shocking velocity discontinuity at that date.

The contrast of Peary's claimed speed with that of Bartlett and previous explorers has probably been, over the years, the single major criticism of Peary's claim. However, the most serious speed improbability is not Peary versus mortal explorers but Peary versus Peary. Even more interesting than his April 1 speed-up is the fact that, on the return over the already broken trail, *Peary suddenly slows down by a factor of about two after passing southward through the April 1 Camp* (April 9-10), the very camp where he is forced, by Bartlett's certificate, to come back to reality. It should be no surprise to learn that Peary had an excuse for this peculiar change of pace. He said in his book and repeated at his hearings that his dogs looked a little bushed, so he simply had to slow down. Of the 23 camps on Peary's route after April 1, this is the *only* one at which he mentions choosing to slow down. Furthermore, the next 57 miles of sledging were to be over a region of thin frozen-over leads (fast going on smooth ice, as Peary says), which gave him "a great deal of concern [due to its vulnerability to possible storm] until we had passed it." This was a most peculiar time to slow down.

If the ice after April 1 had suddenly become smooth and thus made the northward going easy, as Peary said, then the importance of traveling over a pre-pickaxed trail, during the return over it, should be diminished; thus, the homeward pace (April 7-9) over this final-leg ice should differ little from the upward rate on it (April 2-6), about 26 miles per day. But such was not the case at all. After 58 miles on April 7 (26 of it near Camp Jesup, eight over new trail), Peary claimed to have traveled 53 miles on April 8 and 45 on April 9. Thus the 5-to-3 return-vs.-outward speed ratio (characteristic of rough ice) is not only maintained but exceeded.

From April 10 to 16 (after which the upward trail is temporarily lost), with ever lighter sledges (as the food is consumed) he can only average about 25 miles per day. Despite the (story's) slowdown (to a speed much like Bartlett's over this ice). Peary reached land before midnight on April 22, only four and a half days after Bartlett's arrival (April 18 — published as 17), though his post-April 1st distance was half Peary's. His seeming inconsistency the helpful Captain explained away in his book, published 19 years later: "I didn't make much of a march [April 1, going south] and there was

159

no incentive to go fast. Our dogs went well with their light sledges but I didn't want to hurry. I felt like lingering a little in case anything happened to those north of me." (But in a contemporary letter to MacMillan, Bartlett cast a different light on his return. He wrote that (from March 20): ". . . I got on fine. . . .reached ship in splendid condition. But it was drive her, boy drive her."

Peary, practically on his heels, pulled into Cape Columbia the morning of April 23. "I have got the North Pole out of my system," he wrote,". . .and it has been accomplished in a way that is thoroughly American." Then he crawled into his igloo and slept for most of two days.

Two more days later, Peary reached the *Roosevelt*, perhaps still unsure not only of what story eventually to put in writing, but of whether or not to go through with this final exploring hoax, the greatest not only of his career, but in all the history of science.

Bartlett, who had returned to the ship only three days before, greeted him and, before Peary had uttered a word, shook his hand and said, *"I congratulate you, sir, on the discovery of the Pole!"*

Well, if it was going to be *this* easy. . .!

12. Arranging the Results

Not possessing real proof of a trip to the Pole, Peary now settled down in his private quarters aboard the *Roosevelt* and began the task of figuring out how to make the best of his situation. Presumably still unsure of the story he would ultimately present to the public and the societies, he told no one on the ship of even the bare fact of success, except for Bartlett — though in the absence of any details other than Bartlett's above-quoted recollection, it may justly be wondered exactly who told whom. Peary systematically avoided Henson, who recalled: "From the time of my arrival at the *Roosevelt*, for nearly three weeks. . .I could catch a fleeting glimpse of Commander Peary, but not once in all that time did he speak a word to me. . . .Not a word about the North Pole or anything connected with it." When Dr. Goodsell asked directly if he'd reached the Pole, Peary replied "I have not been altogether unsuccessful."

As always, Peary was excused for his odd behavior. Mac-Millan speaks of Peary's "promise to the loyal men of the Peary Arctic Club that they should be the first to know" to be the cause of his reticence. One wonders how Bridgman, the Club's secretary, who publicly guessed in September, 1909, that Borup or MacMillan might have gone all the way, could have expected Peary to keep his attainment of the Pole a secret from men who were standing on it. So obviously, any such promise, if made, couldn't have been meant to cover expedition members. (In fact, the first telegrams went to Mrs. Peary and the newspapers.)

161

For weeks Peary kept to himself; "This was the first time in all my arctic expeditions that I had been at headquarters through May and June." Now that the work was done, he deemed it time to "arrange the results," a job that required long and doubtless agonizing deliberation before commitment. Finally, in June, Borup and some Eskimos had to sledge about 170 miles roundtrip, to place a written cairn record at Cape Columbia — all because Peary had at the same spot neglected this non-private ceremony on his April 23-25 stopover, apparently being too busy writing in a diary no one would see until many months later. The monument erected contained a written statement, dated June 12, of various details of the expedition, including the fact that it "in the spring of 1909 attained the North Pole." (As the whole expedition saw this document before it left the ship, what became of that promise to the Peary Arctic Club?) A wooden guidepost was erected over the monument, one arm of which pointed north and evidently read "North Pole, April 6, 1909, 413 miles" — Peary's first public commitment to a date of discovery. (In 1906, it also took Peary 'til June to commit himself in public writing, regarding the fact of his farthest.)

On July 18, Peary left forever the sight of the Arctic Ocean that had beaten him so often. At Etah, on August 17, Cook's two North Pole Eskimos were interviewed by Peary's men, who had sweated, fought, and risked their lives against hundreds of miles of the hellish Arctic Ocean ice, the sort of journey Cook was ready to fake entirely. In an incredulous fury at this, Borup scrawled in his journal *"Dr. Cook is a damn liar."*

Presumably pondering the now inevitable upcoming controversy, which would surely throw an unprecedentedly strong spotlight on his own 1909 story, Peary lingered at Etah for four days, ostensibly for overhauling the ship and helping the Eskimos lay in walrus meat for the winter. But, finally, on the evening of September 5th, 1909, the *Roosevelt* arrived at the wireless station "Smoky Tickle" near Indian Harbor, Labrador. Now, at last, Peary could tell the world how he had conquered the Pole. His pace here, as all through this period,

162

contrasts interestingly with Green's account, which assumed what one with an honest tale, out to head off a fraud, *would* do: "All breathlessly down the Labrador to the first little telegraph station. . . ." Not too breathlessly. Perhaps the imminence of the moment of truth, or whatever, brought home to Peary the magnitude and difficulty of what he was about to attempt. In any case, though the ship arrived at the station (which remained open all night) at 10 P.M., Atlantic Time (9 P.M., Eastern), still early enough for his news to make the American morning papers, he waited until morning to row ashore with Bartlett to the actual telegraph key.

Peary's revealing first telegram, only censored versions of which appear in all the histories, was sent to Jo. "Have made good at last. I have the D.O.P. [damned old pole] Am well. Love. Will wire again from Chateau." Then, after asking Bartlett to go ahead and send a telegram to his mother, Peary finally buckled down to the irrevocable business at hand. To the New York *Times* (to which he was in debt, and who owned rights to an account of his success): "I have the Pole April 6. Expect to arrive Chateau Bay September 7. Secure control wire for me there and arrange expedite transmission big story." To the Associated Press: "Stars and Stripes Nailed to the Pole." To the Peary Arctic Club, via Bridgman: "Sun," which was a pre-arranged code for "Pole reached, Roosevelt safe." Other cables followed — at least 15 were published — to bankers, lodges, yacht clubs, etc. But still no details of the trip. A station that could carry all these wires certainly could have transmitted Peary's main story, had he chosen to file it.

A newspaper story of September 6 described events at the expectant Peary home. A smiling reporter called at Eagle Island, and Marie (almost 16) inquired:

"Have you any news?"

"Yes," he said, "Indian Harbor."

The young woman leaned forward eagerly. "Oh! What is it?" she asked breathlessly.

"Your father has nailed the Stars and Stripes to the North Pole," said the man.

163

. . .Mrs. Peary ran swiftly down and approached the reporter with outstretched hands. Again he repeated the news. Mrs. Peary covered her face for an instant with her hands. . ."God bless you!" and then, "It is too good to be true."

At this happiest moment of her life, Jo could not help reflecting, in a truly pathetic way;

". . .What he has accomplished represents the best years of his life. It doesn't seem to me that we have lived at all. Sleeping and waking, that is all he has thought about, all he has worked for. . . . How many months we have waited for him, worried about him. But it is all worth while."

On September 7, despite yesterday's statement to the N.Y. *Times*, Peary decided not to go on right away after all.

Bridgman, heading north by rail, talked to newspapermen on the 7th, stating that he expected to meet Peary in Sydney on Wednesday the 8th. The P.A.C. Secretary's anticipations provide unsettling comparisons with actual future events:

I expect that Commander Peary will leave [Sydney] with me by the end of this week [for]. . .Maine, where his wife is waiting for him. . . . It has been a long, trying wait for her. . . . [It's] quite possible that he will be at his old home in Maine by the early part of next week. He will probably stay there for a few days, and then will come on through to Washington. I do not think he will tarry in New York on his way through, as he has an official message to communicate to the Washington authorities.

When the *Roosevelt* finally moved ahead, it was not to Chateau Bay and the secured control wire — apparently because telegraphic facilities had been closed down there — but to the Battle Harbor station, a 35 mile shorter trip, arriving September 8. And still no "big story," just a short itinerary of 250 words. He also wired the State Department: "formally took possession. . . entire region and adjacent for and in name of President." To President Taft: "Have honor to place North Pole your disposal." Light reply: "Thanks your generous offer. I do not know exactly what to do with it. I congratulate you sincerely. . . ."

About now, usually cheery Borup told his diary: "Gee I wished it was a year ago. I hate to get back."

On September 9, the big story of 3500 words was finally communicated, at least half of it was. The critical post-April 1 part was sent on September 10. Thereafter followed another delay, of nine days, explained years later by Bartlett as due to his own wishes for some ship cleaning and defumigating: "Our ship was worse than a Chinese stinkpot . . . for nearly twelve months she had harbored seventy-seven Eskimos . . . who had never had a bath since their birth . . . two hundred dogs and fifty tons of rotten whale meat and blubber. If we had entered New York at the time, I think the Board of Health would have rushed out and sprinkled us with lime and put us to sea again." Even so, Peary was the Commander, and a ship can be cleaned while on the move, and had already been so at Etah anyway. Rumors grew of crew discontent at the unexplained delay, and Bartlett's excuse was not forthcoming at the time. If Peary's hope was to avoid curious newsmen by his peculiar reticence, he was to be quickly disappointed. By September 13th, a tug full of Associated Press reporters and Harper's Brothers representatives arrived at Battle Harbor, followed three days later by a bigger load yet of eager inquirers.

Finally, on September 18, the *Roosevelt* moved ahead, reaching Sydney, Nova Scotia, on the 21st, where Peary was reunited with Jo and their two children, who had come north more than a week earlier. That afternoon, he received a telegram from the Peary Arctic Club and then announced that, on the advice of its president, Thomas Hubbard, and secretary, Bridgman, he would refuse public celebrations or lectures "until the present controversy has been settled by competent authority." At this point, Peary left the *Roosevelt* to continue by train to Eagle Island, his Maine home. On September 23, Peary handed Hubbard some original documents, "papers of extreme importance"; however, these were entirely relative to debunking Cook's fraud, not to establishing his own claim. Hubbard then suggested, in a newspaper interview, that Cook place his records before a competent authority for examination, and added, "I may say that Commander Peary will also be expected to turn over his data and observations for the same purpose." When was not mentioned.

Meanwhile, Cook was developing his own elaborate stall, saying that some of his original observations were not with him, but had been left in Greenland in a box with Arctic sportsman Harry Whitney, whom Cook expected back in the United States in mid-October, toward the end of Cook's lecture series. Whitney instead arrived in New York at virtually the moment of Cook's September Carnegie Hall lecture series kick-off, but without the records or any knowledge of them. Cook thereupon said that he wasn't sure he'd told Whitney the papers were in the box; besides, he reassured believers, he'd kept copies with him all along.

Peary commented: "I cannot conceive it possible for a man under the circumstances to have left such priceless things out of his sight for an instant." Records or no, Cook raked in rewards from a hero-hungry public while Peary fumed at the galling situation: "I pulled the thing off finally," he later confided to the Royal Geographical Society, "and then have the whole matter soiled and smirched by a cowardly cur of a sordid imposter." Peary's ego had been badly bruised by negative public opinion, a conspicuous example being a newspaper poll published on September 26 by the Pittsburgh *Press*. Of the 76,052 readers sending in votes on the Polar controversy, 96 percent favored Cook, a commentary on the value of prevailing opinion as a guide for establishing the truth. The statistical breakdown:

73,238 believed Cook discovered the North Pole in 1908
2,814 believed Peary discovered the Pole in 1909
15,229 believed Peary was second to the Pole in 1909
2,814 believed Cook did not reach the Pole in 1908
58,009 believed Peary did not reach the Pole in 1909

As the figures indicate, almost four-fifths of those who believed in Cook totally rejected Peary's claim, with only one Cookite in five convinced that Peary even came in second. And not *one* of the 2,814 who disbelieved Cook's claim could bring himself to doubt Peary as well. No one — of more than 75,000 readers voting — indicated a belief that *both* claimants could be phonies. This might be laid to the public's rejection of the odds against two near-simultaneous fakes. Regardless, there is nothing unusual about the American people's being presented with two frauds to choose between; indeed, it happens just about every election year.

George Borup and D.B. MacMillan (in center) flanked by Eskimos.

Camp Morris Jesup. Below, driving through rough ice on the trail.

13. Eager for Impartial Judgment

It is obvious that if Peary ever really had any proof of his discovery, his first act on his return should have been immediately to place his records (or certified photographs of them) as sealed *lettres de cachet* with some established geographical society and then to challenge Cook to mutual disclosure before an international body of impartial experts. That some such plan had been thought of is evidenced by Bridgman's statement, written before Peary's first Labrador wire, on what should be expected of Cook: "Records, diaries, notebooks, locations, courses, and all indicia so well-known to explorers will be produced and placed with . . . the principal geographical societies of the world." Also, the President of the Paris Geographical Society had, on September 12, recommended

> . . . that all documents should be submitted to a scientific society which would name a commission composed of explorers, astronomers, and navigators, and polar experts. Every document should be produced in order that the conclusion may be definite. The commission should have the right to summon witnesses and cross-examine. Naturally, in the selection of a commission, the United States should be excluded. One cannot be both judge and party.

Finally, on October 1, Peary Arctic Club President Thomas Hubbard, Peary's lawyer-supporter, telegraphed the National Academy of Sciences: "Peary willing and desirous to submit

169

all his records and data to National Academy committee or other scientists impartially selected."

That same day, the National Geographic Society board of managers announced that the Society could accept the bare report of neither explorer, "without investigation by its committee on research or by a scientific body acceptable to it." Cook and Peary "were urged speedily to submit their observations to a competent scientific commission in the United States." Also on October 1, Peary told reporters that he would be "governed largely by developments in the next few days."

The Hubbard-Peary move was not as simple as it seemed on the surface. For over a week the presidents of the friendly American Museum of Natural History and the American Geographical Society had been privately communicating with the National Academy of Sciences regarding the appointment of a Peary examining committee, and Hubbard had been communicating with them. On September 29, lawyer Hubbard, with Peary at his side had sent American Museum President Henry Osborn a private wire that has the distinct smell of jury tampering about it: "Please defer final arrangements of Committee until you see Peary. Give Peary acceptance, and declination of other party, to Associated Press."

On October 6, the explorer echoed Hubbard's October 1 telegram, with a major alteration: Peary would submit to a committee of *"American* scientists . . . impartially selected" [emphasis added], a contradiction in sampling procedure if ever there was such. And it was no accident. In a private handwritten note of October 7. Peary spelled it right out for Bridgman, stating that his records were strictly "for home, not foreign examination."

On October 11, the National Geographic board and the American Museum of Natural History jointly requested Ira Remsen, President of the National Academy of Sciences,

to appoint a commission to pass upon the records of Commander Peary and Dr. Cook. This plan for an early examination failed, as Dr. Remsen stated that he would not be able to appoint said commission unless authorized by his council, which meets late in November, and unless also requested to do so by both Commander Peary and Dr. Cook.

Commander Peary was willing to abide by such a commission, but Dr. Cook stated that his observations would go first to the University of Copenhagen. In view of the fact that Commander Peary had been waiting since his return, in September, to submit his records to a scientific commission in the United States, the National Geographical Society believed it should receive his papers without delay.

Gilbert Grosvenor later gave another version of the National Academy of Sciences withdrawal, stating that Remsen, during a private Baltimore conference with National Geographical officials on October 12, had been reluctant to involve himself and the N.A.S. because so much bitterness and temper was swirling around the Cook-Peary affair.

Where the involved parties can not even get their stories straight, a bit of speculation seems permissible. At this meeting, might not Grosvenor, realizing the rich stakes involved for National Geographic if it could become Peary's judge, have done some nudging of Remsen into such a shy course? As will be seen below, it was on this very date that the National Geographic secretly initiated the negotiations with Peary which led to his certification solely by the Society.

In any case, as its report makes clear, National Geographic had, by mid-October, taken over entirely and publicly the business of judging Peary.

Well over a month had now passed since the intrepid explorer's return, and yet he had not been so bold as to expose a single original observation sheet to the gaze of a single human. There was no reason why Peary or Cook should not have brought their data straight to scientists without delay. Eventually, the reluctant Cook promised to send his records to the University of Copenhagen, which had already conferred on him an honorary degree. Peary, on the other hand, was determined to present his data only to an American group. The National Geographic and other societies tried to get access to Cook's data so as to conduct a joint examination in a United States scientific arena, where sentiment and influence were strongest for Peary. This inevitably led to a great deal of fruitless delay, thus giving Peary the leisure to wait for the right society to offer itself up for his purposes, at which time his September 21 stalling excuse (waiting for Cook) might be instantly shelved (as it was on Oct. 13).

The attempts to get at Cook's records were to culminate in November, with the sending of a delegation from the National Geographic, led by Vice President Henry Gannett and including co-founder Professor J. Howard Gore and Secretary and Editor Gilbert H. Grosvenor, to the State Department. This diplomatic ploy to obtain Cook's data for its initial review was all very hush-hush, as the New York *Herald* revealed:

> The order of silence was imposed upon the members, little was spoken above a whisper, and "Sh-h-'s" were frequent. One newspaper reporter recognized a member and went over to shake hands with him, calling him by name. But the scientist promptly denied his identity and appeared annoyed at being recognized.

The effort failed to do anything but offend the University of Copenhagen. Cook held fast to his refusal to put his material before United States authorities, as Peary biographer Hobbs describes it, "On the ground that they must first be submitted to the University of Copenhagen; but to more and more urgent demands from Copenhagen, he replied that he would require at least a month to prepare them, though such records are of value only in their original form and not subsequently produced." Hobbs does not, of course, see anything odd in the fact that the reclusive Peary had had by mid-October over a month to prepare *his* records, too. Again, like Cook, he was to stretch it to nearly two before producing the crucial material, all the while complaining to his friends of the suspiciousness of Cook's two-month delay!

As the time ran out before he was due to finally face his Copenhagen judges, Cook became frantically desperate for some way to extend his grace period. Not sure if his written ex-

172

cuses to the University of Copenhagen rector would work, not trusting his hired mathematician, he was, by late November, in such a state that, like Peary at Camp Jesup, he had insomnia. For further delay, what possible excuse could he use? Under the circumstances, the only thing for it was a nervous breakdown. So, on November 24, he fled the country, his last words to his faithful secretary being: "Now I'll be able to get some sleep!" Coincidentally, it seems that Peary, during his Maine seclusion of early autumn, 1909, while stalling for time before his own judgment, was also having a case of nerves.

Perhaps it was his knowledge of Peary's frail condition that made biographer Green's blood boil at the National Geographic Society's "cruel" examination of the broken-down old explorer:

> It was but another of the shameful trials that Peary had to undergo as a result of the grotesque position a cruel Fate had put him in. Yet he submitted willingly and with good grace. For the aching bitterness in his heart one could not blame him. Through nearly the whole of his lifetime this man had played the game as cleanly as it could be played. And now in the hour of his triumph he was being cross-questioned like a common rogue. Yet he had no dignified alternative. So he went before the tribunal selected by a Society whose officers have always been largely distinguished Government officials. According to the official record:

> "At a meeting of the board of managers of the National Geographic Society, Wednesday morning, *October 20,* 1909, the records, observations and proofs of Commander Robert E. Peary *that he reached the Pole* April 6, 1909, were submitted to the Society. The records and observations were immediately referred to the Committee on Research, with the direction that the chairman appoint a subcommittee of experts, of which he shall be a member, to examine the records and report on them to the board." (Emphasis added)

173

Such red tape! Such superfluous circumlocution! Such persiflage! When this man on trial had not it in him to commit the crime at which all this procedure was aimed. Yet Peary knew there was no other way. And the members of the Society knew there was no other way.

"Mr Henry Gannett, Chairman of the committee on research, immediately appointed as the other members of the committee Rear Admiral Colby M. Chester, United States Navy, and O.H. Tittmann, Superintendent of the United States Coast and Geodetic Survey. This committee of the society will personally examine the notebooks and original observations made by Commander Peary in his march to the Pole and see all the papers as brought back from the field. The committee will report the results of its findings at a special meeting of the Board to be called for that purpose."

And so on through reams of foolscap and pitiable weeks of time.

The whole thing was finally accomplished and an itemized report produced that fully and finally established the scientific accuracy of Peary's claims.

As always, when Green's imagination takes over, he unknowingly damages the case for his hero, by indicating how things *ought* to have been done.

Unfortunately for Green, the official National Geographic Society report from which he launched his flight of fancy is guilty of a few falsehoods. Its intimation that Peary was eager to have his records examined as soon as possible is obviously contradicted by dates.

A more important misleading National Geographic statement was that the material received on October 20 was evidence of Peary's reaching the Pole. It was about at this critical point (Oct. 20) when Congressman Roberts swung into a review of the National Geographic examination, that Peary began suffering from fearful fits of amnesia (Peary hearings):

174

Mr. Roberts. I understand you first sent [the National Geographic Society] through a Mr. Nichols [Charles J. — another Peary lawyer] a statement of some sort, sent it from. . . Maine. . . .

Captain Peary. I sent them papers; yes.

Mr. Roberts. Do you object to telling us what those papers were?

Captain Peary. Well, I will suggest as to that that the members of the [National Geographic Society] subcommittee who had those papers — and it is probably on their records — could give that information with absolute accuracy. I don't know if I have a memorandum of what those papers were.

At the time these papers arrived, one could read of them in the *New York Times* (Oct. 21), something never appearing in the official report, namely, that Peary himself would not be asked to appear "unless some unforeseen tangle over the records should arise." In the *New York Times* of November 1 a slightly less prominent article appeared, relating that Peary was being summoned after all and was expected in Washington that day:

. . . to appear in person before the [National Geographic Society sub]committee. . . . The explorer will bring with him additional data asked for by the committee, . . .

National Geographic Society Vice President (soon to be President) Gannett was quoted publicly: "The committee wants to make a complete and impartial report, and that is all I can say as to our reasons for awaiting the rest of the data." Contradicting these reports of more information being requested, Gannett and Peary testified that Peary had not expected the October 20 material to be insufficient. This allegation was backed by no written document, and contrasts curiously not only with the *New York Times* October 21 article, but also with the wording of the announcement of receipt of the Peary records on the opening page of the November *National Geographic Magazine* and with the mid-October exchange of telegrams that had brought in the data

175

in the first place. National Geographic to Peary (October 15):

> Board of National Geographic Society wishes to act on your expedition at regular meeting next Wednesday [October 20th]. Can you not immediately forward us sufficient records to justify action then?

Peary to National Geographic Society (October 16):

> Will have material in Washington by Wednesday. That I trust will serve the society's purpose.

No mention of Peary's supposed expectation that these records were insufficient. In the *New York Times* interviews of November 1, "members of the [National Geographic Society committee] made it plain today that in asking for further enlightenment as to his data they were not dissatisfied with the data already submitted by Commander Peary, but that *certain* documents had been omitted from the first [October 10th] installment *by inadvertence*." (Emphasis added.) The October 20th records were carried personally from Maine to Washington by Peary's old friend and Lawyer, Nichols. Recall (above) that Peary had remarkable difficulty remembering for the Congressmen just what this material comprised. No wonder. Gannett in 1910 under cross-examination made the crucial admission that a little something had been left out of the "voluminous" material submitted: "Peary originally sent down a Mr. Nichols with certain papers which brought the record *up to the time that Bartlett left him.* . . . (Emphasis added). Thus, contrary to the National Geographic report, nothing relating to the North Pole arrived Oct. 20.

Apparently Peary had to be explicitly urged to submit anything further. Again he had stalled, saying he would bring the rest of his material personally. Gannett: ". . . but he was not able to leave his home at that time in order to attend the committee." (Actually, by October 13, Peary had said he was "ready for departure" — but this was before any request for proofs.) Peary and the North Pole data did not arrive at the National Geographic until November 1.

Why was he "not able" to come to Washington for two more weeks? (Recall that Bridgman had expected him and his report there by mid-September). No official reason is on record, but two possibly proffered excuses may be induced: 1. Hobbs later claimed that Peary spent this period writing his magazine story (untrue); 2. An excerpt from an October 28 letter (toward the close of this last delay) from Peary to National Geographic Society secretary and friend Grosvenor indicates how simple it was to exploit pity for his exhausted condition (while he was furiously corresponding with Bridgman, Hubbard, et al. on how to stop Cook).

The quiet, undisturbed time which I am now having is very pleasant to me. It is particularly agreeable to have this opportunity after so many years of effort, of being with my wife and children in our little island home, with no thought of the future to disturb either of us, and with the feeling of intense satisfaction and content that results from having done the thing that one has started out to do, and has put one's whole life into.

By the time Peary arrived in Washington, the subcommittee members must have been ashamed of themselves for putting him through an ordeal such as an examination. Indeed, both Gannett and Chester later spoke as if doubting Peary would have been almost immoral.

Evidently, Peary was trying to see just how little material he could get away with submitting, a gambit he later tried with Congress, delaying almost a year before appearing with his diary. That original diary was dynamite. If it contained anything revealing, he could not blame the error on memory, since it was supposed to have been written nearly contemporaneously with the events described; so it was best that it be carried personally to Washington and whisked back to Maine the same evening. Granted that one would understandably wish to protect such a document, Peary appears to border on the fetishist. For over a month, he would not even *show* it to anyone at all, nor would he entrust it to Nichols and the National Geographic Society committee. Even as late as January, 1911, when the Congressmen politely asked him to leave the diary with them for a while to let them look at it unhurriedly, Peary suddenly bristled: "I do not care to leave it with the committee or anyone. I do not care to let it out of my possession; it never has been."

On November 1, 1909, Peary arrived in Washington to be "cross-questioned like a common rogue. . . ." Gannett recalled that Peary

brought his records in a gripsack and his instruments in a trunk. First he met the committee at the office of the [National] Geographic Society and we appointed a [luncheon] meeting at the house of Admiral Chester. . . .We simply sat down with him and read his journal from his original records. . . . We also had his astronomical observations recomputed, examined them, not recomputed, for he had already computed them on these [data] sheets. . . .Admiral Chester recomputed [a set of observations]; I do not know whether Mr. Tittmann did or not. . . we had his line of soundings. . . .

And the instruments? Gannett: ". . . they started with Peary [in Maine] in a trunk. . .and his trunk did not get here until evening, and we examined the contents of it, examined the instruments down at the station that evening without moving the trunk" — while seeing Peary off on his hasty return to Maine. Simple enough, but Peary could not remember very much of it for Congressman Roberts:

Mr. Roberts. What did you do when you arrived in the city [Washington]; where did you go?

Captain Peary. I do not recall what my movements were.

Mr. Roberts. Perhaps I will ask some leading questions, as the lawyers say, and suggest in my question the answer. You went to the [National] Geographic Society's rooms in the forenoon?

Captain Peary. I do not remember when I went there. The members of the board can tell.

Mr. Roberts. It was the same day you got in?

Captain Peary. Yes.

Mr. Roberts. You went to the Geographical Society's rooms?

Captain Peary. No; I think not. The Geographical Society's rooms? [Where Peary had met the subcommittee.]

Mr. Roberts. Yes; on Sixteenth Street.

Captain Peary. That I can not say.

Roberts made a little progress, but Peary's memory had to be led along, especially concerning the examination of the instruments. Only because Roberts appeared to know all the answers ahead of time, anyway, did he get any information at all from Peary:

Mr. Roberts. After you reached the station and found the trunk what did you and the committee do with regard to the instruments?

Captain Peary. I should say that we opened the trunk there in the station.

Mr. Roberts. That is, in the baggage room of the station?

Captain Peary. Yes.

Mr. Roberts. Were the instruments all taken out?

Captain Peary. That I could not say. Members of the committee will probably remember that better than I.

Mr. Roberts. Well, you do not have any recollection of whether they took them out and examined them?

Captain Peary. Some were taken out, I should say; whether all were taken out I would not say.

Mr. Roberts. Was any test of those instruments made by any member of the committee to ascertain whether or not the instruments were accurate?

Captain Peary. That I could not say. I should imagine that it would not be possible to make tests there.

Mr. Roberts. Were those instruments ever in the possession of the committee other than the inspection at the station?

Captain Peary. Not to my knowledge.

179

The committee's decision to approve Peary's claim was made that very evening (Nov. 1); thus, the entire examination of the *vital* evidence (beyond Bartlett) had not extended through Green's "pitiable weeks of time" — from October 20th into early November, as the official National Geographic Society report states, but rather (at most) a few *hours!* At no time was any other member of the expedition — Henson, Bartlett, etc., called to be cross-examined.

The subcommittee report to the National Geographic Society Board of Managers was accepted without "the slightest" question. Official National Geographic Society approval was made ublic on November 3 the same day that saw another timeless judgment make *New York Times* column headlines: "Mars Digging More Canals, Says [Percival] Lowell. Appearance of New Ones Suggests System is Undergoing Construction or Adaptation."

Part of the text of the subcommittee report to the National Geographic Society Board of Managers makes almost as interesting copy as Green's:

> Commander Peary has submitted to this subcommittee his original journal and records of observations together with all his *instruments* and apparatus and certain of the most important scientific results of his expedition. These have been *carefully examined* by your subcommittee, and they are unanimously of the opinion that Commander Peary reached the North Pole on April 6, 1909.
>
> They also feel warranted in stating that the organization, planning, and management of the expedition, its complete success and its scientific results reflect the greatest credit on the ability of Commander Robert E. Peary and render him worthy of the highest honors that the National Geographic Society can bestow upon him. (Emphasis added.)

Henry Gannett
C. M. Chester
O.H. Tittmann

180

Since the National Geographic Society's certification was to be the most impressive official stamp of verity on Peary's trip, it is enlightening to see how alert the Society was to signs of exploration fraud. President Moore's reaction to doubts of Cook was printed in the New York *Herald* of September 6, 1909, just before Peary's first wire:

I regret that there has been in some quarters, since Dr. Cook's discovery of the North Pole, an attempt to revive the discrediting of his ascension of Mount McKinley. Our Society had Dr. Cook lecture before it on the subject of Mount McKinley, and I assure you we would not have invited him if there had been the slightest doubt of his integrity, courage and ability.

Moore on Cook's North Pole story:

After having read it there can be no question of Dr. Cook's success or the accuracy of his findings. It is stamped with the genuineness of his work.

Moore's opinion of Cook's Polar claim is not so indicative (being then based on early reports and later revised under fire) as is his and the Society's complete swallowing of the Mt. McKinley fake, then hardly fresh. In both cases, he well typifies the prevailing gullibility of the societies and the public. The same optimist's approach was evident even in the statements of some scientists, including Dr. Otto Tittmann, Henry Gannett, and Frank Perkins, the former two comprising a majority of the National Geographic Society committee that later approved Peary. On September 3, 1909, the *Times* reported their reaction to skeptics: "In their opinion even if Dr. Cook were not an explorer of the utmost veracity, it would be almost inconceivable that a man of any knowledge of the requirements of scientific proof should deliberately try to palm off a fake discovery on the world." Tittmann was further quoted as saying: "what he [Cook] says will have to be accepted until the contrary is proved." Which it never was by any geographical society. Such an attitude, of course, gives carte blanche to any Polar faker who disappears from civilization for awhile and can avoid gross Cooklike math incompetencies in the story he brings back.

Similar kindly first impressions had their effect on the official judgment of Peary by the National Geographic committee. Peary's peculiar stall regarding the post-Bartlett data not only did not engender suspicion— to the contrary: both Gannett and Tittman were convinced of the truth of Peary's story just on the basis of the first installment (up to April 1)! This they admitted before Congress, Gannett echoing his colleague thus: ". . . it is hardly believable that a man would sit down within 130 miles of the North Pole and [fake observations] after he had undertaken the uncertainties, the dangers, and the risks to life. . . ."

Why was he so easy to convince?

Mr. Gannett. Everyone who knows Peary by reputation knows he would not lie; I know him by reputation.

Mr. Roberts. A fair inference would be that you believed his statement when it first appeared in the press and before you saw the proofs?

Mr. Gannett. I certainly did.

Peary showing proofs of his discovery of the North Pole to the subcommittee of the National Geographic Society, November 1, 1909. Left to right, Gilbert H. Grosvenor, Otto H. Tittmann, Willis L. Moore, Peary, Henry M. Gannett, Colby M. Chester.

14.   See No Evil

The November 3rd National Geographic pronouncement unlocked the fiscal sluice-gates. The very day following the decision, Peary contracted with *Hampton's Magazine* for $40,000, for a serialized version of the recounting of his achievement. A similar figure was soon after agreed upon with Frederick A. Stokes Co. for a book. Lecturing followed at $1000 per day.

The National Geographic Society blessing was also the single major key to subsequent near-universal acceptance, down to the present, of Peary's claimed attainment of the North Pole. Any examination of that claim must necessarily include a scrutiny of the men who judged it, calling into question not only their actions but their ethics, to determine if the public was handed a decision tainted by a conflict of interest. The members of the subcommittee — Gannett, Tittmann, and Chester — were most likely to carry the prejudices of the Society, since all were on its Board of Trustees (then called "Board of Managers"). Gannett, like Tittmann, was one of the founders of the Society and, in 1909, became an associate editor of its magazine. He was also vice president — later president — of the Society and chairman of its Committee on Research; in fact, all three men were members of that committee when, in 1907, one thousand dollars from the Society's Research Fund was voted as a contribution toward the very expedition they were destined to judge. Though they were capable scientists, they were not im-

183

partial judges. Indeed, at the 1906 National Geographic Society award ceremony for Peary, all three were on the dinner committee.

Tittmann was the only member of the trio who was not a personal friend of Peary's, but even he, as Superintendent of the United States Coast and Geodetic Survey, under which Peary had served on his 1908-1909 expedition, was bound to be predisposed to a positive verdict. Witness the *New York Times* account of the Survey's reaction to Peary's initial report: "The Coast and Geodetic Survey is very proud of Commander Peary's achievement in reaching the Pole. . . . the entire service feels that it will receive some reflected glory from the result. . . ." The feeling was mutual. Peary to Tittman in 1910: "Kindly remember me to my friends in the Coast Survey. . . ." Despite such manifestations of good fellowship, Tittmann influenced the final decision less than the other two members of the subcommittee.

Chester, a wheeler-dealer on an international level in using political influence for private fiscal gain, was a good friend of Peary's, so good that Cook accused him of sharing in Peary's fur profits. Though an October 26, 1909, letter from Chester to Peary Arctic Club Secretary Bridgman seems to have attempted a little formal firmness during Peary's final stall, the demands made are rather lax. It is quite clear that Cook's claim is the sole target of Chester's doubts.:

> Our Committee understands that Commander Peary will be in Washington next Monday and so I shall not come to New York as expected. I hope he can bring all of his instruments on for inspection. . . . Can you get for me a memorandum that Captain Bartlett said he would make regarding his first view of the midnight sun and I would like also the records from Professor MacMillan and Mr. Borup. This has an important bearing on the *other* case. . . .The date and latitude is all that is necessary but if it is in the form of a quotation from Note Books it would be well. Very truly yours, C.W. Chester (Emphasis added.)

184

Subcommittee Chairman Gannett, in response to a Congressional question on his relationship with Peary, did not mention their common associations (He was Dr. Gannett by virtue of an honorary degree from Peary's alma mater, Bowdoin College), saying:

... I think it is fair to say I was a friend of his, but I do not think I had met him a dozen times in my life; I knew him, had an acquaintanceship with him, and that was all. ... I do not think that if Peary's evidence were found to be insufficient or faulty the committee would have had the slightest hesitation in turning him down.

This public pretext to impartiality doesn't square with Gannett's private sentiment. The day after Chester wrote Bridgman, Gannett penned a similar letter to Peary, prefacing it thus: "I want to extend to you personally my heartiest congratulations on your success." Having thus reassured Peary of the purely formal nature of the upcoming "exam," Judge Gannett went on to say (Oct. 27):

I am in receipt of a letter from Mr. Charles J. Nichols written at your suggestion in which he states that you will be in Washington on November 1st with your records and asking whether our subcommittee desires to see your instruments. In reply I would say that it is the desire of the Committee to see all original records and your instruments in order that the fullest possible presentation be made, this for reasons which of course you understand.

The subcommittee will be glad to meet you at Hubbard Memorial Hall. ...

Had the records and instruments Chester and Gannett seemed so anxious to have officially "presented" actually been given a substantial inspection, the perfunctory nature of the whole examination might have been better obscured by the largely correct tone of the two letters. These notwithstanding, the National Geographic committee succumbed to the manifold pressures of partiality.

How else can one explain Admiral Chester's lack of curiosity at Peary's failure to share his Camp Jesup observations with Henson, whom Chester estimated to be capable in such matters? And how else explain innocently that Gannett, a Harvard trained engineer, did not just ignore the significance of Peary's lack of controlling observations for transverse position en route, but later actually defended this omission on (effectively) the remarkable grounds that such steering for the Pole is not possible! — a bit of information which will surely interest all the explorers who have since done it. And how could Gannett, the author of a study of compass-variation in the U.S., close his eyes to the 1909 trip's complete blank in this useful area of scientific research?

In fact, the incredible enormity of their apparent blindness suggests the possibility of something exceeding mere bias, namely that the Geographic trio might have deliberately stifled private doubts while publicly certifying Peary's "unquestionable" Pole victory. But is there any reason to suppose that any one of these eminent gentlemen could be so dishonest? Let us examine the record.

Indeed, an untruth by Gannett appears right in the official National Geographic report (to Congress and the public) of its actions in the Cook-Peary evaluations (Gannett being the responsible chairman of the Peary end of this). The report was personally handed to Congress by Gannett during the Peary Hearings in March, 1910 (where the truth came out during cross-examination) and repeatedly published without correction thereafter. This document identifies Gannett impressively as "chief geographer of the United States Geological Survey since 1882" — a falsehood, as the Geological Survey itself (where Gannett had been only semi-employed since 1882) explicitly stated upon inquiry on the point in 1914.

As for Chester's deceitful behavior in connection with the Peary case — direct knowledge on this will be reserved for our appendix on the Ward Papers. However, a measure of Chester's character can be induced from his shady, multi-million dollar Persian oil dealings, which, though begun in

186

1908, only became public 15 years later, ironically, at the same time Cook's relatively piddling operation got him arrested.

The "Chester concession" was a sensation when news of it broke in 1923, the N.Y. *Times* noting that it could "place Americans virtually in economic control of the new Turkey" and, in an editorial "The Golden Fleece," calling it "the most valuable trophy brought back from the Near East since Jason. . ."

Compared to Chester and Gannett, Tittmann was a minor influence in the 1909 certification of Peary, but even he was demonstrably deceitful while assisting Peary with his Congressional recognition, as will later be seen.

The National Geographic trio's excesses were indeed exceptional. Of course, some shade of over-friendliness to Peary was by no means restricted to this one ultra-loyal group — though one must wonder whether any other society could have enthusiastically endorsed, first-hand, such a pseudo-scientific attainment. Indeed, the American Geographical Society, the nation's most eminent center of geographical scholarship, has never recognized it.

To see why Peary stipulated that his judges be American, it might be well to look at the three major societies as the returned explorer must have seen them in October, 1909. The American Geographical Society was actually a contributing member of the Peary Arctic Club in 1905. Its late President, Charles Daly, was commemorated in North Greenland by Daly Land, a region discovered and named by Peary in 1892. Five years later, Peary was awarded the first Cullom gold medal by the American Geographic Society, and five years after that, he was the first recipient of its Daly gold medal, having discovered the Daly Mountains on his last trip. For a time (1903-1907) Peary was himself the American Geographical Society's President. The American Museum of Natural History was hardly less involved. Morris K. Jesup, the major fiscal instigator and first President of the Peary Arctic Club, had helped found the Museum, and had contributed and bequeathed to it about two million dollars. He was also its

President for some years. The Museum owed many animal exhibits and sledges as well as the world's largest meteorite to Peary, who in 1897 had removed the latter from Greenland to New York. Peary's chummy Indian Harbor telegram to Museum officials would have read like a brazen bribe-offer had they later directly refereed the Cook-Peary bout:

> The Pole is ours. Am bringing large amount of material for the Museum.

There were no isolated geographical societies in the United States. Just as honorary National Geographic Society member Jesup had been President of both the American Museum of Natural History and the American Geographic Society, so Gannett, in 1909 the Vice President of the National Geographic Society, was simultaneously associate editor of the *Bulletin* of the American Geographic Society. The connecting web was more than intellectual and social. Just after Cook's exposure, United States geographer and explorer Henry Bryant wrote:

> The occurrence is bound to dis[credit] American scientists abroad . . . there is more or less jealousy of us abroad, and this Dr. Cook incident will give that sentiment an opportunity to crystallize. . . .

All the American societies would naturally take pride in an American conquest of the Pole. A more serious bond between them was that they all drew from the same general pool of contributors. They not only had a common fiscal stake in the maintenance of public heroes like Robert Peary, but stood to lose more than just an Arctic demigod if Peary were discredited. By late October, 1909, it was clear to the National Geographic Society, both from the Mount McKinley scandal and the tenacity and power of the Peary Arctic Club's anti-Cook campaign, that Cook was probably a goner. If Peary went too, the drop in contributions the Society could expect for future ventures in Polar exploration would be catastrophic. Even as things were, Bartlett failed in an attempt to put the touch on a millionaire in the summer of

1910 for a Polar Sea drift scheme he had in mind. "Chuck it, old man!" a wealthy friend advised him, "Don't you realize that this Polar game is all off? Cook put the ki-bosh on it. Why I wouldn't dare to be associated with you Arctic explorers after all that mess!" This common popular view doubtless contributed to the poor response to the 1910 National Geographic Society-Peary appeal for funds to support a United States Antarctic expedition. Gannett, in confiding to Hubbard, admitted as much:

> For every letter we received containing a subscription we received one abusing our friend Peary. . . . Of course Peary must never hear of this matter, for he [sic] would break his heart.

The National Geographic Society's particular connections to Peary's influence were less obvious than those of the American Geographic Society or American Museum of Natural History but nonetheless quite strong. Peary had been a star lecturer at the National Geographic for years. At Peary's death, Gilbert H. Grosvenor, National Geographic President (Secretary in 1909) and longtime friend and admirer of the explorer, recalled (not entirely accurately — e.g., Peary's first 1906 lecture was in N.Y.):

> Peary's first address to the [National Geographic Society] was in the Fall of 1888, when the society was only a few months old. . . . He had been actively associated with its work ever since those early days, and on his return from each of his expeditions to the far north his first public address was to the National Geographic Society. . . .[Peary] later [after 1909] was a member of the Board of Managers for years.

This sentiment was echoed by Peary's daughter Marie: "Even farther back than my memory serves there has been an unusually strong bond of admiration and affection between the [National Geographic Society] and the Peary family." In July of 1892, Peary proudly flew an American flag donated by the National Geographic at Navy Cliff, the farthest point of his pioneer crossing of northwest Greenland. In 1906, he received the first Gardiner Greene Hubbard gold medal awarded by the Society. His 1908-1909 expedition profited from National Geographic fund-raising efforts, the Society itself being a contributor. All of which may explain the tone of Peary's little-known telegram from Indian Harbor to the National Geographic Society: "Have won out at last. The Pole is ours." Ours? National Geographic President Moore sent the following reply to Peary's wire:

> In answer to your telegraphic report to this Society that you have reached the North Pole the National Geographic Society, through the action of its Board of Managers, today extends to you its heartiest congratulations on your great achievement.

It may seem bad form to use a group's generosity against it, but such acts, psychologically if nothing else, act as an investment and render difficult an objective view of the beneficiary. Moreover, the altruism was not unalloyed. The National Geographic Society was, and is, a business, a profitable — "nonprofit," for tax purposes — publishing concern. The Society's gain in its approval of Peary's claim is not a matter of mere conjecture. In his official history of the organization, longtime Society President Gilbert H. Grosvenor paid Peary his due:

> The National Geographic Society's championship of this distinguished American naval officer always will be a glorious chapter in the history of the organization. The Committee's careful, scholarly vindication of Peary's claims won world-wide approval and clearly established The Society as a potent force in the fields of exploration and scientific research.

Grosvenor undoubtedly realized from the start what prestige and commercial possibilities the opportunity of honoring Peary's discovery held for the National Geographic Society. Yet the published cable of October 15, 1909, to Peary inviting him to submit his records to the Society for judgment

190

seems perfectly proper and uninvolved. Equally proper: only after the "careful scholarly" approval of these records in November was it announced that the Society would host Peary's first lecture. But since this plum had previously been promised to New York, the question arises: Was a *quid* arranged behind the scenes, before an October 15 *quo?* The Society, in a letter to the author in 1968, stated that it was "unable to locate" any 1909 correspondence with Peary. So, how can the truth be determined? Fortunately, the texts of pre-October 15 cables have been obtained, despite the Society's inability to find anything on the subject in its archives. It is not difficult to see why the cables were never published:

Grosvenor to Peary, October 12: "National Geographic Society has been anxiously waiting your appointment of date for your address. Will give you a tremendous welcome."

Peary to Grosvenor, October 13: "Telegram received. Pardon inadvertence. Was under impression everything off under existing circumstances. [Cook controversy.] Delighted come to Washington. Will fix date after conferring General [Thomas] Hubbard. Illustrations under way now. Regards."

With this lucrative commitment in its pocket, the Society was still perfectly ready to pose on October 15 as an impartial examiner of Peary — brass topped only by that which demanded at the same time that the National Geographic Society pass judgment on Cook as well.

What was good for Robert E. Peary was, demonstrably, good for the National Geographic Society. And that included the denigration of the "cowardly cur." Peary said: "I put my views in regard to the [Cook] matter as clearly as I knew how, up to Admiral Chester and Grosvenor, while I was in Washington [November 1]." On November 3, the responsive Society, immediately after handing Peary the Polar prize, appointed a committee to find out "whether or not anyone reached the North Pole prior to 1909. . . ." Predictably, the committee found that no one had. Reported committee spokesmen Professor James Howard Gore and Rear Admiral John E. Pillsbury: ". . .we deem it wise to endorse the

191

opinions expressed by the University of Copenhagen to the effect that there is no evidence to show that Dr. Frederick A. Cook reached the North Pole." They concluded with a statement more meaningful than they probably intended:

> The committee furthermore invites the attention of the board of managers of the National Geographic Society to the conscientious and fearless position taken by the University of Copenhagen in giving wide publicity to a decision which, in the minds of so many, seems incompatible with its earlier attitude. By this act the University of Copenhagen has emphasized the fearless quality of truth and given to the world an example worthy of emulation.

And so it had. But the National Geographic Society did not choose to follow it. Instead, the Society associated itself irrevocably with one of the great frauds of all time.

The North Pole! — photographed from the airship *Norge,* May 12, 1926.

15.   The Making of a Hero

Except for Scandinavia and Paris, there was never much question concerning Peary's recognition by professionals and the established societies — most of whom quickly accepted his word. By contrast, the general public was at first reluctant to accept Peary's claim, because he had denounced the likable Dr. Cook. A hero hungry populace that reasoned at such a level was not going to be hard to manipulate, and Peary's newspaper friends wasted no time in getting to the task.

Because of Cook's nationwide lecture tour, starting on September 27, 1909, at Carnegie Hall in New York, and his 25,000-word newspaper series, "Conquest of the Pole," appearing every other day from Sept. 15 through Oct. 7 in the New York *Herald* and reprinted in newspapers all over the country, the Doctor had an initial advantage. Had he returned to civilization in 1908, a year before Peary's claim, or had Peary never existed, Cook might have fared better. There were, in fact, numerous insiders who were willing to say nothing of Cook's 1906 fake — some even hypocritically praised him — until Peary's 1909 charges forced them to choose sides. But in the jealous Peary camp, Cook had a powerful enemy, and all the underdog sympathy in the world could not long withstand the nags and onslaughts of a largely hostile press.

Though the New York *Herald* was committed to Cook, and the New York *Evening Telegram* and the Paris (France) *Herald* were under the same owner — James Gordon Bennett

193

— Peary otherwise had Cook well beat in the papers. The *New York Times* had contracted for Peary's story; Peary Arctic Club President Hubbard was part owner of the New York *Globe*, among other papers, and Bridgman was business manager of the Brooklyn *Standard Union*. Alfred Harmsworth (Lord Northcliffe) had been a Pearyite since 1898, when he contributed generously, including the ship *Windward*, to Peary's great four-year expedition, during which the explorer christened Harmsworth Bay in Bache Peninsula. As owner of London's *Evening News*, *Daily Mail*, *Daily Mirror*, *The Observer*, and Manchester's edition of the *Daily Mail*, as well as being chief stockholder in the London *Times*, Northcliffe was a good fellow to have on one's side. In England Cook never had a chance.

Moreover, British exploring circles were at least as pro-Peary as were American ones, the Royal Geographical Society having awarded him a gold medal in 1897 for his Greenland labors. British geographers and explorers, while reserved, sardonic, and sometimes openly skeptical about Cook's claim, immediately and unreservedly accepted Peary's a few days later, creating a contrast that was meant to draw note, and did. It being crude etiquette for geographers to accuse a peer of fraud, many simply made known their disdain for Cook by now heaping praise on Peary. British explorers Nares and Shackleton personally wired him their immediate congratulations, and Royal Geographical Society President Leonard Darwin immediately sent the Society's "warmest congratulations." A reporter, on finding that it was already planning a gold medal for Peary, commented: "In striking contrast with this prompt action by the Royal Geographical Society in recognition of Peary's feat, taken even before the publication of the detailed report. . .is the total silence which the society has maintained regarding the claims put forward by Dr. Cook."

Professional opinion in Washington was reported similar to that in London, though naturally a little easier on countryman Cook: ". . .there have been many references [to Cook's need for producing immediate proof.] No such remarks greeted the announcement of Peary this afternoon. It was taken for granted at once...that the documentary evidence will not only be complete but unquestionable."

Every fall in Cook's stock aided Peary's acceptance psychologically. And the Doctor's troubles, much to the consternation of those who tend to trace them to Peary persecution, began even before the latter's first telegram. Philip Gibbs, a correspondent for the London *Daily Chronicle*, a paper which had no ostensible cause to play favorites, chanced to be the first reporter to greet Cook on September 4 as he returned to civilization. Gibbs wrote a series of articles suspicious of the Doctor, and the *New York Times* reprinted the dispatches with great relish.

Naturally enough, doubts of Cook's Mount McKinley claim were recalled upon the receipt of his first North Pole telegram, the *Times* immediately reprinting Cook's earlier devastating reply to the 1906 skeptical remarks of a supporting member of his own expedition (Herschel C. Parker, of Columbia University): ". . . Prof. Parker was not there [at the attainment of McKinley's peak] to witness the act." As if in answer, two other members of Cook's 1906 party, Edward Barrill (who *was* Cook's lone companion on the last leg of the climb) and Fred Printz, both mountain guides of Darby, Montana, were reported in the New York *Sun* of September 6 as having said that "Dr. Cook did not place a foot on Mt. McKinley, but. . . lower peaks were climbed and photos taken. . .in order to deceive the public."

Whereas it would be difficult to trace these attacks to pro-Peary influence, the remarks of Admirals Melville (U.S.) and Nares (England) probably stemmed from a prejudice for Peary that was widespread in the geographical community. Melville called Cook a faker straight out, mainly for claiming to have maintained speeds such as 14 miles per day over the Arctic pack. Nares, skeptical of Cook's sudden good fortune with *smooth ice*, agreed: Cook "may, as Admiral Melville has suggested, have turned back at once and imagined the rest of the journey. Such a thing has been done before in Arctic exploration. . . . There is so much that Dr. Cook might have told us and has not." Gibbs' story the next day also remarked on the unprecedented sustained pack-ice speed, adding that Cook had returned with no geological specimens and, in effect, no witnesses. Apparently not a single newspaper in the English-speaking world volunteered a few days later to admit that many of these criticisms were at least as applicable to Peary, who, for example, had claimed speeds far greater than Cook had. *Le Temps* (Paris) alone was concerned by Peary's lack of useful witnesses.

Peary himself refused to go into details on Cook because: "I intend to wait until Dr. Cook has issued his full authorized statements. Up to the present time there have been only newspaper accounts of Dr. Cook's alleged Polar trip, and these may or may not be accurate." How about Peary's own "authorized statements"? Other than the bare North Pole claim, what details would *he* have to stick by at this point? It is the most extraordinary fact that, while in seclusion, getting his records straight, all the way until October 18th, Peary issued absolutely no details of his great victory over his signature. But surely he must have sent a written report to the United States Coast and Geodetic Survey or to the United States Navy, the two national scientific institutions he represented. Besides a telegram to the Navy, telling of nothing beyond hoisting the Navy Ensign at the Pole, Peary claimed to have sent "a telegram to the U.S. Coast and Geodetic Survey, stating so many days tidal observations. . ., the line of soundings. . .a summary of the work." Curiously, of all the twenty plus telegrams Peary sent, that was the *only* one that never arrived. When the Survey got on him, and the Navy on the Survey, he promised data shortly in an October 7th telegram. Finally he sent a brief written report on October 18th, 42 days after first reaching Labrador, but he asked that the soundings not be published at the time. The 1911 Congressional subcommittee naturally was a little curious about this:

Mr. Dawson. You have [still] made no report to the Navy Department since your return — that is, no extended report of any kind?
Captain Peary. No, sir.

196

The Acting Superintendent of the United States Coast and Geodetic Survey, Francis Perkins, had said in September, 1909: "The first service which the [Survey] will expect of Mr. Peary after his arrival will be the preparation of a detailed report of his expedition." The Survey never got it, any more than the Navy did. After finally dragging the sounding profile out of him, Perkins noticed that no longitudes for Peary's positions were specified between Cape Columbia and the Pole. This must have intrigued him, so he wrote back asking not just for the longitudinal results of observations en route, but the actual data: "The Hydrographic Office of the Navy Department has asked for your soundings, which I shall send them as soon as I shall have received the data for determining their positions." Peary waited a few days and then simply avoided the request by misconstruing it: ". . .will say that these soundings were made on the meridian of Cape Columbia; and plotting on that meridian at the latitudes [shown] will give their position." Perkins gave up, and no data were ever sent.

Saying as little as possible, Peary won his prestigious National Geographic Society endorsement on November 1, a minor news item, actually, as all suspense then hung on Cook's upcoming presentation to the University of Copenhagen. By December 15, in time to make the National Geographical Society Annual Dinner and medal presentation a thoroughly happy affair, Peary knew Cook's downfall was certain. The Doctor had disappeared on November 24 and was dropped from the Explorers Club not long after Peary had been re-elected its president. And, on December 9, the *New York Times* had published the December 7 sworn confession of Cook's data fixing mathematician. Public opinion, high and low, naturally swung to the man who had faced his judges and was now left in possession of the field. During the 1909 Christmas season (and subsequent ones), United States post offices received thousands of children's letters to "Santa Claus, North Pole, c/o Mr. Peary." At the close of Peary's triumphant year, the editors of *The Nation* well expressed the nationwide sympathetic reaction to Peary's woes at the hands of Cook:

Peary. . .has been defrauded of something which can never be restored to him. . . .False as it has been proved, the claim of the cheap swindler has dimmed the lustre of the true discoverer's achievement. He will receive the full acknowledgment that his work merits, in the form of recognition from scientific and other bodies and of a sure place in history, but the joy of the acclaim that should have greeted him at the triumphant close of this twenty-three years' quest can never be his.

Cook had tried his best to take advantage of similarly misty-eyed sentiment, but — as in everything but charm — he just couldn't come up to Peary, who topped off his lectures by saying his discovery meant "that the splendid, frozen jewel of the North. . . is won at last, and is to be worn forever, by the Stars and Stripes."

The patriotic platitudes that filled explorers' speeches and writings then were typical of the times. However, in that star-studded field of flag-wavers, one stood out. In *The North Pole* Peary described how his wife had given him a "silk American flag . . . fifteen years ago. . . . I carried it *wrapped around my body* on every one of my expeditions northward . . ." (Emphasis added)

How could Cook ever top that one?

16. Moral Gulfs and Capers

[The Eskimos] called him [Peary] their father; he called them his children. A theme could be written on this one text, and yet how little it is understood except by those who have been Peary's companions.

—Admiral Colby Chester

Peary's fury at those not content to take merely his word as proof of his achievement, is reminiscent of the ire of an ancient hero whose veracity was publicly called into question. The Roman general Scipio Africanus had been accused of rifling the Roman treasury of four million sesterces, and the books were about to be examined for shortages. Tradition recounts his wondrous public performance: "when he had directed his brother Lucius to bring the account-book, he had himself, with his own hands, torn it up. . . ." Peary couldn't be quite this bold; but his anger at being questioned shows that he had a lot of Scipio in him and would meet doubt by huff instead of evidence whenever given the chance.

No one can assume a man is telling the truth just from his reputation or apparent personality; such trust is what every con artist feeds on. A deceiver may, in fact, believe in his own essential honesty. After the painful trauma of losing his toes in 1899, after giving more than 20 years of his life, after fighting and wearing himself down and twice risking his neck far out on the pack, Peary probably figured he at least *deserved* the Pole. Besides, his word was above question — as the N.Y. *Times* printed: "There was a moral gulf between Cook and Peary." And, as National Geographic president Henry Gannett said: "Every one who knows Peary by reputation knows he would not lie. . . ." Anyone will lie under enough pressure, and Peary was a man constantly pressed. He, in fact, deceived his major financial backer, his most trusting political booster, his wife, and his public on various non-trivial points, even leaving aside his exploring fantasies.

Ordinarily, airing dirty laundry would have no place in a scientific discussion, but keeping it clean was rejected long ago when Peary and Cook first began trading epithets. Cook initially offered to share the North Pole honors, declaring: "There is glory enough for us all." Peary, who knew very well what the second place share would be, publicly labeled Cook's story a "gold brick" and called its author "the greatest imposter of the present generation." Even before Cook returned from the Arctic, Peary was spreading rumors, even to President Theodore Roosevelt, about the Doctor's sources of revenue:

John R. Bradley, Dr. Cook's backer in this enterprise . . .is a well known gambler, known in certain circles as "Gambler Jim." I have heard that he was formerly a card sharp on the Mississippi River until driven out, and it is a matter of actual fact that he runs a gambling hell at Palm Beach, where both men and women gamble.

Such gossip probably helped inspire a top British explorer's delightful first reaction to Cook's Pole claim: It must be "either an American gambling scheme to make money or a medical project to test the stupidity of the public."

Even five years after Cook's claim was first announced, Peary's hired lobbyist was secretly busy sending anonymous bundles of smear propaganda to every town in which Cook was scheduled to lecture. Cook became no less a character assassin, as present-day Peary biographer John E. Weems wrote in 1960, when cataloging in his *Race for the Pole* the insults Peary suffered:

As for the rumor about Peary's Eskimo wife, that originated with Cook. The Doctor also said in lectures that Peary had left two Eskimo children to perish in the frozen North, and in his book he reproduced a photograph of an Eskimo woman and a child, captioning it, "Polar Tragedy - a Deserted Child of the Sultan of the North and its Mother." This story was to be repeated by many other persons.

Eventually including Weems, who, when he wrote the above remarks, was prone to attribute criticism of Peary just to spite. Imagine his shock when, a few years later, he researched the Peary papers (for his 1967 biography) and found that Peary *did* have a common-law Eskimo wife and fathered at least one child by her. But Weems' surprise was nothing compared with Jo Peary's back in 1900. She discovered the truth about her husband in one of those improbable coincidences that are more customarily associated with a Hollywood bedroom farce. As Weems tells it:

Unknown to Peary, the *Windward* [his ship, with Jo aboard, unannounced] had returned [from the United States to Etah], Greenland. [While Peary stayed, over 200 miles north, unawares, at Fort Conger] . . ., ice now [late summer, 1900, unexpectedly] imprisoned the ship, and it was held in the Arctic for [the] winter. . . .[Early during this unanticipated stay] an Eskimo woman, Alla-kasingwah - or "Ally" . . . and her baby [came aboard]. The woman innocently boasted of her relationship with Pearyarksuah [Eskimo for "the Great Peary"], not realizing the enormous difference in mores.

Immediately Jo wrote Peary a letter, mentioning among other things, "You will have been surprised, perhaps annoyed, when you hear that I came up. . .but believe me had I known how things were with you here I should not have come." The hapless adventurer did not learn of this ghastly contretemps until the following spring. Hobbs' retelling, from an account by Peary's daughter Marie, of the moment is delightfully innocent of its pregnancy:

> On April 30, 1901, at Hayes Point Peary ran into a party of Etah Eskimos bound for [Fort] Conger in search of him, and so met with a pleasant surprise.

The interview with the Eskimos from the ship well brings out their racial characteristic of imparting news only when requested:

> "Peary. 'Did the ship get up last year?'
> 'Yes.'
> Peary. 'Who was the captain?'
> 'Captain Sam [Bartlett]. . . .'
> Peary. 'Who was the steward?'
> 'Old Charlie.'
> Peary. 'Anyone else on board that I knew?'
> 'Mitty Peary and Ahnighito'" [Jo and Marie]

[After registering his shock, Peary] put another question.

> "'When did the ship go back?'
> 'Oh,' said one of the men very calmly, 'didn't go back. Right. . .in Payer Harbor.'"

Then Peary without waiting a moment struck out for the ship, leaving the amazed Eskimos far behind and greatly upset by this to them extraordinary behavior of a man usually so calm and self-possessed.

Both Weems and Marie Peary Stafford Kuhne deserve much credit for not hiding an embarrassing facet of a man each greatly admires. As is often the case, honesty turned out to be not only the most admirable policy but the wisest. For, ironically, less than a year after the publication of Weems' frank biography, a freak accident would have brought the truth to light anyway. Early in 1968, when the United States Strategic Air Command was fishing for hydrogen bombs lost in a plane crash off Etah, Greenland, one of the curious spectators was a man appearing to be mostly Eskimo. *Life* magazine published a photograph of him on the scene, with the caption: "Greenlander who claims to be the grandson of explorer Robert E. Peary. . . ." How many children Peary himself left in the North is hard to say. Peary's son, Kahdi, and Henson's, Ahnowka, were of known lineage, but Kahkotchingwa was fathered by an unspecified member of Peary's expeditions. Considering the ubiquity of wife-swapping among Greenland Eskimos and the orgies they like to throw — participant Freuchen provides an account of such — it's little wonder track was lost regarding who was whose.

Prior to the controversy with Cook, the nearest Peary's secret life ever came to being uncaped was in his fight with Dr. Thomas Dedrick, 1898-1902 Expedition surgeon, who had resigned his post in 1901. Unlike some, Dedrick was revolted, as Weems states, by the "purely sexual relationship available from Eskimo women," and longed "for the companionship of his wife." He felt more money was owed him than Peary was prepared to pay after their return to the States in 1902, so Dedrick fed to the press veiled references to Peary's carryings-on and even sent copies to various societies. John Keltie, Secretary of the Royal Geographical Society, wrote Bridgman: "he hints mysteriously at some nameless conduct on the part of Peary which made him leave. . ., but does not state explicitly what it was." But, of course, "I in common with all who know Peary give no thought to Dedrick's vague charges." Peary, though outwardly cool, must have had fits at the thought of Jesup's learning of any of this; so, at the first sign of Dedrick's game, he wrote Jesup in hopes of forestalling the nightmarish possibility of the Doctor's making direct contact. In other squabbles Peary was happy to have Jesup's help; but, as for handling Dedrick, he'd rather do that himself. "I hope you will waste none of your valuable time on him," Peary said, suggesting that Jesup send him any letter received from Dedrick. Four days later, Peary, still fretting, wrote Jesup again: "My only fear. . .was that [Dedrick] might annoy you with his letters."

Evidently, a quiet deal was eventually worked out with

203

the Doctor, since Weems reports that "Dedrick's original diaries later were turned over to Peary. . . ." However, presumably as insurance against reprisal, Dedrick for years kept a locked file of incriminating documents in the public library of Washington, New Jersey.

The possibility of Dedrick's tattling to Jesup about Peary's moral character *had* to be headed off, for Jesup, "financially a tower of strength in the work" and "an intimate personal friend" of the explorer, stood foursquare against wickedness. In 1852 Jesup had helped found the Young Men's Christian Association in America, through which he discovered in 1872-3 an earnest young zealot whom he immediately promoted, bankrolled, and protected — Anthony Comstock. With Jesup's backing, Comstock successfully pushed for Federal legislation against the mailing of obscene matter, declaring that lust "is the constant companion of all other crimes." The crusader once actually boasted of having driven to suicide no fewer than 15 dealers in contraceptives and unapproved art. When the YMCA couldn't take any more Comstockery, Jesup founded and largely funded the bigoted Society for the Suppression of Vice for Saint Anthony. He served as its vice president for a quarter of a century, to about the time he founded the Peary Arctic Club, the birth of which (1899) roughly coincided with another, farther north.

"I trust Peary," professed Jesup, the explorer's most powerful financial backer. "I believe in you, Peary," echoed Teddy Roosevelt from the political heights. In 1907 the President lauded Peary for ". . .setting an example to the young men of our day which we need to have set amid the softening tendencies of our time." Peary himself had something to say about his exemplary conduct in Greenland. His book *Northward Over the "Great Ice,"* published in 1898, recounts how in late 1894 the departure of his male companions from their cabin

> puts me in the somewhat embarrassing position of being left, alone and unprotected, with five buxom and oleaginous ladies [one of them Ally], of a race of naive children of nature, who are hampered by no feelings of false

modesty or bashfulness in expressing their tender feelings. My years, and at present semi-crippled condition from a fall on the rocks, will, I trust, protect me.

Peary then described an impetuous 20-mile, starlit hike by one of those oleaginous children of nature, only 14 years old, he remarks. Her photograph is provided with her name: Alakasingwah. At another point, Peary writes longingly of his "bright-faced Alakasingwah." And he actually adorns his book with nudes of Ally. He makes it clear that his purpose is not prurient but scientific, "to show physique and muscular development." And, if the reading public's interest in structural anthropology should happen to spur the sales of the book, where was the harm?

Incidentally, this lesson in how to popularize science was, one may suppose, not lost on enterprising young Gilbert H. Grosvenor of the formerly staid *National Geographic Magazine*. Appointed editor and director in February, 1903, he initiated in the May issue the oft-lampooned *National Geographic* policy of publishing photographs of nubile natives in scanty costumes. Perhaps coincidentally, at about this time the magazine's sales (memberships) began a climb not to be equaled until Hugh Hefner unveiled his bunnies. Like Peary's, the *National Geographic's* reason for displaying pictures of undraped women was strictly scientific, to show things as they really were.

While the *National Geographic* could go its own merry way, poor Peary, increasingly under Jesup's domination, unfortunately had to keep the clothes on his Eskimos in his next book, *Nearest the Pole*, published in 1907. It was a financial flop. But even if he could no longer share his pleasures with the public, Peary could at least continue to enjoy them himself while in the North; and he could revel in the irony of the situation. Cast in the hero mold, Peary has never been sufficiently appreciated for his fine sense of humor. One of the most exquisite expressions of it: Overlooking the "wide" bunk, the result of "long experience in the Arctic regions," which he shared with Eskimo girls, hung an autographed photograph of inspirational Teddy Roosevelt as well as a portrait of Peary's vice-crusading mentor, all-seeing Morris K. Jesup.

Weems has written that "Peary's personal papers have provided even greater proof [than available before] that his recognition as the discoverer of the North Pole is proper. . . ." On the contrary, much of the material he has unearthed indicates that the 1909 fake was not merely aberrative, but natural, and, indeed, almost predictable.

To delve into Peary's writings is to be struck by the fact that, for all the man's admirable qualities — intelligence, romanticism, curiosity, a free spirit and a sometime kindness — his values were simply too externally oriented.

As a student at Bowdoin College, his greatest joy in solving a math problem was not an intellectual or even aesthetical one; rather, it was his teacher's approbation which made him "completely rewarded for my labor." In 1880 he was stuck in a routine job with the Coast Survey in Washington still looking for "the main chance," as Weems phrases it, and feeling at the time that it lay south rather than north. He wrote his mother:

> I want to have a good long talk with you on a subject that I have been thinking of for a long time, and that is in regard to going to the isthmus. . . .What good will fame or a name do me if it comes when I am an old man? . . . It will not be long before I am thirty and if I remain here I may be drawing two-thousand as a draftsman, a machine, working so many hours a day and known only on the payroll of the department. . . .I feel myself already thirty or forty years old with nothing accomplished, . . .is it the restlessness of ambition which spurs men on to be in front of their fellows, or is it an ineffective uneasiness productive only of unrest to its unfortunate possessor? . . .there are more opportunities for a lasting fame to be obtained on the little strip of land called the isthmus, in an area about half as large as the State of Maine, than anywhere else on the globe.

Many men have made themselves world known by

looking forward, seeing something sure to be of importance in the future, making the subject thoroughly their own, and then when the right moment came, stepping forward as the chief or only authority on the subject. . . .

I do not strive for money; but for fame, though money as a secondary consideration would be no objection.

Whether Peary found his fame in the equatorial zone or the Polar was apparently then immaterial. In 1886, he sailed for Greenland ". . . impatient to reach that northern region which holds my future name. . . ." Then back to Nicaragua where "They [the canal company] will have to give me something special or give me up." In 1888 he returned to marry Jo; but when the honeymoon was over, he began thinking of the need to soon reinvest the measure of fame he had won in Greenland in 1886, and to develop more: "I consider it a matter of importance not to let myself drop out of sight." In 1902, toward the end of a series of abortive Polar attempts, he was seized by the same fear:

I seem to have reached the end of the lane. What I gained in Greenland I am losing in Ellesmere Land. Soon they will call me a fake, say I am just hoarding what I can mint from the public's credulity.

What was it then that Peary achieved in 1906 that enabled him to write instead in his fund-appeal of May 2, 1908: "It has been my good fortune to meet with more success than any of my predecessors." Even though they were, as he adds humbly, "some of the ablest men of the most enlightened nations of the world [over] three centuries." By then Peary had found simply that cheating paid. And it was the payoff, not the Pole, that he was really seeking; he had always been less interested in achievement than in reward, because reward doesn't depend upon what one achieves, but on what others *think* one has achieved. His backers, as hungry as he for fame, hastened his ethical decay with their incessant demands for signs of *continual* achievement; and that led inevitably to a blurring of the distinction between means and ends. Thus Jesup Land, "farthest North," Crocker Land.

In his later years, deceit evidently became as regular a part of Peary's creative flow as doodling is to an artist. For instance, he thought so little of lying to the Secretary of the Navy and to the United States Coast and Geodetic Survey that he didn't even bother to hide the truth from Jo. His final northward report to both these Government superintendents of his last expedition stated that he had just ordered "two men landed with supplies for the relief of Dr. Cook," then unheard from for many months and presumed to be wandering near Ellesmere, low on supplies. In his eventual book Peary repeated the same tale of his charitable purpose. The instructions he apparently gave the men he left there spoke of the depot as being for the relief of Dr. Cook. Yet, in a simultaneous letter to Jo, he revealed:

> I have landed supplies here, and leave two men ostensibly in behalf of Cook. As a matter of fact I have established here the sub-base which last time [1905] I established at Victoria Head, as a precaution in event of loss of the Roosevelt. . . .tell "Mister Man" [Robert, Jr., then almost five] to remember "straight and strong and clean and honest,". . .

Like Daddy? In a 1910 letter, he boasted: ". . .I have put my life into the effort to accomplish something which seemed to me a thing worth doing, and because it had the great attraction of being a clean, manly proposition." On December 15, 1906, Peary had spelled out his credo, as Hobbs termed it, in his speech to the National Geographic Society:

> The true explorer does his work not for any hopes of reward or honor, but because the thing he has set for himself to do is a part of his being, and must be accomplished for the sake of the accomplishment. And he counts lightly hardships, risks, obstacles, if only they do not bar him from his goal. . . .

Could this be the same person who wrote randomly in his 1909 diary? "Present sextant and horizon to the Navy Museum" . . ."Have my North Pole eyeglasses mounted for

208

constant use. Have extra pair ditto as present to someone?" ".. .monument for mausoleum? Faced with marble or granite, statue with flag on top; lighted room at base for two sarcophagi? Bronze figures, Eskimo, dog, bear; musk ox, walrus, etc., etc. Or bronze tablet of flag on North Pole and suitable inscription. Bust." Could this be the same person who exploited his North Pole fame in advertised endorsements of tobaccos, disinfectants, gunpowders, cereals, rifles, pencils, cameras, cooking utensils, razors, watches, maps? "I am indebted to the United States Tobacco Co., both on this expedition and the last, for some specially packed North Pole smoking tobacco for the use of the expedition," Peary huckstered. "This tobacco was most highly prized by both members of the party and the Eskimos, and assisted materially in passing many an hour of the long, dark winter night at Cape Sheridan." Yet, both in his first book (1898) and his last (1917), Peary said he avoided tobacco users when selecting his parties, Bartlett being the lone exception. "Tobacco is. . . objectionable in Polar work," Peary wrote. "It affects the wind endurance of a man, particularly in low temperatures, adds an extra and entirely unnecessary article to the outfit, vitiates the atmosphere of tent or igloo, and, when the supply gives out, renders the user a nuisance to himself and those about him."

It is clear that Robert Peary was not quite the same person he generally appeared to be to his contemporaries. To use his heroic image as an argument for his achievement, as Gannett did and Weems does, is no longer effective today, for it is an article of fact if not faith that more is known about Peary now than his Victorian era backers would have cared to know then.

Allakasingwah, Peary's common-law Eskimo wife. Below. looking to the rear — the trail in soft snow.

17.   Purer Than Pure

Early in February, 1910, the idea of granting Peary official Congressional recognition began to become remarkably
contagious in Washington. On the 2nd, Representative Amos
Allen introduced a bill into Congress with this intent, and the
very next day, Senator Eugene Hale did likewise. Republi-
cans, both men were from Maine, Peary's home state, and
both attended Bowdoin, Peary's old school. But this is not to
imply that Peary sentiment was entirely provincial; in the next
few weeks other Congressmen introduced similar bills. Fitzhugh Green asserts that this was not Peary's idea but that of
his "wide circle of influential friends" — and probably, had
Peary suspected what its outcome was to be, he would never
have gotten tangled up with Congress in the first place. However, he likely expected that the recognition would be another
virtual rubber stamp, so he went along with the idea and even
hired a lobbyist and distributed a pamphlet to help push the
thing through.

Certainly Congress looked like a pushover. The Republi-
cans ruled the country, and Peary had a flock of powerful
friends among them. Over a decade earlier, he'd employed
pull with Republican President William McKinley to get his
leave for the 1898-1902 expedition, and later had similarly
used McKinley's successor, Republican Theodore Roosevelt.
While his successor, Republican William H. Taft, was not as
close to Peary personally as was T.R., Taft, a cousin of
National Geographic Society Secretary Grosvenor, was
friendly enough to grant Peary a private personal audience on

211

November 24, 1909 — something Cook could never have managed.

To one accustomed to requesting favors of men, there is no friend so loyal as one beholden. Peary writes openly in such a vein when describing his gift giving among the Eskimos: "I have made it to their interest to do what I want done." One of the essentials of success for his expedition he lists as being: "To have the confidence of a large number of Eskimos, earned by square dealing and generous gifts in the past. . . ." It seems likely that Peary obtained by similar means the confidence of a large number of influential Americans. For example, he sent expensive Arctic trophies (fox skins, walrus and narwhal horns, etc.) to Teddy Roosevelt and Herbert Bridgman; it was common gossip that he did the same by many others, including National Geographic officials. Whether done out of the most altruistic or the most cunning motives, the effect would be to create a useful loyalty and trust among important people, the sort of people Peary had been associating with for years via the wealthy membership of the Peary Arctic Club.

As far back as 1902, Bridgman was suggesting the idea of Congressional recognition for Peary, and Jesup promised to "cooperate in any reasonable way to bring it about. . . ." On Christmas Day of that year, Peary wrote Bridgman a letter containing a sentence that comes out a kind of classic: "Do you happen to know anyone whom I know, that also knows Congressman Lessler. . .member of the House Naval Committee?" Not by chance, one would imagine, at the very time the 1910 Peary bills were flooding Congress, there was held on February 8 in New York what Hobbs rightly called:

> . . .one of the most remarkable testimonials ever given to a citizen of the United States, when the municipality of the city of New York received Peary in the Metropolitan Opera House. The occasion was national in character, and the President of the United States, Honorable William Howard Taft, sent a long message of congratulation to the explorer. The Governor of the state of New York, Hon. Charles Evans Hughes [1916 Republican candidate for President], presided. . . .

An honorary committee, formed of 31 leading United States millionaires, including Carnegie, Fish, Dodge, and Morgenthau, presented Peary with a gift of $10,000. Hughes read the wire from Taft, which helpfully said: "I sincerely hope, as is now proposed, Congress will take some substantial notice of the great achievement which has reflected such great credit on American enterprise, persistence, courage, and endurance."

Two weeks after the Met spectacular — which kicked off Peary's well-greased campaign to stampede Congress into certifying him without proof — Gov. Hughes was to celebrate Washington's Birthday by telling a trusting Philadelphia audience that corruption in public office was decreasing, declaring; "that the sentiment of the country was purer than ever before and that the right was coming steadily into the ascendancy."

The very day after the New York affair, without opposition in the Senate, the Peary bill was referred to the House Committee on Naval Affairs. At this highwater mark, Peary's woes began.

The House Committee on Naval Affairs' Subcommittee on Private Bills was composed of Chairman Thomas S. Butler (Republican, Pennsylvania), Arthur L. Bates (Republican, Pennsylvania), Ernest W. Roberts (Republican, Massachusetts), Albert S. Dawson (Republican, Iowa), William F. Englebright (Republican, California), Alexander W. Gregg (Democrat, Texas), and Robert Bruce Macon (Democrat, Arkansas). On March 4, before these seven men, the Peary Hearings officially opened.

Hobbs called the hearings "one of the most discreditable proceedings in the history of [the House of Representatives]." Perhaps this was so. But not for the reasons imagined. The biographers' tears have dimmed the fact that, if anything, the odds were well stacked in Peary's favor. His lobbyist, Lucien Alexander, of Philadelphia, had evidently been hard at work; for, even before the hearings commenced, Chairman Butler and Representative Bates, both from Pennsylvania, had openly introduced pro-Peary bills. Retiring Representative Dawson (recently invited to be President Taft's private secretary) and lame duck Representative Englebright were also well lined up in advance, it would appear, though both were to contribute an occasional probing question.

On the other hand, a minority of three — Roberts, Macon, and Gregg — wanted to know just what they were approving. Roberts and Macon, to whom so much of this book is owed, were former attorneys, Macon even having been a district attorney for four years; but there the resemblance about stops. The former was a Yankee Republican, later a regent of the Smithsonian Institution; the latter a Dixie Democrat, highly suspicious of scientists and academia in general. (Orphaned at nine, he was a good deal self-taught.) Yet, for their different reasons, Roberts' respect for science, along with Macon's disrespect, they prepared to let loose their curiosity and logic on the explorer. Without their joint efforts, the heart of the Peary affair would have inevitably remained forever uncertain.

The battle was joined even before the hearings began, as soon as the subcommittee began seeking expert guidance. On February 18th, some members pondered submitting Peary's records to the University of Copenhagen, but undoubtedly this was dropped as unpatriotic. A week later the *New York Times* learned that a judging panel of experienced explorers in Washington was being considered:

> According to the tentative plans of the subcommittee of the Naval Affairs Committee, this board of scientific investigation will be composed of Rear Admiral Melville, U.S.N., retired; Rear Admiral Schley, U.S.N., retired, and Major General A.W. Greely, U.S.A., retired, all of whom have won recognition at the hands of Congress because of their attainments in the Arctic ice fields.
>
> Members of the committee will communicate with Commander Peary to ascertain if the three experts suggested are acceptable to him. The explorer's friends on the committee believe that he will welcome an investigation in order that there may be no technical quibble whatever as to any action taken by Congress. . . .

Commander Peary was asked by the correspondent of

the *New York Times* this evening if the appointment of such a board would be agreeable to him. He declined to discuss the matter in any way, saying that he had nothing whatever to do with it or any opinions to express.

Peary did his "nothing" right away, through lame duck Representative De Alva Alexander (Republican, New York), a good friend of fellow Bowdoin alumnus Thomas Hubbard and, as Green explained, "a medium through which the Peary Arctic Club could keep its finger on the pulse" of the subcommittee, of which he was not a member, though he was on the larger Naval Affairs Committee. On February 27th, Alexander wrote Chairman Butler a letter, which, like Hubbard's September 29 cable to Osborn, further reveals Peary's use of connections to avoid submitting his records to actual explorers and/or skeptical professionals for an official judgment:

My dear Tom:

I am counting upon your kind treatment of Commander Peary, not, of course, because of your personal friendship for me, which, as you know, I doubly reciprocate, but because I know you love to be fair and just. . . .

There are two reasons why Admiral Schley, Admiral Melville, and General Greely should not be asked to pass upon these proofs. First, it would be a reflection upon the National Geographic Society. Secondly, it would be manifestly unfair and unjust, for Admiral Schley is known to be unfriendly, while General Greely is scarcely less undesirable. On the other hand, Admiral Melville has been so pronounced in favor of Peary that any verdict he rendered might not be called impartial. . . .

As to Peary's own personal position in the matter, Alexander let loose a cascade of falsehoods:

He has *never* suggested or mentioned to *anyone* the matter of official Government recognition. As far as he is aware, *none* of his friends have ever written or suggested the recent move in Congress in this direction. As far as

215

he knows, this move was spontaneous and voluntary. He has not been seeking official recognition, though he and his friends would be intensely gratified if it came in suitable form. Action having, however, originated in Congress, the effort has been made to have that action crystallize in the form suited to the deed, and in the form desired by Peary and his friends. (Emphasis added.)

The Senate bill, as introduced by Senator Hale, and passed unanimously by the Senate, embodies that form. In this connection, it should be made entirely clear that Peary is not looking for the financial part of it, the retired pay or pension aspect.

The fact is that on February 9, Senator Hale's February 3 bill to retire Peary as a rear admiral was specifically amended to make the promotion effective "at the highest pay in the grade."

Because of Peary's stubbornness or caution, and his friends on the committee, the expert examination of his records that might have been performed never was, with the ultimate result that all computational testimony at the Peary Hearings was friendly to him. It should have been; he paid hard cash for it.

The official hearings opened on March 4th with testimony by Tittmann and Gannett. Admiral Chester was abroad in connection with his private investments, so he never appeared before the Congressmen. Tittmann did so only long enough to admit that he had seen no original records of the depth soundings, just a prepared chart of results, and that he had not bothered to examine Peary's solar observation data sheet paper for signs of fresh or worn paper, perhaps because, as he says, he did not believe, to begin with, that anyone could fake figures, or would have to, when so "near" the Pole on April 1. Tittmann replied "Surely," when asked if he was satisfied that Peary had reached the North Pole, then recited his reasons for believing so:

. . .Mr. Peary's expedition differed from all previous expeditions in this, that when he got within striking distance of the Pole — that is, within about a hundred and

216

forty miles of the Pole — he had with him a large party of men and Captain Bartlett; that up to that time he had kept himself in absolute reserve, allowing the hard work — the pioneer work — to be done by a younger man and a stronger man, and when he reached, as I say, a point which I considered within striking distance, his position was so different from any previous explorer who had ever gone — usually when they get to — well, nobody had been so far before — anyhow, when the people did get there they were single or exhausted or minus provisions, but Peary got within a hundred and forty miles of the Pole and had with him his sleds in perfect condition, plenty of provisions, and it was a holiday jaunt to go there, unless some accident happened, like a great rift, which he was not able to pass; so it would have been absurd if he had not gone there.

Contrast this to the recollection of MacMillan (who, incidentally, was never asked to testify at the Peary Hearings; nor were Peary's other expedition members):

As a matter of fact it cannot be stated too emphatically that a trip over the Polar Sea is not a holiday. . . .When I saw so strong a man as Bob Bartlett break down and want his mother as we shivered and shook together on a snow bed in the Far North, his underclothing wringing wet, his clothing a mass of ice, his face scarred with frost, his fingers hard, horny, and cracked, his body chafed by sores by walking, plodding endlessly on. . . ."

When requested to tell "all the facts" leading to the National Geographic committee's conclusion, Tittmann explained that

. . .I was very busy and went only to the last meeting of that committee, and at that meeting Captain Peary showed me the actual observations — the astronomical observations that he made when he was at the Pole. . . . He showed me the actual papers on which he did this, and I asked him to explain it to me, so that I looked at his astronomical observations, saw the form in which they were kept, and his reductions, and felt perfectly satisfied as did other members of the committee who had an opportunity to go over the details that I did not have, because I was very much occupied with other matters.

Mr. Gregg. Those that he showed you, then, were they the original entries made at the time?

Mr. Tittmann. Yes; made at the time *on loose slips of paper.* (emphasis added)

Pressed by Gregg on the condition of the paper, Tittmann flippantly ". . .couldn't say whether it was watermarked or not." Asked for details on the observations and instruments, Tittmann said: "I think Mr. Gannett could give you all of that, as you have him here. I am really due before the Appropriations Committee."

Gannett, now President of the National Geographic, contributed few details, and some of these were inaccurate. He could not remember how many days were required to travel from Bartlett Camp to the Pole. He and Gilbert H. Grosvenor, at his side, each volunteered that this took six days — although Peary's own bookkeeping indicates that if was four and a half. Responding to Roberts' queries about equipment and personnel on the Polar dash, Gannett stated that Peary took two sledges (he actually took five), and two Eskimos (actually four).

A few further questions by Roberts quickly exposed the superficiality of the National Geographic examination chaired by Gannett.

Roberts. Was anyone, other than Mr. Nichols [Peary's lawyer] and Mr. Peary, before your committee. . .?

Mr. Gannett. No.

Roberts, who later characterized the National Geographic committee's examination as "perfunctory and hasty," asked if any effort was made ". . .to interrogate Henson to verify in any way any of the statements made by Peary?"

Mr. Gannett. No.

Mr. Roberts. Or the time it took him to make his different journeys, the number of miles per day?
Mr. Gannett. No.

Checking Peary's statements was unnecessary; as Gannett testified, "Every one who knows Peary by reputation knows he would not lie; I know him by reputation."

Gannett, though declaring his confidence in the committee's ability to be objective, as much as admitted that Peary's reputation counted more with him than any scientific evidence. When asked if he could rely on astronomical data without knowing the man responsible for it, he honestly confessed the obvious: "No; I don't think I could."

Mr. Gregg. The personal equation and confidence in the man would cut a considerable figure in aiding you to come to a conclusion?
Mr. Gannett. Yes. . . .

To render a judgment based on impersonal scientific data — as the University of Copenhagen did — was not the way the National Geographic worked.

Mr. Roberts. Was any question whatever raised [by the National Geographic Board of Managers] as to its acceptance [the committee's favorable report on Peary]? Did anybody question the findings or ask for information?
Mr. Gannett. Not in the slightest; the vote was unanimous in favor of acceptance.

The National Geographic might buy a Pole in a poke, but not Macon. "I want [Peary's records] brought in," he demanded; "this Congress belongs to the country, and whatever we do as its Representatives ought to be done in the open and not in secret. If we are doing anything to be kept back, I propose to make it public myself. . . ." Bates and Butler asked Gannett why Peary would not let the subcommittee make a perfectly open review of records, which the National Geographic Society had not done. Gannett said he'd rather Peary explained that. Representative Alexander, the Peary

219

Arctic Club's friend, said he would ask Peary whether his records could be aired in a public hearing. The subcommittee reconvened on the afternoon of March 7 to hear Alexander deliver Peary's negative reply: ". . .it would be breaking faith with his publishers. . . ." Perhaps Peary at last realized that some of the subcommittee meant business, or possibly he feared that public hearings might let the world in on the ridiculous nature of his scientific case. Regardless, his excuse is far from convincing, for he certainly worried little enough about his publisher's feelings on other occasions, and there was no written agreement specifying secrecy regarding his records (the scientific ones being of little value to a publisher anyway).

The next meeting was scheduled for March 9 but came to naught because the subcommittee perversely continued to insist on seeing the records before approving a bill based on them. How much of his data Peary preferred to divulge publicly is clear from his reaction to the subcommittee's rebuff. He simply launched a propaganda barrage to pressure the group to accept the National Geographic judgment without question and thus to approve the bill without seeing any records at all. On March 11, another Pennsylvania Republican, Representative Joseph Hampton Moore, a lifetime National Geographic Society member — whose main contribution thus far had been his February 16 bill to give the thanks of Congress to Peary alone, not to his expedition's members (since this would give a black "the privileges of the floor of the House") — got a notion to introduce a resolution reading, in part:

Whereas since the [National Geographic Society] report of. . .American scientists and trusted officials of the United States was made by them in their capacity as committeemen of the [National Geographic Society], credence has been given their findings by all the great scientific bodies of the world, to the great honor and glory of the [United States of America]: therefore be it

Resolved, That this Congress accepts the [National Geographic Society] report. . .as a true and competent

220

statement, to which shall be accorded the same consideration and respect . . [as] if made officially to the Congress. . . .

Simultaneously, the order was gotten underway for a pamphlet: *How Peary Reached the North Pole. An Expedition Over the Ice That Went to its Mark with the Precision of a Military Campaign and Reached the Goal Sought for Centuries.* Merely a reprint of his New York *Times* cable story of the previous September, it was distributed to members of Congress as fast as possible. On March 15th, Representative Moore spoke for Peary on the floor of the House. His address was also printed as a pamphlet and distributed. A few excerpts may prove enlightening (emphasis added here and there):

. . .neither the Department of the Navy nor the United States Coast & Geodetic Survey has any doubt of the success or value of his achievement. . . . For this reason, Mr. Speaker, it would seem a gracious thing for Congress to settle the controversy *upon the reports of the departments alone.* If we fail to do this, it would reflect not only upon the authenticity of the departmental reports and records, but *upon the findings of the scientific world.*

. . .I have asked that Congress [certify and promote Peary]. . .not only for his sake and the patriotic impulses it involves, but for the sake of *scientific America,* which through *its* National Geographic Society *has staked its reputation upon the work of the man.* To discredit Robert E. Peary, after all his years of endeavor. . .*must necessarily discredit* American scientists who have put the stamp of their approval upon his labors.

. . .But it is still contended by some of the discontented and disturbed minds amongst our 90,000,000 people that the report to the [National Geographic Society] was prejudiced. . .that his exploit was impossible, and so forth. Are these excuses for delaying action by Congress tenable? Are we, by delay, to gratify the *grievances* of Peary's opponents. . .?

221

. . .[The National Geographic Society subcommittee was] better qualified than any committee of Congress to pass upon the Peary instruments and records. . . .Who were these three men? Independent scientists who dared to stake their reputations upon a falsehood or upon a *superficial examination* of the facts? . . .Henry Gannett . . .president of the Geographic Board, a proven, trusted geographer and geologist; O.H. Tittmann. . .the honored and respected Chief of the [United States Coast & Geodetic Survey], under whose direction the coast lines of our country are surveyed and inspected; and C.M. Chester, an honored and respected. . .rear admiral (retired). Who will dispute the integrity of these men, even though they acted. . .[unofficially]? Surely no associated body of foreign scientists. For the verdict of the [National Geographic Society] which passed upon the report of these distinguished Americans *has been accepted without question* by the Royal Geographical Society. . . . , the geographical societies of Berlin, Paris, Geneva, Rome, Brussels, Antwerp, Vienna, Dresden, Madrid, St. Petersburg, Tokyo, Mexico, Lima, . . .Chicago, New York, and Philadelphia, and practically every geographical society in the world.

Moreover, in addition to [United States Admirals] Melville and Sigsbee, Peary's achievements and the report of the National Geographic Society have been received *without question* by Nansen, The Duke of Abruzzi, Greely, Shackleton, and Scott. With this strong array it would seem that the only thing for Congress to do would be to accept the verdict of the National Geographic Society *without further humiliation of the American explorer.* . . .

The March issue of *National Geographic Magazine* reprinted Moore's hint suggesting acceptance without question, but no amount of propaganda could erase what the subcommittee had learned on March 4 during Gannett's testimony, namely, that the National Geographic Society exam *had* been superficial.

The demand by the press for Peary's swift acceptance by Congress was so fierce that it was even mentioned in the eventual official report of the subcommittee. The *New York Times* and the New York *Post* attacked those subcommittee members who wished to be shown proofs; on March 19, *Outlook* bemoaned the ingratitude of Congress to an American hero. As the heart of the scientific spirit is the individual's reliance on evidence, as against blind truckling to authority, one might expect the scientific community, at least, to take the Congressmen's side. Alas, not necessarily when the authority being questioned is a scientific one, as witness the umbrage taken in *Scientific American's* lead editorial of April 9:

> The hearty recognition which Shackleton has accorded Peary for the discovery of the North Pole, coming as it does from a man who knows something of the rigors of Polar exploration, ought to shame the Congress *which refuses national honor to Peary without proof of the North Pole's discovery.* The *doubt* which has been foolishly cast on Peary's exploit by a Congressman [Macon] whose "farthest north," as one Washington correspondent phrased it, is the semi-tropical cold of Omaha, Nebraska, is more than extinguished by the cordial deference which Shackleton has shown toward Peary on the occasion of their many public meetings. (Emphasis added.)

(Shackleton's ultimate view is as ironic in this context as is the fact that Peary himself had just finished working through Representative Alexander to keep Arctic explorers off any judging board.)

Despite all pressure, the subcommittee was as adamant as Peary regarding his records, so the Congressional session closed without further action on the promotion.

On April 26, Peary sailed for Europe, commencing a European tour that would see him honored by virtually all the British and Continental geographical societies, an invaluable boost to popular acceptance of his claim, though of little aid with the subcommittee, which was well aware that every last one of these societies had simply accepted the National Geographic Society judgment without question. The only honoring society forming any sort of exception to this pattern was England's Royal Geographical Society, which privately asked that Peary submit his North Pole records to them for examination. As the Royal Geographical Society judgment is often cited as unbiased, one ought to keep in mind not only the general British climate of opinion on the controversy, but a recollection of the Royal Geographical Society's instant congratulatory telegram of September 7. In January, 1910, the Royal Geographical Society voted Peary a special gold medal for "having been the first man to lead an expedition to the North Pole," months before seeing the data supporting the claim. Peary could not very well refuse the friendly Royal Geographical Society request for data without arousing suspicion, so, in May, 1910, he took his records to England with him. But, even with all sorts of British prejudice going for him, Peary was, characteristically, playing it mighty coy: he waited until *after* the Royal Geographical Society medal was presented and then submitted just copies of some of his records.

Peary returned to the United States in June and resumed lecturing *daily,* at a thousand dollars per performance. By early fall, his magazine series had run its course and his book released (with a foreword by National Geographic's Gilbert H. Grosvenor), so no excuse remained for withholding his records from Congress. Though Peary must have known that the farcical navigational methods of his tale might at last come out before a partly skeptical group; still, these had been hidden from the public during the crucial first year, when most of his North Pole profits went safely into the bank. There was no cause for panic now, especially as he was an expert facing amateurs. As Roberts, perhaps over innocently, said: "No doubt the members of the Committee wouldn't be able to tell anything about Mr. Peary's records even if they were submitted to us, for we are not scientists. . . ."

18. On Trial

On December 6, 1910, in the Annual Presidential Message to Congress, President Taft referred to "the unparalleled accomplishment of an American in reaching the North Pole, April 6, 1909, approved by the most expert scientists. . . .I recommend fitting recognition by Congress of the great achievement of Robert Edwin Peary." The President subsequently could not remember whether his favoring the bill was or was not due to the influence of Peary Arctic Club President Thomas Hubbard. Macon responded four days later that he would fight the proposal to "the last ditch."

On January 7, 10, and 11, Peary himself was now questioned by the Naval Affairs subcommittee as if he were "a criminal on trial for a crime"(Green). Chairman Butler opened the hearings:

Captain Peary. . . , the subcommittee suggested that you should be invited to come here. . .and tell us anything you may see fit bearing upon your trip to the North Pole.

. . .Take your own way and drift along, and, for one member of the committee, I shall be greatly pleased to sit here and listen.

And later

Mr. Butler. We have your word for it, and we have these observations to show that you were at the North Pole. That is the plain way of putting it — your word and your proofs. To me, as a member of this committee, I accept your word; but your proofs, I know nothing at all about.

With such treatment, Peary had little to fear from Butler, Bates, Englebright, or Dawson, except when they blundered into the embarrassing matter of magnetic variation. The episode started with Englebright asking Peary to point out on a map the location of the North Magnetic Pole.

Mr. Englebright. And practically wherever you are on the earth the needle is pointing toward the magnetic pole?

Captain Peary. It tends to do so.

Mr. Butler. The needle tends to point toward the magnetic pole?

Captain Peary. *It does point near it,* until you get [too close to the magnetic pole]. . . .

Mr. Butler. Was there anything in the action of your needle that would assist in determining whether or not you had been to the Pole?

Captain Peary. No, sir; except so far as you used a compass.

Mr. Butler. I understand, but in the pointing of the needle?

Captain Peary. It would assist you with the magnetic pole. That is the distinction. One is a geographical pole, which is the point where the magnetic attraction is.

Mr. Englebright. In using a compass in the northern regions you use it with a calculated variation?

Captain Peary. You use it, checking [the variation] by observations *wherever you can* [!] To give you an idea of what those variations are, here at [Cape Sheridan] (indicating on map) the variation is approximately 95° west. [This is really obsolete British 1875-1876 data.] In other words, the north end of the needle points a little south of true west, and *as you go west* that increases.

Mr. Englebright. Is not that all charted by the Coast Survey and by the maritime nations of the world?

Captain Peary. They have the lines of certain variations, but, of course, the greater the number of observations, the more accurate the data.

Mr. Englebright. Did you have such a chart with you?

Captain Peary. No, sir; I did not have such a chart.

Mr. Dawson. *Did you make any observations in the locality which would tend to throw any additional light on the variation of the needle?*

Captain Peary. *I did not* on this last expedition, I did on the previous ones; when I went along this coast (indicating). I should say that on this trip that I had what I called a double team of dogs, twelve, and a light sledge. The usual team was eight dogs, although we started from Columbia with seven. . . . (Emphases added.)

The lack of a single 1909 discovery, implicit throughout these remarks, is as obvious as is their uncomfortable evasiveness. Here is a claimant to the discovery of the North Pole telling how the compass behaves as one goes — west! The simple, deadly question, asking for *any*thing new learned on the 1909 journey about the compass variation in the region he claims to have discovered, yields nothing; then an abrupt and uncalled-for change of subject. By contrast, Peary is quite garrulous and volunteering after diverting his questioners onto a less sore point.

Just before adjournment of the January 7 session, Roberts asked Peary about the pamphlet, *How Peary Reached the North Pole . . .,* which had been distributed to members of Congress back in 1910.

When the subcommittee reconvened on January 10, Peary replied that he had had the pamphlet printed, after "a suggestion," by Judd and Detweiler, the printers of the *National Geographic Magazine.*

Soon after, Gregg initiated a critical and revealing exchange.

Mr. Gregg. . . . have you any data by which some one else could go to the Pole along your route?

Captain Peary. Nothing that would help them.

Mr. Gregg. Then the North Pole is just as much lost as ever?

Captain Peary. Yes, sir. Of course, the term discovery of the North Pole is a misnomer. It should be the attainment of the Pole.

. . .

227

Captain Peary. With Cape Columbia as a starting point and with their instruments and their time and their compass they could follow my course.

Mr. Gregg. You have left the data, then, by which they could use those instruments?

Captain Peary. They would not need any data I have.

Peary's testimony amounted to an outright admission that his trip had been fruitless, thus unverifiable. In short, he had no hard evidence to back his claim — the very same formal grounds on which the University of Copenhagen had denied recognition to Dr. Cook.

Butler unwittingly soon had Peary in new difficulty.

Mr. Butler. Were you paid for your services?

Captain Peary. I was not.

Mr. Butler. All the rest were paid?

Captain Peary. Yes, sir.

Mr. Macon. Was not the Government paying Captain Peary's salary?

Macon had scored again. Peary was indeed being paid by the United States Navy, thanks to a special deal worked out *sub rosa* in late June, 1908, at Teddy Roosevelt's insistence.

The big payoff, however, was to come from publishers; and their alleged rights of priority to Peary's story, over those of the United States Navy, the United States Coast and Geodetic Survey, and this United States Congressional subcommittee, vexed Roberts.

Mr. Roberts. . . .[Rep. Alexander in March, 1910] said that you felt that you could not come then [March, 1910] because you were under contracts to publishers . . . that forbade your disclosing any of the results of your recent trip.

Captain Peary. My position at the time was that I was willing to come before the committee and show all my papers and my journal and answer all questions, but I was not ready to have the results of my work published.

Mr. Roberts. The reason you did not wish them published was because you were under certain contracts?

Captain Peary. Yes, sir.

Mr. Roberts. Those contracts have now expired?

Captain Peary. Yes, sir.

Mr. Roberts. You were bound by the contract with your publishers not to make known or disclose, without their permission, any of the results of your trip?

Captain Peary. Yes, sir; *in a general way,* I should say so. [Emphasis added.]

With that lame attempt to make the publishers the whipping boy for his own procrastination, Peary was excused from further questioning until the following day. When the hearings resumed (Jan. 11), Roberts picked up where he had left off, starting with a question about Peary's diary:

Mr. Roberts. Captain Peary, when you returned from your dash the first people you saw were those at the ship?

Captain Peary. Yes, sir.

Mr. Roberts. You, of course, told them of the trip?

Captain Peary. No, I did not. I did not go into any details in regard to the trip.

Mr. Roberts. Did you tell them you had reached the Pole?

Captain Peary. I told Bartlett; no one else.

Ostensibly, Peary had been unwilling to confide to his own diary of the journey, with particular reference to the title information on the cover.

Mr. Roberts. Have you any objection to my reading what is on the outside of it, simply to identify it?

Captain Peary. No sir.

Mr. Roberts (reading): "No. 1. *Roosevelt* to _____ and return, February 22 to April 27, R.E. Peary, United States Navy."

How strange that Peary had not filled in the blank with the words "North Pole." He had noted the dates of his departure from the ship and his return to it; why omit any mention of the Pole? Evidently, three weeks after the discovery, Peary still wasn't certain he'd made it. There were symptoms of at least temporary uncertainty at extremely critical points *inside*

229

the carefully guarded diary, too, as Roberts recounted:

"April 6, forty-third day, twenty-seventh march," the record covers two pages, and has a *marginal* entry and additional writing. Then follows *two loose leaves.* Without careful reading I can not say whether or not they are part of that day's record. Then follows two blank pages. "Wednesday, April 7, forty-fourth day, first return march." No record on that day. None on the next page. None on the next page. None on the next page. Then comes "April 8, forty-fifth day, second return march." No record. "April 9, forty-sixth day, third return march" [at the camp where Bartlett turned back], the record covers a page and a half. . . .

The diary, observed Roberts, "shows no finger marks or rough usage, a very cleanly kept book."

Macon had let the other subcommittee members go ahead of him, perhaps in the hope that he would be able to conduct his own uninterrupted examination. He got out one complete sentence before Butler broke in briefly. Macon, uninterrupted for a while, then managed to elicit in detail Peary's incredible claims regarding navigation, perhaps the most crucial testimony in the whole literature of the Peary affair:

Mr. Macon. . . .You said, I believe, that you took no longitude observations [in effect, observations for transverse position] at all?

Captain Peary. I took no observations for longitude at any time on the trip.

Mr. Macon. I am advised by astronomers and geographers and explorers and scientists that it is impossible for any one in a broad field as you were going over on your explorations of the North Pole, to tell exactly the direction they were traveling unless they took longitude observations. What do you say about that?

Captain Peary. I should say that would be an opinion to be left to experts.

Mr. Macon. What is your opinion about it?

Captain Peary. My opinion is that we were able to

230

keep our course. My opinion also is that at the time of the year, and under the conditions existing there, any attempt at taking longitude observations would have been a waste of time.

Mr. Macon. Why so?

Captain Peary. In the middle part of the journey the altitude of the sun was so low that presumably any longitude observations would have been unnecessary, and in the neighborhood of the Pole it is generally recognized that longitude observations are not practicable with any degree of accuracy. [Gannett actually bought this evasion of the early April omissions. No judge wondered why the moon was not sextant-shot for longitude at April 1 noon.]

Mr. Macon. Then, you do not hold to the teachings of other scientists, which is to the effect that unless you take the longitude observations you can not know exactly the direction in which you are traveling? [Longitude uncertainty on such a Polar trip is at all times equal to the traveler's uncertainty as to which way it is to the North Pole.] . . . Then, you took no observations, longitude or otherwise, for a distance of 133 miles after you left Bartlett at 87° 47'?

Captain Peary. No, sir.

Mr. Macon. And without that you managed to make a straight course to the Pole without anything except conjecture or estimate to guide you. Is that it?

Captain Peary. I leave the [April 6-7, "Pole"] observations to answer that question. . . .

After this patently circular response (Macon's whole point was that Peary's steering story invalidated these uselessly rendered "observations"), Peary over-expanded on the dead reckoning accuracy of which he said he was capable:

Captain Peary. I have crossed the Greenland ice cap, a distance of five hundred miles, on two occasions, and was within ten miles and, on one occasion, within five miles of my objective point, but we will say ten miles. . . . I made a cache on this ice in the fall at a distance that I

231

would call forty or forty-two miles from the edge of the ice cap, going in and estimating my distance by paces. The fall and winter of that year were particularly stormy with a great deal of snow and wind. In the spring, when I was starting to make the trip northeast across that ice cap, I went in to find this cache, and after reeling off my forty or forty-two miles, whatever the distance was, and that distance was again estimated by pacing. . .and that . . .cache was not over a hundred yards from my sledge. I do not pretend to say that I could do that every time, but it shows that I was fortunate that time.

Aside from the fact that Peary rode so much in 1909 that he could not have determined mileages by pacing, his *The North Pole* states that: "On the inland ice of Greenland my [distance] dead reckoning was. . .the reading of my *odometer*, a wheel with a cyclometric registering apparatus. This could not possibly be used on the ice of the Polar Sea, as it would be smashed to pieces in the rough going." (Emphasis added.)

Mr. Macon. Did you submit any observation of temperature for air, water, barometer readings, wind velocity, and the direction of the water?
Captain Peary. Meteorological reports were submitted to the United States Coast and Geodetic Survey. I took no water temperatures on the sledge journey. . . .The direction of the wind has not, as far as I know, been compiled separately from the notes of the party. . . .The data as to the direction of the wind and general water conditions at different points on the same day has not been compiled and worked up, but that could be done.

His scientific sloppiness exhibited, his credibility under attack, Peary could not have been anything but relieved when sympathizers burst into Macon's questioning with increasing frequency. At two separate points these interruptions may well have obscured revealing testimony relating to compass variation at the April 1st Camp and Camp Jesup. Macon got increasingly touchy and the quality of the hearing declined:

Mr. Macon. Can you prepare a map showing the exact location [of Camp Jesup, etc.]. . .?

232

. . .

Mr. Englebright. . . .we have gentlemen present who prepared such a map from the observations. . . .

Mr. Butler. If the committee want the map, they can have it. I do not want to see it; I would not understand it if I saw it.

Mr. Macon. Mr. Chairman, we are making a record here —

Mr. Butler. That is all right, if the gentleman wants the map —

Mr. Macon. and we want to have Captain Peary's knowledge —

Mr. Butler. It is your privilege to question him, Mr. Macon.

Mr. Macon — about these matters.

Mr. Butler. Yes; that is right.

Mr. Macon. [At the North Geographic Pole] did the [compass] needle answer to the primary or secondary magnetic pole?

Captain Peary. The direction of the compass was fairly constant there.

Mr. Butler. Will you tell me, please, what that means?

Mr. Macon. I asked him whether the needle answered to the primary or secondary magnetic pole.

Mr. Butler. What are they?

Mr. Macon. Oh, they are known in science.

Mr. Bates. Where did you find that question?

Mr. Macon. They are known in science.

Mr. Bates. But I am not a scientific person.

Mr. Dawson. I would be glad if the gentleman from Arkansas [Macon] would explain.

Mr. Macon. The gentleman from Arkansas is going to ask questions, and he is not going to ask any foolish ones, either.

Mr. Englebright. Is he trying to test [Peary's] knowledge on science by asking such questions — ridiculous questions?

Mr. Macon. I have asked no ridiculous questions.

. . .

Mr. Butler. I will ask the members of the subcommittee not to further interrupt you.

Mr. Macon. I am advised by a school of scientists that it is a physical impossibility for man or beast to reach the North Pole, for the reason that. . .the diminishing centrifugal action and, in proportion, the increasing center of gravity near the Pole causes a complete failure of man and animal energy that produces a kind of paralysis of the senses and of motion, a paralysis of sensation in any part of the body, including the exercise of the faculty of the mind. . . .So that it would be almost impossible for them to exercise their independent functions so that anybody could ascertain a real fact. . . .You never heard of that before?

Captain Peary. Never heard of that before.

The fact that Macon's latter remarks are distinctly crank has doubtless encouraged many to entirely discount his' questions. The journals *Scientific American* and *The Navy*, as well as Green and Hobbs, deplore Peary's having to bear such pointless badgering. Both of Weems' books quote from the foregoing passage to show how ignorant Peary's inquisitors were of the matters under discussion. In fact, however, Macon's question on a secondary magnetic pole was a perfectly legitimate and relevant one, especially in the light of Peary's attempts to obscure his ignorance of the variation by vague statements about how the needle "tends" to point to "near" the magnetic pole. As mentioned earlier, at the North Pole the compass needle does *not* point to the north magnetic pole. The common notion (which misled Cook and Peary) that the earth is a single magnet has been known for centuries to be erroneous, a matter on which Weems clearly is still entirely ignorant.

As early as 1692 Edmond Halley proposed a partial solution: a theory of multiple terrestrial magnetic poles, and though some of the rest of his paper was as wild as the Arkansan's talk of centrifugal effects, this has not caused his valid reasoning to be forgotten, any more than Macon's ought to be. The notion of a double magnetic pole is naturally an improvement on the single magnet as a description of the earth's complex and secularly varying magnetic field — though still itself just an approximation to reality.

Macon labored ahead — a few excerpts from the close of his attempted questioning will make clear that if Peary was suffering harassment he was not alone in his ordeal:

Mr. Macon. . . .a scientific society right here [the National Geographic Society]. . .said that your observations were not any good without your narrative?

Mr. Bates. I object to that.

Mr. Macon. I believe you said, Captain, that the Eskimos that you selected to go with you to the Pole would walk through hell with you if you said so . . . and that they, and Henson, the colored man you took with you for witnesses, were as pliant to your will as the fingers of your right hand. . . . Do you   really think those men would walk through hell for you, or was that just a figure of speech?

. . .

Mr. Butler. Of course the statement presupposes that there is a hell.

Mr. Macon. And it presupposes that they would say whatever the Captain told them to say and abide by it.

. . .

Mr. Bates. I think that last remark better be struck out.

. . .

Mr. Hobson. I ask that he withdraw it.

Mr. Macon. No; I do not want to withdraw it. I want to ask another question. . . .

After the irrepressible Macon had finished with Peary, Roberts tried to clear up a few final points. Long before it became the fashion to invoke the Fifth Amendment, Peary was avoiding, if not actually refusing to answer, questions of the most elementary nature that Roberts put to him, namely those pertaining to his arrival in Washington for the National Geographic Society examination. He, the man who claimed he found his way to the North Pole by an intuitive dead reckoning bordering on the psychic, could not, for the life of him, recall when he arrived in Washington, what he did, or whom he met.

Mr. Roberts. What time did you reach the city [of Washington], Mr. Peary?

Captain Peary. I could not say.

Mr. Roberts. Did you get here in the morning?

Captain Peary. . . .what time I got in I could not say.

. . .

Mr. Roberts. What did you do when you arrived in the city; where did you go?

Captain Peary. I do not recall what my movements were.

Mr. Roberts. . . .You went to the Geographical Society's rooms sometime in the forenoon?

Captain Peary. I do not remember when I went there. . . .

. . .

Mr. Roberts. I would like to have the best recollection you have about when you first saw any of the members of the committee, and where.

. . .

Captain Peary. I do not recall about that, about my meeting any members of the committee.

Mr. Roberts. You would not want to say that you did not meet two of the members of the committee at the rooms of the Geographical Society, would you?

Captain Peary. I would not want to say I did or did not.

The Peary forces' major argument for approval had been that the validity of the National Geographic Society exam was beyond question. However, since Roberts' 1910 quizzing of Gannett had shot down that position before it was even taken, before the subcommittee the Peary lobby readied two new stratagems for the afternoon of the final day of the hearings. The first was sprung toward the end of Macon's questioning.

Mr. Macon. . . . Captain, have your proofs been submitted to any geographical or scientific society to be passed upon except this National Geographic Society?

When Peary answered "Yes" and forthwith produced two letters of support from officers —including Leonard

Darwin, President — of the Royal Geographic Society, the most prestigious of all the world's geographical societies, Macon was noticeably surprised and flustered.

At the very end of Peary's appearance, Roberts brought the matter into perspective a little, at least:

These documents must have had their effect. But it would have been impossible for the committee to tell from them that, in fact, the originally well predisposed Royal Geographical Society was, after seeing Peary's records, badly split on him. Even the sending of Darwin's restrained private letter was approved by the 35-member Royal Geographic Society Council only by a vote of eight to seven, with two not voting and 18 absences.

Mr. Roberts. Just one question or two I forgot. You spoke of submitting copies of your records to the Royal Geographic Society of London. . . . That was after the award of the medal?

Captain Peary. Yes.

Mr. Roberts. Has any other geographic or scientific body requested you to submit proofs?

Captain Peary. No; not that I recall.

Mr. Roberts. Have you volunteered to submit them to any other body?

Captain Peary. I do not recall that I have.

This completed Peary's less than impressive testimony. The final ploy of his forces followed. Tittmann now introduced, as "unsurpassed anywhere in ability or experience," his United States Coast and Geodetic Survey employee, computer Hugh C. Mitchell. Mitchell presented a written report by himself and a diagram done by his colleague Charles R. Duvall (based on their reduction of the expedition's solar data, using ship's chronometer comparisons made in New York), testimony riddled with misstatements, computational inelegancies, and optimistic assumptions, which were naturally not picked up by the untrained legislators. But the crucial testimony was Mitchell's professional opinion on the genuineness of the data:

Mr. Englebright. Now [considering the factors involved: declination, refraction, chronometer ratings], do you consider it possible that anyone could have faked those observations?

Mr. Mitchell. No.

The chairman, with commendable curiosity, returned to this theme later:

Mr. Butler. Suppose these figures submitted to you by Captain Peary had been made here in Washington or New York or Boston, how could you have detected it. . .?

Mr. Mitchell. Well, that is a rather difficult question to answer. I believe it is altogether a matter of experience that any dishonesty in observations or computations will show up in the reduction of [them]. . . . At some point of the work it will come out; yes. That is a belief. That is not a mathematical demonstration.

So concluded Mitchell's testimony, and the Peary Hearings came to an end. Though utterly false, Mitchell's opinion weighed heavily with some members of the committee. It might have counted less had they known who the secret boss of the work was. None other than Captain Peary! For, Tittmann's glowing introduction had omitted to mention that the computers' reduction of Peary's data was not government work but was paid for by Peary (a fact that did not come out until 1914). Later that day, Peary phoned Mitchell to thank him for what he had done.

On January 21, 1911, the subcommittee's report was sent to the House of Representatives.

Things were going well at this point, but Peary was a worrier by long experience and so presumably not ready to feel out of the woods until President Taft's ink was drying on the bill.

It certainly gave Peary no extra sleep to be reminded of the vastness of the "moral gulf" between himself and the society and statesmen who were honoring him. He could hardly have missed the page one news story of January 28, 1911, that Taft was forcing Rear Admiral Barry to resign, the action being the "outgrowth of charges affecting the moral character of the naval officer." Peary must also have realized that Dr. Cook (now back in the U.S.), privy to the details of Peary's double life, probably had seen the item; would it give Cook ideas? Peary's experience with thin ice had not ended upon his return from the Arctic.

Macon was not giving up as easily as Roberts. On February 16, he spoke of his own minority report on the floor of the House. While occasionally reminding one of William Jennings Bryan's 1925 finale at Dayton, Tennessee, some of Macon's skepticism would have done defender Darrow proud — though Macon's was the unenviable role he knew best, that of the prosecuting district attorney. But perhaps all that needs to be said is that this remarkable speech defies classification (as do the laughs it drew):

. . .I have the combined influence of the [Taft] administration, a paid lobby of the Peary Arctic Club, and the National Geographic Society to contend with, but having right upon my side as I see it, I am going to do everything in my power to defeat [the bill]. . . .

I know that we can not afford to heed the importunities of a paid lobby that has haunted the Capitol for days and days in the interest of the bill. . . .

. . .I have always been skeptical concerning many of the scientific theories. . .[of] the various schools of scientists. . . .[Many persons] pretend to accept any kind of a so-called scientific statement or discovery without question, because they are so weazen-brained (laughter) that they think they will be classed as scholars if they do accept them at first blush — a thing devoutly sought after by the ignorant — or because they fear some unblushing, know-all, or titbit editors of yellow journals, like the *New York Times* or the New York *Post* (laughter), will call them ignorant blatherskites. (laughter). I pity a man who is so ignorant as to be terror stricken all the time for fear he will be called ignorant by some saphead (laughter). . . .

. . .the Congress. . .is being asked to jump the writer of *[The North Pole]* over the heads of many true, able, and efficient naval officers. . .upon the self-told and unbelievable exaggerations to be found between its lids, the unreliable data for which was collected while our hero was loafing around in northern latitudes gathering up furs to sell and to bestow upon the members of the Peary Arctic Club (laughter) and the National Geographic Society. . . . that virtually accepted his discovery of the North Pole before examining his proofs, [all the] while drawing his pay from the government with great regularity.

The burden of proof is upon him to prove his claim by a preponderance of the testimony, if not beyond a reasonable doubt.

Some of us who have tried to plow a straight furrow. . . across a ten-acre field without stakes to guide us, or who have undertaken to ride across a broad prairie without a path or other object to direct our course, know how impossible [Peary's] contention is when he insists that he could rush pell-mell over a rough, rugged, and broken ice course for a distance of 130 miles without an observation or object to guide him and go directly north to an imaginary point.

It is. . .contended by [a school of] scientists. . .that the North Pole is located in an open sea that never freezes over. . . . Another school. . .insist that the thing that they call the "North Pole" is a hole that extends into the interior surface of the earth, and their reasoning about the matter is as sound as that of another school that tells us that Mars is full of canals that were dug by human hands and that the nights in Saturn are seven years long. Ah, gentlemen, we cannot afford to pin our faith to all of the mythical contentions and bogus discoveries of theorizing scientists and fake explorers. If we do, we will soon be as crazy and unreliable as many of them are.

Scientists tell us that such mighty mountain chains as [the Rockies]. . .are nothing [but] volcanic upheavals of the earth, but common reason teaches us that they are as much a part of the original creation as Mount Ararat, . . .and certain schools of [scientists] tell us that man does not possess a soul. . . .I insist that to accept such scientific teachings as that as true would either run us all

240

crazy or convert us into a vicious set of murderers, grafters, and fakers, for, without the belief of the existence of a soul, there would be no hope of a future reward and hence no incentive for living a correct life. . . .

. . .It would be impossible to use the [compass] needle with any confidence unless its variations were tested on the way, and. . .if the tests were made by the sun. . .an error of the chronometer would give a wrong direction.

. . .If I were to walk into the House some morning. . . and inform Members that I had walked to Baltimore and back since breakfast, and were to exhibit a copy of the Baltimore *Sun* as proof. . ., no one would believe [it]. . .

It is much more reasonable to believe that instead of Peary going to the Pole and back. . .that he actually turned back [toward] Cape Columbia the day after Bartlett left him.

I am advised by explorers, navigators, and scientists that [a reduction of Peary's data] would be no evidence of where he had been. . . .Then why all the gentleman's pretense of secrecy about his proofs that he would not allow Congress to see until some "cashing in" arrangement had been made?

[Regarding Peary's inability to recall the circumstances of his National Geographic Society exam:] Do you really believe that this man knew nothing of a positive character about the matter, or, rather, do you believe that he was afraid to make a positive statement, for fear he would be flatly contradicted by others, and in that way his whole story repudiated to the letter?

I have given more time and thought to this alleged discovery than I have to any other public question that I remember to have undertaken in my whole life, and the more I have investigated and studied the story the more thoroughly convinced I have become that it is a fake pure and simple.

At the conclusion of his speech, Macon was cross-questioned by Representative Moore.

Mr. Moore. . . .I ask him whether he has been in communication with the Arctic traveler upon whom he seems to pin his faith, Dr. Cook?

Mr. Macon. I never had a line from Dr. Cook in my life. . . .The gentleman could not believe him to be a greater fake than I believe him to be.

Dr. Moore. Did not the gentleman, coming from that section of the country which boasts of its Anglo-Saxon blood, have at first a little touch of pride, as a native American, when he read that an American had discovered the North pole?

Mr. Macon. I did not believe it.

Moore then made a short, emotional speech for Peary; Representative Edward W. Sanders (Democrat, Virginia) followed with another, twice mentioning the vouching for (the genuineness of) Peary's data by Mitchell, "expert computer . . .of astronomical observations, from the Coast and Geodetic Survey of the United States. . . ."

On March 3, 1911, the bill finally came to a vote. Speeches preceded the roll call. After several accolades for Peary, Macon addressed the House. His full remarks will probably never be known, as they were accorded the rare distinction of total deletion from the *Congressional Record*. He is said to have called Peary a "wilful and deliberate liar, dirty little pilferer of words, and contemptible little ass."

After several more pro-Peary speeches, Representative Dawson moved the passage of the bill. Macon demanded a roll-call division, which yielded: 154 ayes, 34 noes. The bill had finally passed. The "disgraceful wrangle" (as Hobbs called it) seemed done, and Robert Peary's greatest battle at last finished. His daughter Marie broke the glad news to him on his return from a Washington walk with Jo. For this, Peary gave Marie a ring with three diamonds. Next day, President Taft signed the bill and Peary was a rear admiral, with a lifetime pension, and acclaimed the *official* attainer of the Pole, with a certificate of the Thanks of Congress.

Peary's later comment on the Congressional investigation is one that may bear second thoughts: ". . .I saw the humor of it."

19. Snake in the Grassroots

Few copies of the Peary Hearings were originally printed. Apparently none ever existed at the Library of Congress or the National Archives. In 1916, Representative Henry Helgesen (R.,N.D.) could hardly find a copy anywhere: "The public never saw this published hearing. It was practically suppressed. The Senate library has not a copy of it; the members of the [1911] Naval Affairs congressional subcommittee have none [highly exceptional]; Senators and Congressmen have tried in vain to procure copies." Helgesen thereupon entered the entire Hearings verbatim in the *Congressional Record*.

Still, the general public of 1911 might never have seen, or having seen might have ignored, or having noticed might have forgotten, the revelations of the Peary Hearings but for the reappearance of a certain familiar reptile, bearing the fruit of inside knowledge.

Dr. Cook came out of hiding in mid-December, 1910, and returned to the United States. As part of his promotion for the publication of his emotional confession to having some mental doubts of his Polar attainment, he pleaded for mercy from the public, apparently thinking this the only way left for him to garner publicity for future projects of then indeterminate nature. But, to his amazement, he found that many of his followers still believed in him, and so within a month he was preparing to seriously reassert his claim.

243

On January 7, the opening day of Peary's 1911 testimony, Greely's savior, Admiral Schley, wrote Cook a supporting letter: ". . . I have never varied in the belief that you and Civil Engineer Peary reached the Pole. . . ." Neutral judge Gannett phoned Schley immediately in shock at this. On January 10, Cook wrote a letter to the chairman of the Naval Affairs Committee urging Peary's recognition: ". . . I ask for nothing. Within my own bosom there is the self-satisfying throb of success. . . ." By January 26, he was already "more positive than ever" that he had been to the Pole.

Back in September, 1909, Cook had responded to Peary's announcement of attaining the Pole by publicly praising him, acting on the assumption that Peary would follow the polite custom then in vogue and respond in kind. Peary's necessary failure to play the game caused Cook eventually to jettison the orthodox share-the-wealth-and-glory approach in favor of throwing mud back at Peary. A major ingredient of Cook's dirt was predetermined, since Peary's Eskimo offspring were an open secret among exploration professionals. Arctic Club of America Secretary and Cook-believer Bradley Osbon recalled that in 1909

> One of the things seriously proposed to him [Cook] was to send north for the Eskimo wife and family of a well-known explorer, who were to be placed on exhibition in this country. A vaudeville impresario offered him a huge sum for the first call on the family's services.

Cook would have none of this, reports the admiring Osbon. But, in the discontentful winter of 1910-1911, while Peary was being nationally celebrated and proposed for rear admiral and Cook was simultaneously being treated as simply an American embarrassment, the Doctor suddenly began to feel that it was his moral duty "to uncover the leprous spots of one's accusers," so, "I changed my tactics." As Peary before him had done, Cook went right to the top with his gossip, cabling Taft, on the very day the President signed the Peary-promotion act, one of the most unusual communications ever received by a Chief Executive:

The President
The White House   Omaha, Nebraska
Washington, D.C.   March 4, 1911

When you sign the Peary bill you are honoring a man with sin-soiled hands who has taken money from our innocent school children. A part of this money I believe was used to make Arctic concubines comfortable. I am ready to produce others of the same opinion. Thus for twenty years while in the pay of the Navy, supplied with luxuries from the public purse, Peary has enjoyed, apparently with National consent, the privilege denied the Mormons.

There are at least two children now in the cheerless north crying for bread and milk and a father. These are growing witnesses of Peary's leprous character. Will you endorse it?

By endorsing Peary you are upholding the cowardly verdict of Chester, Tittman, and Gannett, who bartered their souls to Peary's interests by suppressing the worthlessness of the material upon which they passed. These men on the Government pay-roll have stooped to a dishonor that should make all fair-minded people blush with shame. This underhanded performance calls for an investigation. Will you close these dark-chamber doings to the light of justice?

In this bill you are honoring one, who in seeking funds for legitimate exploration, has passed the hat along the line of easy money for twenty years. Much of this money was in my judgment used to promote a lucrative fur and ivory trade, while the real effort of getting to the pole was delayed seemingly for commercial gain. Thus engaged in a propaganda of hypocrisy he stooped to immorality and dishonor and ultimately when his game of fleecing the public was threatened, he tried to kill a brother explorer. The stain of at least two other lives is on this man. This bill covers a page in history against which the spirits of murdered men cry for redress.

Peary is covered with the scabs of unmentionable in-

245

decency, and for him your hand is about to put the seal of clean approval upon the dirtiest campaign of bribery, conspiracy, and black dishonor that the world has ever known.

If you can close your eyes to this, sign the Peary bill.

(Signed) Frederick A. Cook

By the summer of 1911, Cook had published his book *My Attainment of the Pole*. In it he not only renounced his confession and now soberly defended his claim, but laid before a wide public much of the damaging evidence relating to Peary. Cook then took to the lecture trail, vaudeville and Chautauqua, and made tens of thousands more converts and dollars. Early in his new lecture campaign, he realized that the audience's greatest response was not to his trial in the North but to his condemnation of Peary. Cook obliged his listeners' preferences. Attending one of the very first talks, a press reporter related: "Probably no person in the small audience that greeted Dr. Cook ever heard a more scathing denunciation of a public man, and fearful charges bearing on Admiral Peary's character were made with apparently no regard whatever for the outcome of such statements." By 1913, Cook was starring in a pack-'em-in Chautauqua road show, aided by skilled press agent gimmickry that included another telegram to the President (Woodrow Wilson), twice as long and thrice as florid as the last, e.g.: "The American Eagle has spread its wings of glory over the world's top. . . . The graves of our worthy ancestors are marks in the ascent of the ladder of latitudes. . . ." Postcards denouncing Peary and asking for a redress of the injustice done Cook were printed by the thousands and distributed at his talks for rapid signing and mailing to United States Government officials. For example, Mr. Josephus Daniels, Secretary of the Navy, read:

Rear Admiral Peary wears the stripes of the Navy, he is drawing a pension of $6,000.00 per year from the taxpayers—the National dictates of honor compel such a man to be clean morally—honest and upright officially. Dr. Cook has publicly made charges against Peary which relegate this Naval Officer to the rank of a common thief

246

and degenerate. In his book "My Attainment of the Pole" (Mitchell-Kennedy, New York) there are specific charges made which call for an investigation. These charges have remained unanswered for three years — *Why?*

In the Polar controversy the Flag has been dragged through muck, and this dishonor seems to rest upon a man for whose actions you are responsible. The American people have a right to demand an investigation into the intrigue of the Peary Polar Propaganda, and as one believing in justice at the bar of public opinion, I ask that you take steps to clear this cloud in the eyes of the world.

Peary rode out these personal attacks by the old reliable beneath reply approach, and so, as with Dedrick, no one of any importance believed the charges. As if Peary's guardian angel were its muse, *Living Age* indignantly condemned Cook's ". . . unwarrantable attacks upon Admiral Peary . . .; it says much for the recovery of self-control in that gallant explorer that he has had the strength of mind to ignore these charges and refrain from giving the author further notoriety by bringing him into a court of law." The Cook cause, which Peary, like most other observers, even Cook, apparently, had thought dead in 1910, was so powerful by 1914 that Congress was petitioned (90,000 signatures) and lobbied for *his* recognition as attainer of the Pole. Within Congress the movement found enthusiastic backers in Senator Miles Poindexter (Republican, Washington), Representatives Caraway (Democrat, Arkansas), Charles B. Smith (Democrat, New York) and William J. Fields (Democrat, Kentucky), among others. Early in 1915, a private Congressional hearing, set up by Cook's lobbyist Ernest C. Rost (Congressman Helgesen's secretary), was held on the matter. Some of the talk in Congress inevitably cast doubt on Peary's claim, and the Admiral must have gradually realized that he was in for another fight, this time just to maintain the status quo. By January 30, Representative Moore was attacking Cook in the House.

As part of the Cook movement, Representative Helgesen introduced on February 25 a Congressional resolution for the

247

correction of U.S. Hydrographic Office maps containing Peary's non-existent Peary Channel, East Greenland Sea, and Crocker Land. Just five days after this direct attack, Peary's lobbyist Lucien Alexander was back in action in Washington; and two days later, Congressman Simeon D. Fess (Republican, Ohio) debunked Cook, with Helgesen rebutting. At this point, just when serious Congressional scrutiny seemed imminent, Cook typically took off for faraway parts.

Helgesen did not return to the controversy for almost a year. But in January of 1916, he again attacked Peary, this time avoiding any position with regard to Cook's claim, and closing with a defense of Greely's discovery of Schley Land. A few days later Helgesen really unloaded, entering 25 pages of often highly intelligent critical analysis of the Peary Hearings, plus the original text of the Hearings, into the *Congressional Record*, concluding: ". . . in view of the facts . . . presented . . . I . . . make the unqualified statement that Robert E. Peary never reached, discovered, nor was approximately near to . . . the North Pole." On July 21, Helgesen entered 21 more critical pages, this time picking apart Peary's book and magazine serial.

On August 2, Helgesen unveiled the ultimate: He actually introduced before Congress a bill to repeal the original 1911 Act of Congress which had given Peary his costly promotion, pension, and recognition. Two weeks later Helgesen publicly branded Peary "the greatest faker which . . . ever disgraced the nation." On September 4, after rather over-disclaiming any original belief in Cook's claims, Helgesen introduced 29 *Congressional Record* pages blasting Cook's pretensions. At about the same time, Helgesen's secretary, Ernest C. Rost, sued Cook for almost $3,000 non-payment of lobbying fees.

Peary was plenty concerned by this time. On September 10, he had written out a court martial threat to Helgesen, but it is not recorded that it was ever delivered. Peary must have known that another hearing was the last thing his case needed; for the same reason, he decided at this time against running for United States Senator in Maine. Yet, on the other hand, Helgesen, if unopposed, might be encouraged to make new sallies. What Peary finally would have done to bluster down this threat will never be known, for on April 10, 1917, Helgesen died.

If luck had just saved Peary, the score was shortly to be evened. By the end of the year he was ill with what was diagnosed as incurable pernicious anemia, for which a control was not known until 1926. Peary's condition worsened rapidly in early 1920, and on February 20, he died. Burial took place at Arlington National Cemetery before the leading statesmen, geographers, and explorers of the nation. In 1922, on April 6, the 13th anniversary of Peary's arrival at Camp Jesup, an equally distinguished gathering attended graveside ceremonies for the unveiling of a white granite monument, whose inscription reads, "Erected by the National Geographic Society. Dedicated April 6, 1972, [by] the President of the United States [Harding], the Chief Justice of the United States [Taft], the Secretary of State [Hughes], the Secretary of the Navy [Denby], the Dean of the Diplomatic Corps [Jusserand], and the Board of Trustees of the National Geographic Society." To: "Robert Edwin Peary, Discoverer of North Pole, April 6, 1909."

Transferring the airship *Norge* to Norway, March 29, 1926. Left to right, Mussolini, Calant, Nobile, Amundsen, Ellsworth, and Thommessen.

The *Norge* group en route from Nome to Seattle. Sitting (left to right) Amundsen, Ellsworth, Nobile. Standing, (left to right) Riiser-Larsen, Ramm, Gottwaldt, Wisting, Omdal, Malmgren, Strom-Johnson, Allesandrini; (in back) Cecioni, Horgen, Arduccio and Caratti. Below, the *Norge* arriving at Kings Bay, Spitzbergen, May 7, 1926.

20. The Silent Majority

Though quiescent for years at a stretch, the Cook-Peary controversy has never quite died and probably won't for a long time to come. Cook's sentencing in 1923 to almost fifteen years in jail, for selling phony oil stock ads through the mail, was probably seen at the time by many hopeful Peary believers as the absolute end to the Polar question. To the contrary, Cook, before his first year at Leavenworth was up, had become the storm center of another public dispute on his and Peary's claims.

On January 20, 1926, Roald Amundsen, then between his 1925 and 1926 air attempts at the North Pole, stopped by the prison to see his old friend. Exactly what were the actual events is now hard to say, but three days later Amundsen was lecturing in Fort Worth, Texas, where Cook's oil headquarters had once been; and a newspaper story came out of there that Amundsen had said "Dr. Cook may not have discovered the Pole, but Commander R. E. Peary also may not have and the former has as good a claim as the latter." When a howl instantly arose from the United States exploring establishment, Amundsen sent a telegram to the *New York Times,* with which he had contracted for his past flight and the upcoming *Norge* airship expedition, stating that he had been somewhat misquoted: "I did not commit myself to any opinion as to the respective achievements of Peary or Cook. What I said was that the only evidence I could accept would be the publication of their complete observations." Not suffi-

251

cient recantation for the *Times:* "It was bad enough for [Amundsen] to seek to rehabilitate Dr. Cook, but it was worse and almost unforgivable for him in the same breath to discredit Peary." Shortly afterward, National Geographic Society President Gilbert H. Grosvenor canceled a lucrative lecture invitation to Amundsen, who rightly called the action infantile. Grosvenor explained on March 4:

When on January 24, 1926, the newspapers printed a statement by Amundsen seriously reflecting on Peary, I felt compelled on behalf of the society to withdraw an invitation to Amundsen to speak.... [Amundsen's later] telegram to the *New York Times,* which was read to me by [Norwegian] Minister Bryn, was not a retraction of his reflection upon Peary.

Amundsen had originally planned to be in the United States until March 19, but now he planned immediate embarkation for Europe. Though he protested publicly that he was not foreshortening his lecture tour, there was evidently a rupture with his lecture manager, who feared Amundsen's opinions on the Cook-Peary affair would hurt business. To understand the effect of this, of the *Times* rebuke, and of Grosvenor's spitefulness, plus the serious threat of future similar treatment, one must realize that Amundsen at this time was bankrupt and thus dependent on United States lecture and writing fees for his survival. On March 6, just as he sailed, Amundsen was asked point-blank by a reporter whether he believed the North Pole had yet been reached by anyone. "We could hardly get into that," replied Amundsen, "it is so late." Yet this poor persecuted man's subsequent tongue in cheek genuflection to the Peary myth is offered in all seriousness by MacMillan, and repeated by Weems, in support of Peary's claim.

Eager to excuse, daring to doubt, Amundsen was all but ostracized in the United States for his candor. From 1926 on, the lesson was clear to those who had not already understood the realities: Any Peary skeptic inclined to speak his mind must expect to offend the wealthy power brokers of the geographical societies. How many explorers could dare risk that?

One would expect that an organization dedicated to "increasing and diffusing geographic knowledge and promoting research and exploration" — as the National Geographic Society professes in its charter and each issue of its journal — would moderate such hidebound attitudes over the years, and that its old emotions and old prejudices would finally give way to a modicum of introspection, if for no other reason than to reassert proprietorship over the glamorous institution of Polar exploration. The National Geographic Society had a fairly recent opportunity to exhibit such maturity when, in 1953, a young historian at Ohio Northern University, Russell W. Gibbons, submitted to the Society a set of questions regarding the debatable aspects of Peary's Polar journey. The reply, inspiring a pro-Cook book by Gibbons, was, as he understates, "a classic in thinking":

Dear Mr. Gibbons:

I trust you will not take offense when I say that the officers of the National Geographic Society and Magazine have much more of importance to attend to than waste time with this ancient absurdity.

It is cowardly, yet easy, to attack a dead man!

You will find an interesting article in the forthcoming October issue. Sincerely,

John Oliver La Gorce
Vice President, National Geographic Society

This writer received a more responsive reaction to similar queries in 1968. The Society launched an immediate investigation — of the writer! Essentially, then, little has changed in 60 years, the logical attacks on Peary's claim are not really being met by his defenders, but are either ignored or brushed aside as unimportant.

This protectionist policy has long prevented the public from realizing that the majority of Peary's peers eventually came to doubt his claim, including many who had at first accepted it. The dean of the world's geographers, retired Royal Geographical Society President Clements Markham, formerly a friend and admirer of Peary, wrote in his book

Lands of Silence his explicit disbelief in Peary's success at such near-perfect aiming toward the Pole. He was undoubtedly influenced by his exploring cousin, a former farthest North record holder; the only living explorer of the day who had, like Peary, led a Poleward expedition off North Ellesmere Island, Albert Markham in 1909 publicly stressed at the Royal Geographical Society the necessity even on short journeys for continually checking one's compass variation to maintain a straight course.

Like Clements Markham, retired senior American explorer Adolphus W. Greely had little to fear, financially, by offending powerful institutions. Though having at first written his acceptance of the claims of both Cook and Peary, by 1916 he had publicly rejected each. Contemporary explorers were less direct. The United States' Anthony Fiala and Denmark's Ejnar Mikkelsen were properly tactful, but let their doubts show anyway. Aside from Amundsen, two of the greatest explorers of the day were Fridtjof Nansen, effusive admirer of Peary, and Ernest Shackleton; both had at first accepted Peary's success, Shackleton even wiring his congratulations. However, once the details of the Peary claim began to leak out, neither man was willing thereafter to offer a word in its support. Reading meaning into an explorer's silence may seem unwarranted guesswork, but in these two cases there is plenty of reason to make a definite interpretation, by analogy with their behavior regarding Cook. Though both had by September 11, 1909, already concluded, as had Robert Falcon Scott, that Cook's claim was baseless, they nonetheless remained silent. When Cook was finally exposed, Nansen admitted that he had never believed his story:

> I therefore preferred to keep silent. As for Peary, I never doubted his veracity, although I did not approve of his behavior [calling Cook a fake] after his return. However, it is easy to understand his indignation. At least he is a man and there is no comparison between him and Cook.

Even at this time Shackleton said that he would not criticize Cook. During Peary's triumphant 1910 European tour,

Scandinavia did not award him a single medal or citation. Even the silent Shackleton ultimately expressed private doubts of Peary's attainment; in fact, by 1920 he was planning a full-scale Arctic expedition to clear up the controversy. At the time, and for years thereafter, Shackleton's view of Peary's claim was perhaps the majority one in formerly pro-Peary England, but almost no critic would put his views into print. The Royal Geographical Society, which in 1910 had provided Peary with politically valuable private supporting letters by President Darwin and Council Member Douglas Freshfield, was by 1930, with the concurrence of Darwin and Freshfield, taking the judicious official position that their judgment of Peary was based on the National Geographic Society examination, which Royal Geographical was pleased to take on faith.

Other prominent skeptics include Royal Geographical Society historian Hugh Mill, Canadian Arctic explorer Joseph E. Bernier, Polar scholar Reverend James Gordon Hayes, Scott Institute founder Frank Debenham, Ellesmere explorer Edward Shackleton, and contemporary Polar explorers Vivian Fuchs, Ralph Plaisted and Wally Herbert. This is not to say that Peary didn't have his defenders. Aside from the understandably biased 1909 expedition members MacMillan and Bartlett, pro-Peary explorers whose opinions some would consider authoritative include Stefansson, Lauge Koch, Jean Charcot, Peter Freuchen, Knud Rasmussen, and Richard Byrd, "Admiral of the Ends of the Earth" — as the National Geographic Society dubbed him. Promoted by special act of Congress, pronounced by National Geographic judges as the first air-borne attainer of the North Pole, Byrd had a lot in common with Peary.

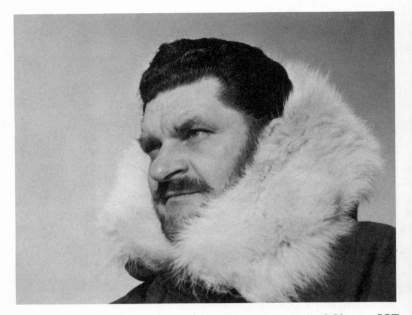

Polar explorer Ralph Plaisted. Below, history being made, 9:30 a.m. CST Saturday, April 20, 1968, as an aircraft of the U.S. Air Force Weather Service, 9th Air Force, flies over the Plaisted Polar Expedition and verifies its position as 90 degrees north, the geographic North Pole, "on the nose." This made the Plaisted Expedition the first surface expedition to have its location at the exact geographical North Pole confirmed by an outside source. Four members of the expedition reached the North Pole on Ski-Doo snowmobiles at 3 p.m. CST Friday, April 19, 1968, becoming the first to get to 90 North by overland mechanized travel. Above photo was taken by expedition navigator Gerry Pitzl.

21.   Götterdämmerung

By the 1920's, the romantic era of heroes walking and sledging over Polar wastes was rapidly giving way to the age of flying machines. In 1925, two flyers destined soon to be rivals led the field in separate parts of the Arctic — Roald Amundsen and Richard Byrd. Amundsen's decade long attempts to fly deep into yet unexplored Arctic regions had bankrupted him; but now his efforts first bore substantial fruit, thanks to a sudden $85,000 boost through Lincoln Ellsworth, the adventure seeking son of a United States millionaire.

In autumn of 1924, Ellsworth had telephoned Amundsen in New York without introduction. On May 21, 1925, the two men took off from Kings Bay (79° North, 12° East), Spitzbergen, in two Dornier-Wal amphibious airplines. Each machine was powered by centrally placed Rolls Royce twin engines and carried three occupants. Both planes were piloted by Norwegian Naval First Lieutenants: Amundsen's by Hjalmar Riiser-Larsen (later a major Antarctic air explorer and subsequently commander of the Norwegian World War II air resistance); Ellsworth's by Leif Dietrichsen. The expedition headed north over the 600 miles of sea ice between Spitzbergen and the Pole, "as a reconnoitering trip for [a] coming transpolar flight." At 1 A.M. on May 22, after eight hours of flying, Amundsen's plane circled for a landing — then a sudden rear-engine failure forced an immediate set-down. Instead of finding smooth ice in the central Arctic Ocean, as

257

Peary's false reports had led them to expect, the flyers found "Ice blocks standing on edge or piled high on top of one another, hummocks and pressure-ridges. . . . It was like trying to land in the Grand Canyon." Sextant observations showed the position of the party to be 87°44'N., 10°20'W., short and to the left of the Pole, (despite the use of a sun compass and drift measurements for most of the flight) due to a wind from the northeast. Only 136 miles from the Pole, the men had attained a genuine farthest North (since Peary's highest 1909 latitude is unknown). Two soundings were taken, and two determinations of compass variation were performed before the end of May. It took the six men more than three weeks on thin rations, during which time the civilized world presumed they might never return, to smooth out a takeoff ice strip one-third of a mile long. At last, they barely got one of the planes into the air, and then back to Spitzbergen, arriving at an incredulous Kings Bay on June 18. During their long absence, Ellsworth's father, who'd put up the money for the planes, had died, never knowing that his son not only would return but would fly north again and would some day lead his own air expedition in the Antarctic.

Two days after this dramatic return, Richard Byrd sailed on the steamer *Peary* from the coast of Maine for Etah, Greenland, as leader of the United States Navy air arm of Donald MacMillan's Arctic expedition under the auspices of the National Geographic Society. The flagship of the expedition, the schooner *Bowdoin,* was seen off personally from Battle Harbour, Labrador, by Gilbert H. Grosvenor. One of the Navy pilots, previously an obscure aviation mechanic, was named Floyd Bennett.

Byrd was now a lieutenant commander, promoted in early 1925, like Peary, by special act of Congress, except that Peary was promoted *after* his explorations. This advance in rank hadn't been difficult for Byrd — himself an able Navy lobbyist who "enjoyed the work," according to his modern biographer Edwin Hoyt — since the Chairman of the approving Senate Naval Affairs Committee was Claude Swanson (Democrat, Virginia), a good friend of the flyer's brother,

Virginia's Democratic State Committee Chairman Harry F. Byrd, then establishing one of the strongest and most enduring political machines in United States history.

Byrd's aim during the 1925 National Geographic - United States Navy - Zenith Radio Corporation expedition was to seek for land out in the Polar Sea — though Billy Mitchell implied that the trip "was staged to sell magazines and radios." His major navigation instrument was a sun compass designed by National Geographic Cartographic Chief Albert Bumstead. The expedition is described in the official history of National Geographic as if it were an impressive success: "In 15 days, Navy flyers *surveyed* 30,000 square miles of Arctic ice." (Emphasis added.) Actually, the airplane program had been such a dismal failure that MacMillan, who now preferred dirigibles, openly admitted the fact to the press, though *National Geographic's* November article put his view in more diplomatically obscure words. The article under Byrd's name in the same issue gave his excuses but used large numbers in such a way as to imply enormous accomplishment against great adversity: "of those fifteen days [less than four] were good for flying; two . . . fair . . . and one indifferent. More than half the time was . . . dangerous. . . . Yet the three planes flew more than five thousand miles. . . . We *saw* thirty thousand square miles. . . ." (Emphasis added.) (Byrd's less noted initial report to the Society had revealed: "Of course many of the flights were made over the same course . . . extending for seventy miles." In fact, he never once got 80 miles from his Etah base.) *National Geographic* readers doubtless thought that Byrd did a lot of exploring; instead, what he mainly did was a little figuring. A circle of a mere hundred miles radius has an area greater than 30,000 square miles — and on a good day Byrd could see 100 miles without traveling anywhere but up.

Though both Amundsen and Byrd failed in their 1925 missions, they gained experience for their 1926 exploits. Amundsen had learned that the central Arctic ice made a poor airstrip for planes vulnerable to forced landings due to "small leakage or a loose screw. . . ." Byrd had learned that, in the pages of *National Geographic,* failure might be made to masquerade as success.

When Amundsen, in January, 1926, publicly cast some slight question on the validity of Peary's 1909 claim, the National Geographic Society quickly silenced him. But the nightmarish possibility of Amundsen's reaching the Pole in the spring and then claiming its discovery for himself must have occurred to the Society. Coincidentally, Richard Byrd at this *very* time decided to try to beat Amundsen to the Pole; curiously, despite his closeness to National Geographic and Gilbert Grosvenor both before and after this venture, the Society had not the slightest official connection with its launching. From January to the April 5 departure at Brooklyn, the Byrd expedition was a "crescendo of toil."

By the time of Byrd's first move, plans for the Amundsen-Ellsworth trans-Arctic flight were well along. The idea of ballooning to the Pole had been fatal in 1897, when the Swede Salomon Andree had tried it from Spitzbergen. And it had produced a fiasco as late as 1909, when Walter Wellman of the United States failed for the second and last time to get much beyond his Spitzbergen takeoff point. But after World War I, airships had become quite sophisticated. Even before the 1925 flight, Riiser-Larsen had suggested using a dirigible designed and already proved in the air by Italian Colonel Umberto Nobile. Convinced by experience of the current unreliability of airplanes, the Norwegians before the summer was out had contracted to buy the airship "N1" from Mussolini's government. Amundsen lectured in the United States to raise money; but after National Geographic stanched the flow of this normally rich source of funds, Ellsworth contributed $125,000 of his inheritance to the project. The ship was personally handed over to Norway by Mussolini at Ciampino on March 29 (four days before he escaped an assassination attempt) and christened the *Norge.* Driven by a trio of 250 horsepower Maybach motors, it was 106 meters long with a volume of half a million cubic feet. Departing April 10 under Nobile's direction, the *Norge* arrived on May 7 at Kings Bay, Spitzbergen, carrying among others Riiser-Larsen and

Amundsen's old companion Oskar Wisting, a veteran of the Norwegian 1911 Antarctic exploit.

By this time Byrd's Fokker airplane, the *Josephine Ford,* had already arrived (April 29) at Kings Bay. Forty-three feet long and having a wingspread of 63 feet, the plane was powered by three Wright air-cooled, 200 horsepower motors, any two of which could keep it aloft. Byrd gave out a lot of talk about flying first to Peary Land and back, but it is doubtful he was taken seriously in the Norwegian colony.

The first attempts to get the Fokker into the air on May 3 and 4 repeatedly smashed up the landing gear skis. With the *Norge* reported leaving Leningrad for Spitzbergen on the morning of the 5th, matters were getting desperate for Byrd when, at Amundsen's suggestion, one of the Norwegians, a young Naval Air Force lieutenant named Bernt Balchen, showed Byrd how to fix up effective landing skis from the last pieces of hardwood available. With a load far lighter than would be needed for the Pole flight, a successful takeoff and test flight were accomplished on May 5. Even so, as the *Norge* sat in wait, the fully loaded *Josephine Ford* could not get aloft on May 8 and some equipment and fuel had to be removed. Byrd's previously announced intention to run a roundtrip to Cape Jesup (Peary Land) first was now changed to Spitzbergen to Peary Land to Pole and back to Spitzbergen, non-stop. Then at the last moment this was reversed. He decided to go to the Pole first and hit Cape Jesup on the return. Byrd: ". . . I was not actually racing to be the first man to fly across the North Pole. . . ." But despite "almost no sleep for thirty-six hours" Byrd and pilot Floyd Bennett took off six days ahead of schedule from Kings Bay for the North Pole at roughly quarter to 1 A.M. (all times are Greenwich Civil Time) on May 9, turned toward the sun, and flew out of sight to the north.

The plane returned suddenly just about 4 P.M. (Balchen, whose recorded takeoff time agrees with Byrd's, has it 4:07 P.M.), dripping oil from a leak in the right engine. The landing was so unexpectedly early that it had to be repeated next day for the news cameras. There had not been nearly

261

enough time in the air to hit both the Pole and Peary Land; therefore the latter was dropped from the story and promised for an imminent future flight, which was soon forgotten. There was no denying that an oil leak had scared the flyers into abandoning their intended flight plan. The fifteen and a half hours in the air had not even been enough time to go to the Pole and perform an alleged thirteen-minute maneuver there and return. The plane's sustained speed capability, even without extra air drag from the ski landing gear, was about 70 miles per hour, certainly no higher than 75 miles per hour, as is roughly shown by an analysis of its 1927 United States tour's log and as privately admitted then by Floyd Bennett. Yet the supposed 1330+ mile Pole flight must have averaged at least 87 miles per hour. Had the real plane reached the Pole, it should have returned to Kings Bay nearer 8 P.M., and absolutely not before 6:30 P.M.

But if Byrd did not seize the opportunity to claim victory, he took on a terrific risk. His debt mounting to nearly $40,000, he needed to grab the Pole ahead of Amundsen to recoup his investment or be ruined. Suppose he admitted failure and gave it another try. First, he might not get airborne again at all: "One more smash and it would be all off. We had no more material out of which to make skis. The last pair had been put together by enormously painstaking efforts. . . ." Second, Byrd saw the *Norge* ready to go any day, and he knew that if the airship reached Alaska, there would be no disputing her priority, since the Pole is so near the most direct path to there from Spitzbergen.

He reported success. The rapid speed was explained away by a helpful wind. Of course, as any track runner is aware, a steady breeze *hurts* average speed over a round trip, that is, the help it gives on the half of a lap when one is running with the wind is less than the retardation when going into the wind; and any transverse wind component slows one both coming and going. So Byrd's saving zephyr was not steady but, rather, most obligingly shifty. Virtually non-existent going north, it "began to freshen and change direction soon after we left the Pole. . . ." — thus whisking the *Josephine Ford* back to Spitzbergen (670+ miles by the alleged route) at nearly 100 miles an hour! — a pace Byrd believed possible only from his trust of the plane's exaggerated sales-figure speed. Byrd: "The elements were surely smiling on us that day." But bad luck was present as well. Just after turning back, Byrd's only sextant accidentally fell and was damaged. So — reminiscent of Peary's case — no astronomical data from the wonderfully rapid return leg of the trip were ever available to check its validity.

In his eventual story, Byrd had to put his spotting of the oil leak somewhere near the Pole, because, if it occurred well before, no one would believe that the flyers would have kept on; while if it started during the return trip, some distance toward Peary Land would have to be claimed, and the alleged trip was too suspiciously stretched out for 15+ hours as it was. Thus, in Byrd's reports, the leak was first noted about an hour or less before reaching the Pole. Remarkably cumulative is the improbability of the extraordinary coincidence of events occurring at about 9 A.M. as the story is constructed:
ted:

1. A dangerous-looking oil leak is discovered.
2. The Pole is reached.
3. A homeward wind springs up.
4. Byrd's sextant is damaged.

Aside from internal improbabilities, how about scientific data to support the claim? Sextant altitudes near the Pole are easy to fake and Bennett did not participate in them. As for the unfakable, no soundings were taken, since Byrd feared landing on the ice. Figures for the compass variation — which, in case of fog, could have been a lifesaving aid to navigating a direct return to tiny Spitzbergen — were known by Byrd to be of interest to scientists. Yet Byrd — exactly like Peary before — while providing a hard figure for his compass course within 50 miles of his starting point, gives nothing specific beyond.

As for non-technical proofs: the utility of a visible marker seems — at first glance — out of the question, because of ice drift at the landless Pole. However, remember that Byrd knew the *Norge* was to follow in his track almost immediately, so anything dropped onto the ice at the turnaround point of the *Josephine Ford* just might be spotted a few days later by one of the dirigible's observers, thereby verifying that point's approximate latitude. (Drift is only a few miles a day in the central Arctic Ocean.) In the context of this unique opportunity, it is therefore particularly distressing to learn of a correspondingly unique though long-forgotten aspect of Byrd's expedition, namely that it was the first and probably only one in exploring history to claim a Polar record without leaving a national flag at the conquered goal. The disappointment is only augmented when it is further discovered that Byrd had had the patriotic concern to stuff the *Josephine Ford* with a record number of Star Spangled Banners for dropping upon the Pole: "a hundred small and several large American flags." But somehow, the flyers had been too busy to remember to let fall this red, white and blue blizzard — and the banners all ended up right back in Spitzbergen. Byrd later explained his failure to beflag the Pole somewhat differently: "Peary had done that."

Byrd did, however, possess sufficient presence of mind to remember to take still photos and movies of the monotonously typical Arctic Ocean ice below, during the 13 minutes spent circling the Pole. It is odd that the publicity-savvy Byrd would, all this time, not have thought of the spectacle United States audiences would be most eager and proud to see on film: the American ensign being laid upon the North Pole of the earth. Byrd's book *Skyward* (ghosted by Fitzhugh Green) omitted all mention of the flags in the fusilage — while spending an entire paragraph on a ukelele "secreted aboard by the notorious 'Ukelele Ike' Kontor."

Thus — like scientific verification — contemporary eyewitness checks have been rendered impossible; and so the only remaining test of any worth is that of consistency.

In 1960, Gosta Liljequist, Professor of Meteorology at the University of Uppsala, Sweden, published an analysis of Byrd's claimed speeds. Liljequist first drew on published performance data for the Fokker trimotor to prove that Byrd indeed required assistance from the wind to achieve the southward speeds he reported; and, second, he established that the meteorological conditions of May 9, 1926, as indicated in Polar weather charts of that date (as well as the 8th and 10th) show that the winds could not in fact have aided the return flight appreciably; indeed, there is rather more of an indication that they must have *retarded* it.

With goods of such a stripe for sale, Byrd was in no position to take chances; and so, proving he had indeed (as admiring biographer Hoyt puts it) "learned much" from the Peary Controversy, Byrd would turn, for his official rubber stamp of approval, to the one organization on earth that could be counted on to swallow such a story.

From Spitzbergen, Byrd's ship, the *Chantier,* under command of Captain Mike Brennan, headed south for England, arriving late in the month. Hoyt records:

Byrd was lionized in England . . . [but, in addition to Italian and Scandinavian carping], there was another unfortunate incident: the Royal Geographical Society invited Byrd, since he was in London, to speak before a Society dinner — and he refused , although he was a member of the Society. What happened was that he had been booked elsewhere by his hosts, and had not made the issue of this matter that he probably ought to have made, given the nature of the invitation. He had met with the Society's Secretary [Arthur Hinks] and talked to him about the expedition, but that was not deemed satisfactory by many members and the story that appeared in the press was not totally favorable to Byrd.

Byrd's navigational discussion with Hinks was vague, Hinks being shown no figures at all. As with Peary's 1909 refusal of the Paris Société de Geographie suggestion of international arbitration of the dispute with Cook, it is hard to imagine a man whose veracity is in question, but who has genuinely succeeded and has proof of his success, passing up an opportunity to put his claim beyond doubt. Why should he instead pick an organization whose recently demonstrated attitude toward skepticism was to kick a practitioner of it out of its lecture series? Hoyt:

The years of waiting and the years [lobbying] on Capitol Hill had taught Richard Evelyn Byrd how to handle just such situations. He might not have expected to have his findings questioned so flatly and so quickly, but he was certainly ready for the crisis when it came. He put an end to speculation, at least for the moment, when he told a press conference in England that he intended to submit his proofs to the National Geographic Society in the United States. It was natural for others to question the findings, he said. Let the Society judge. Such open-handedness put an end to complaints, for what else could be said?

In London, Lieutenant Commander Byrd took immediate pains to set the wheels in motion for official acclamation of his "first." He radioed the Navy Department and asked that an officer be sent to meet the ship and pick up the charts and records of the Polar flight and submit them to the Secretary of the Navy, who would then submit them for confirmation to the National Geographic Society.

National Geographic now obliged by appointing, in the 1909 tradition, another of the Society's expert examining committees, consisting largely of (again) three scientists. They were: Albert H. Bumstead, National Geographic Society Chief Cartographer and inventor of the very Bumstead sun compass that was advertised by the Society as having been the instrument of the flight's success at aiming; Henry G. Avers, Chief Mathematician of Geodesy of the United States Coast and Geodetic Survey; and Hugh C. Mitchell, United States Coast and Geodetic Survey computer, who had testified, before Peary's 1911 Congressional examiners, that convincing sextant data could not be manufactured.

Byrd got his NGS approval and gold medal on June 23. The National Geographic Society official report to the Secretary of the Navy and the public, printed in the September, 1926 *National Geographic,* was proud as could be of the Society's caution and the excruciating thoroughness of the appointed three's analysis of Byrd's original records.

Presumably the National Geographic Society was still smarting from the 1911 exposure, by Representative Roberts, of the discreditable details of what he justly characterized as the "perfunctory and hasty examination of [Peary's] records by the [1909 sub]committee of the National Geographic Society."

From the official National Geographic report on Byrd's records, as it appears (full of technical errors) in the September, 1926, *National Geographic Magazine:*

> Prior to his return to Washington [for the National Geographic Society's Hubbard gold medal, June 23, officially certifying his claim to have attained the North Pole], Commander Byrd submitted his records, through the Secretary of the Navy, to the National Geographic Society. The papers were referred to a special committee . . . consisting of its President, Dr. Gilbert Grosvenor; the Chairman of its Research Committee, Dr. Frederick V. Coville, and Colonel E. Lester Jones, a member of the Board of Trustees, who is also the Director of the [United States] Coast and Geodetic Survey.
>
> This committee . . . at the *conclusion* of its investigation and computations reported its findings [to the Secretary of the Navy thus]:
>
> "The committee has examined [Byrd's] original records . . . and found them . . . carefully and accurately kept. In the opinion of the committee, these records substantiate *in every particular* the claim of Commander Byrd. . . . [N.B.: This is an *exact* quote, excepting minor grammatical alterations, from President Grosvenor's June 23 speech, given as Byrd was honored by National Geographic for his supposed success.] . . . experienced calculators [Mitchell, Avers, and Bumstead] have verified *all* of Commander Byrd's computations, devoting *five* consecutive days to the work; they have also critically examined the sextant used by Commander Byrd. . . . (Emphasis added.)

This would be most reassuring were it not for the fact that the above report has been *deliberately doctored,* in order to deceive the public and foreign geographical societies, which

267

it has successfully done, undetected for nearly a half century.

The original report, sent to the Secretary of the Navy in 1926, has disappeared from the Navy's files since. (Brother Harry's pal Swanson became Secretary of the Navy in 1933, while Harry was appointed to Swanson's vacated Senatorial seat.) And National Geographic has somehow misplaced its carbon of the report. But in spite of these convenient disappearances, the writer has found that — due to a fluke — the original text has survived after all. A comparison shows that the September, 1926, *National Geographic* left out one sentence and one sentence only. Belonging immediately after the foregoing quotation, it reads:

"Their [Mitchell's, Avers', and Bumstead's] examination began at 10 A.M. on June *23* [the same day Byrd got his pre-engraved National Geographic Society medal!] and was completed at 5 P.M. on June *28*." [Emphasis added.) That is — five days *after* the Society had publicly certified and honored Byrd's supposed attainment. A pre-approval exam of a few hours, reported publicly as days, seems to be standard National Geographic procedure; only the faked numbers vary from fifteen days in 1909, to five days in 1926.

Of course, National Geographic's getting Byrd's flight records only on the morning before the pre-scheduled award (and first public lecture for the Society) was no accident. If Byrd's May 9 return from the Pole to Spitzbergen seems swift, it was nothing compared with the way he moved into the United States on June 23, 1926. The whole program had been arranged in advance: pre-noon parade in New York and political awards there, followed by afternoon festivities and trip to Washington, the arrival was "only a comparatively few minutes" before the National Geographic ceremonies — i.e., no cross-examination of Byrd or Bennett.

However, Captain Brennan unexpectedly got the *Chantier* across the Atlantic and near New York two days ahead of schedule. So Byrd could easily have got his data to Washington well before June 23. Instead, the ship sat secretly off-shore, as quietly as Brennan's door-slamming ire at the seemingly senseless delay would allow, and only after dark on June 22 did Byrd turn over his records to the Navy men who were to carry them to Washington. Next morning tickertape parade moved up Broadway from the Battery to City Hall, where the explorer exchanged speeches with Mayor Jimmy Walker and received a medal in recognition of his attainment. Senator Swanson was on hand to contribute to a windy luncheon at the Advertising Club. Only Floyd Bennett seemed subdued.

That evening in Washington, as he accepted the National Geographic Society's Hubbard medal from the hands of President Coolidge, Byrd summed up the whole arrangement with masterful understatement [N.Y. *Times*]: "Alluding to the National Geographic Society, [Byrd] said he had never known of an organization so courteous throughout."

In the July, 1926, number of the Royal Geographical Society's *Geographical Journal*, Secretary Hinks wrote:

To technical geographers the great interest of his [Byrd's] exploit lies in the details of his navigation. . . . *We hope that it may be possible for him to publish his track chart in facsimile, with extensive notes.* Nothing could be more instructive, to show the high pitch of skill and concentration required in navigation at a speed of a hundred miles an hour or more. (Emphasis added.)

In the *National Geographic Magazine* of the following September, Byrd's and the National Geographic Society's reports were printed, accompanied by, instead of facsimiles of the original charts, as Hinks had suggested, simply a reproduction of an entirely derivative diagram drawn in June by the National Geographic Society examiners. However, the September *National Geographic Magazine* concluded, very reassuringly, with Byrd's apparent receptiveness to Hinks' proposal; after the National Geographic Society Report to the Secretary of the Navy,

The explorer transmitted certified copies of his data and photographic reproductions of his charts, together with true copies of the Report of the [National Geographic Society] Special Committee, to a number of the leading geographical societies of the world for their archives.

In 1967-1968, the writer attempted to locate these reproductions and thereby discovered that, contrary to the definite
statement quoted above, no other society *ever* possessed such
copies. In 1968, National Geographic admitted to the
National Archives that its archives at least had Byrd's Navigation Report, but then (after phoning back to find out who
wanted to see it) denied possessing it, on this writer's subsequent inquiry. This unpublished document, obtained elsewhere, contains two especially interesting items. One is a
description of a tail wind *near* Spitzbergen on the return
("making white caps beneath us"), in flat contradiction to the
weather recorded at Spitzbergen. The other find concerns the
time Byrd privately told the National Geographic trio he returned to Kings Bay: 4:*34* P.M. — a datum avoided in *all* his
published accounts. It evidently was useful with the National
Geographic committee, since this makes his average return
speed from the Pole (9:15 A.M.) equal to 92 miles per hour,
agreeing remarkably well, indeed, almost exactly, with the
corresponding (but notoriously unreliable, because
barometer-dependent) visual speed estimates given in the
report for the first six hours of the return. Of course this
alleged return time could not be published because it would
have been denied by the recollection of every independent
observer at Kings Bay.

Deceiving the public was easy for Byrd to rationalize. His
purpose for the trip, he was fond of saying, was to promote the
cause of aviation, as he said he had promoted it when
lobbying to defeat Billy Mitchell's reforms. Admission of failure in the 1926 flight, especially from mechanical failure,
would give aid and comfort to those who, like MacMillan and
Amundsen, proclaimed the airplane unreliable. Likewise,
during the 1927 trans-Atlantic competition (won by Lind-
bergh) when Byrd's entry, the *America*, crashed during tests,
he used the same excuse to deceive regarding the extent of the
damage: "It was possible that we might find that we couldn't
fly the distance necessary to go from New York to France.
Should there be a great deal of publicity and then should we
have to admit [this], aviation would be hurt."

Next year he launched the First Byrd Antarctic Expedi-

270

tion, which was to do some productive work and which claimed to have reached the South Pole in 1929 by air over Amundsen's 1911 route. However, it was a commercially oriented operation, Byrd making about $1000 per week in salary, plus royalties, endorsements, movie rights, etc. From the start, he exercised total censorship on all dispatches sent out by Little America's resident New York *Times* reporter, editing and rewriting them. One critically minded flyer's diary mysteriously disappeared; the journal contained, among other things, accounts of Byrd's prayer filled mental battles with his near petrifying fear of dangerous flights. At one point, before six incredulous members of the expedition, Byrd pulled off a cloddishly blatant fake discovery of a territory found by others, naming it Marie Byrd Land (now Byrd Land) and exaggerating the size of the claim to such an extent that even a flagwaver of Hobbs' ilk had to confess privately to the British that it was overdone.

Byrd may not have been an amoral man; but he was, like Peary, perfectly willing to resort to deceit as a means to his desired ends. By the time he died in 1957, he had become a national hero and a member of the Board of Trustees of the National Geographic Society.

In 1956, Bernt Balchen was asked by the Dutton publishing house to write his autobiography. In the resulting manuscript, Balchen at last told some of what he knew of Byrd's exploring career, still top-secret information as far as the public was concerned. However, after 4000 copies were printed, Dutton caved in to political force (which included threats of libel suits, deportation of Balchen, etc.), and the book was censorially rewritten to make it appear that Balchen accepted all the exploring claims of an inspirational leader.

Finally, in 1971, reporter Dick Montague related some of Balchen's revelations on Byrd (a few more are incorporated into the present book) in Montague's delightful history of early aviation heroes, *Oceans, Poles, and Airmen.* Montague's courage was matched by Random House, which published the book without the slightest doctoring. (Also included was a detailed before and after comparison of the hatchet job Dutton had done on Balchen's earlier book.)

Balchen was a close friend of Floyd Bennett from 1926 to Bennett's death two years later. In spring, 1927, in a Chicago hotel, Bennett finally admitted to Balchen (who had kept querying him about the speed impossibility) that indeed he and Byrd had never got near the North Pole.

Balchen also revealed that on each of the two flights he had personally piloted for Byrd (the *America,* trans Atlantic, 1927; the *Floyd Bennett,* onto the South Polar plateau, 1929), navigator Byrd had not taken a single sextant observation to steer the plane. The 1927 flight ended up in a dangerous crash landing as a result. Because of a lack of landmarks in the vicinity of the South Pole, one cannot know how far off the 1929 turnaround point was, suffice it to note that Byrd's sole navigational instrument during the flight was a bottle of cognac.

Leaving Byrd to his post-1926 designs: who then *did* discover the North Pole? The next attempt was launched less than two days after the conclusion of Byrd's flight, as the *Norge* cut her moorings just before 9 A.M. on May 11, with the weather clear and still virtually windless, and the temperature a relatively warm −8° Centigrade. Carrying 16 men, and Nobile's little dog Titina, in its seemingly tiny gondola, the dirigible turned ponderously northward and finally disappeared over the sharp peaks from which Spitzbergen derives its name.

The expedition commanders were Amundsen and Ellsworth, who had the final word regarding geographical courses, objectives, and en-route changes of plan. Other major figures included: navigator Riiser-Larsen, pilot Nobile, elevator helmsman Wisting. The good weather held, as did radio contact with civilization, and the ship, at an altitude of only a few hundred yards, progressed Poleward at about 50 miles per hour over the vast Arctic Ocean ice fields.

Riiser-Larsen handled the sextant, the first time a North Pole expedition leader claimant had shared this duty with anyone; all positions and drift measurements were announced to the commanders and to the steersman at the sun compass in order that the proper instructions be relayed to the helmsman. Progress was radioed to civilization as it was made. Any

272

fakery on such an expedition would require quite a conspiracy. Magnetic records were kept, showing that the theoretically extrapolated lines of constant variation on current maps required serious correction, and steering was further aided by use of radio bearings. Every so often (twice en route to the Pole, more beyond, as is evident from the slightly jagged original flight chart later published) sextant readings gave position lines proving that the steering had been imperfect and required en route correction; likewise visual speed estimates were off, due to barometer error. This is what happens on a real trip. From 7:30 P.M. until 1 A.M., fog became a problem, and the ship proceeded at an altitude of over a half-mile in order to clear it.

With the sun now before the dirigible, Riiser-Larsen depended on radio bearings to check his transverse position so as not to miss the invisible point ahead, and made continuous use of the sextant (for checking forward progress) only as the moment approached. At about 1 A.M. he consulted the *Nautical Almanac* to find the solar declination for the now-expected success time (1:30 A.M., May 12, 1926) and corrected for refraction and parallax. At 1:15 A.M., setting the sextant for the calculated angle, Riiser-Larsen recalls:

... I went down on my knees and measured steadily out through one of the portholes whose coverings had been removed. When the reflection of the sun and the bubble for the artificial horizon lay side by side, sharply touched by the marking-threads, I announced: "Now we are there." The time was 1:25. Under us lay the Polar basin, bathed in sunshine. We slackened speed, and went down to 200 meters altitude. One by one the flags were dropped down, whilst we stood with uncovered heads. Thanks to the special way in which the flags had been fastened to the poles, they went beautifully down, and with good enough speed for the steel points to penetrate the snow and ice. The colors streamed out nicely as the flags [unfurled below]. When the ceremony was over all our hands sought Amundsen's, and then, naturally enough, Wisting's. There stood the only two men who

273

had planted their country's flag at both Poles.

Did Amundsen and Wisting suspect they were first at the North Pole as well as the South? Even if they did, they were undoubtedly more certain of political reality: The world would never know, while they lived, the private truth they shared.

After so much international bitterness and deceit in the race for it, that the North Pole should first be attained by a multi-nation effort is fortunate. That the airship should be named the *Norge* provides, however, a well deserved justice, considering the productive and honorable Norse tradition of Polar exploration culminating in Nansen, Sverdrup, and Amundsen. As the Norwegian colors struck the ice and flew out at the North Pole, Ellsworth recorded the crowning scene of the ceremony: "Amundsen at the same moment turned round and grasped Wisting's hand. No word was uttered; it was unnecessary, for these two men's hands planted the Norwegian flag at the South Pole on the 14th of December, 1911."

The attainment of the goal of centuries was radioed in a fraction of a second to a world that had heard the tale three times before, and little realized that only now, a half-generation late, was it finally getting the goods. How fortunate that, like the first step on the Moon, the moment of truth could be shared with the explorers.

At the Pole, the ship was now well past previously explored regions. The ice seemed more broken than before, as it would for about the next 250 miles. After a very short circling maneuver, the course was set for Point Barrow, Alaska. A sextant position line at 4:20 A.M. indicated that the *Norge* had probably missed the Pole by only about ten miles to the right, coming closest somewhat after 1:30 A.M. Beyond lay the main mass of the unexplored portion of the Arctic, the center of the Polar Sea, the remotest part of the frozen North, sometimes called the "Pole of Inaccessibility" or the "Ice Pole." It had been expected that a large land mass might exist here. To the great disappointment of the *Norge's* men, absolutely nothing but more sea ice was observed, and the hitherto durable theory of an unknown continent north of Alaska was

274

demolished as the ship virtually bisected the region.

Radio communication difficulties commenced beyond the Pole, accompanied by more fog, plus some frightening punctures of the dirigible by sloughed icing violently bouncing off the propellor blades — thus forcing occasional slowdowns of the motors. The Alaskan coast was sighted at 6:45 A.M., May 13 (afternoon of May 12 in Alaska), by Riiser-Larsen. It was reached at 7:25 A.M., roughly 20 miles right (west) of Point Barrow, so close to the desired landfall that the *Norge* was spotted at Point Barrow by Polar competitors, pioneer flyers George Hubert Wilkins of Australia and West Pointer Thomas Lanphier, Sr. (whose son Thomas, Jr., then ten, was to shoot down Japanese supreme commander and Pearl Harbor attack planner Admiral Yamamoto in 1943). The *Norge* was shortly seen and photographed over the town of Wainwright, but the rest of the journey to west Alaska was much delayed and wildly detoured by fog and gale. After growing concern aboard the ship, and by the waiting world at large, the *Norge* set down at Teller, Alaska (just north of Nome) on May 14, with the aid of the town's few inhabitants. Amundsen's last great journey of exploration had ended. Re-marking that the only adventure left to him now was marriage, he announced his retirement.

Having earlier in the year vainly done everything possible to prevent Amundsen's genuine success (all because he'd been so impolite as to doubt an exploring story, one of whose false-hoods had nearly *killed* him), *National Geographic's* response to this unprecedented transarctic aerial feat was to give it late and second billing to Byrd's swiftly conceived and certified North Pole disappearing act — and then to join the Fascist press' attempt to convert Nobile into the commander of the expedition. The August, 1927, *National Geographic* ran a long article under Nobile's name called "Navigating the Norge." While throwing a few modest crumbs to the expedition's conceivers ("Norway . . . with her initiative gave us the opportunity") the article speaks of the *Norge* as "commanded by an Italian officer. . . . Premier Benito Mussolini . . . fostered the undertaking and gave for it the ship and the men to command her." The piece ends: "We are happy and proud that all along this aerial route of eight thousand five hundred miles across Europe, the Barents Sea, the Polar Sea, the Bering Sea, and Alaska, we carried on the front of our commander's cabin the 'fascio littorio,' symbol of the old, eternal Rome and of the new Italy." Simultaneously, Amundsen attacked the intentions of Nobile and Duce, which many felt was uncivil.

After the *Norge's* conquest, a number of other firsts at the North Pole were yet to come. In 1928, in sole command of the new dirigible *Italia,* Nobile led a 16-member Arctic expedition (including six *Norge* veterans), which reached the Pole on May 24 and dropped various patriotic and religious articles there, including the flag of fascist Italy and a large cross presented and blessed by Pope Pius XI. On the return, just north of Spitzbergen, the *Italia* crashed on the ice (May 25). In the summer-long aftermath, half the crew were saved, including Nobile. Mussolini now disowned Nobile as thoroughly as he had formerly taken credit for him.

Radio contact with civilization was achieved in June and an international rescue operation using airplane and ice-breaker began. The recent bitterness was forgotten by both explorers, as Amundsen — who well knew the dangers of airplanes in the Arctic, but who also realized the necessity for speed for Nobile's sake, flew out of Tromso, Norway, in a hurriedly obtained Latham seaplane. Nobile radioed the Italian naval contingent in the Spitzbergen area to "put yourself entirely in Amundsen's hands. . . ." But a reconciliation on the ice was not to be. The Latham crashed at sea, and, while Nobile's party was the center of rescue attentions, Amundsen and those with him were lost forever.

In 1937, a Russian expedition led by Ivan Papanin and the scholarly scientist-explorer Otto Schmidt were flown from Rudolph Island (north Franz Josef Land) to the vicinity of the North Pole and on May 21 landed there, to drift on an ice floe for the better part of a year, taking scientific measurements. In 1959, it was implied by a United States explorer that the Russians had faked something, because their reported depth at the Pole disagreed with the correct figure. However, most of the discrepancy is due to the fact that the critic used the depth taken from the English translation of Papanin's book, a figure which is the result of a gross miscalculation during the conversion of meters to English feet; moreover, the sounding was made more than 50 miles from the Pole. Though Papanin larded his diary with praise of Stalin's glorious purges of anti-Soviet traitors, he was no faker. His expedition was technically competent and productive (e.g., bathymetry and magnetism), and he always openly admitted in his charts that he had landed well to the left of the Pole — at about 89½° North latitude, and that the drift had then taken him ever farther from it. Whether he is to be counted as an attainer of the Pole itself is partly a matter of arbitrary standards of exactitude. In any case, the Russians were the first men to demonstrably stand within the 90th degree of latitude (i.e., north of 89° North latitude).

The first submarine attempt on the Pole was Wilkins' 1931 fiasco near Spitzbergen with his *Nautilus* — named for Jules Verne's fictional undersea machine. It failed — possibly from inside sabotage, suspected Wilkins. But by the late 1950's, United States Admiral Hyman G. Rickover's nuclear-powered subs were capable of the trip. Commander William R. Anderson traveled under the Polar pack in the first of these, also named the *Nautilus,* arriving at the Pole on August 3, 1958, and obtaining the first figure for the Arctic Ocean's depth there: more than 13,000 feet. Another nuclear sub, the *Skate,* commanded by James Calvert, repeated the *Nautilus'* attainment only nine days later. However, neither had surfaced at the spot, for fear of damage from the ice.

Wilkins died that autumn. Late the following winter, Calvert returned to the Pole with the ashes of the father of Polar sub travel, and this time, after much anxiety, the *Skate* was able to surface. March 17, 1959, marks the day man first walked on the place that had eluded so many of the finest explorers. A note was left in a cairn on the spot and a ceremony held in honor of Wilkins' birthplace (Australia), allegiance (United Kingdom), and final home (United States); three flags were flown above the *Skate* during a brief funeral service in a temperature of −26°F., which concluded with Wilkins' ashes being sprinkled to the Polar winds.

The first party to reach the North Pole by surface travel (as Cook and Peary had claimed to have done) was the United States-Canadian expedition led in 1968 from Ward Hunt Island (north Ellesmere), by Minnesotan Ralph Plaisted, which succeeded on April 19, virtually over Peary's alleged route, but at a slower pace despite the use of light, motorized speed sleds and air-dropped supplies. The contrast between Plaisted's real trip and the 1908-1909 fantasies is further driven home when one notes that Plaisted's 400+ mile trip required roughly 300 miles more en route from detouring.

At about the time Plaisted began, British explorer Wally Herbert left Alaska on a dogsledge journey across the Arctic Ocean (using air support like Plaisted) to Spitzbergen via the Pole, but with the intention of wintering on the pack. Herbert's party reached the Pole on April 5, 1969, and made Svalbard a few weeks later on May 29 (after a detouring percentage almost identical to Plaisted's). Thus the first transarctic journey was British — as the first transantarctic trek had been in 1957-58 by Sir Vivian Fuchs, actualizing the last dream of Sir Ernest Shackleton.

Recognition of the *Norge's* priority at the North Pole should not greatly upset anyone's patriotic pride, thanks to the international aspects of the flight. Lincoln Ellsworth of the United States was the major individual purchaser of the *Norge* and was official co-commander of the expedition. Italy's Umberto Nobile was the airship's designer and a key factor in the transarctic flight itself. Norway's Hjalmar Riiser-Larsen, the pilot hero of the narrow takeoff of the 1925 party, was the man who in 1926 navigated the *Norge* across the Polar Sea. But the most fitting outcome of the *Norge's* recognition will be the popular establishment of Amundsen at last in his rightful place as the supreme Polar explorer.

A gentleman is not necessarily a great explorer, as Cook proved beyond question, yet the combination can occur. To both his competitors in his famous Polar races, Amundsen offered and gave what aid he could. At the Bay of Whales, in

1911, he suggested to the visiting British that Scott take his extra dogs, and dogs were the key to the speed that brought victory to Amundsen, while their lack meant defeat and death for Scott. He helped Byrd get into the air in Spitzbergen, and was thanked for the gesture by being defrauded of one of his life's goals. And though Cook had, with Peary, cheated him in 1909, in that he lost financial backing for his proposed 1910 Arctic expedition, he did not forget his 1898 Antarctic winter with the Doctor on the *Belgique,* visiting his old friend even when he was in jail. Contrast Peary's hard excuse for leaving Bartlett on April 1, 1909 — why "divide" with a man who has only worked himself near to death for you? — with Amundsen's sharing of not one but both Poles with Wisting, whom he could easily have replaced in 1926 so as to make himself the first man to both. Finally, Amundsen died a hero, sacrificing his life in attempting to save that of his bitterest enemy.

His sepulchre is the Arctic itself. His monument is not smooth granite propaganda erected in a national cemetery by a publishing outfit, but is instead the geography he first explored at the ends of the earth.

Amundsen's exploring career is incomparable. He was the first explorer to winter in the Antarctic, first navigator of the Northwest Passage, relocator of the North Magnetic Pole, first at the South Pole, first to circumnavigate the Arctic Ocean, first to cross it, the attainer of the last farthest North and first at the North Pole itself. No other Polar explorer could match this record by half. No other was so versatile. Amundsen pioneered via ship (Northwest Passage), dog sledge (South Pole), airplane (farthest North), and dirigible (Arctic Ocean crossing).

Yet, ironically, it is possible that the driving force behind such an extraordinary career is somewhat responsible for its relative obscurity. It may have been Amundsen's eagerness to be recognized as being first at the North Pole that led to the 1926 tiff with the National Geographic Society. There is no doubt that his outracing England's Captain Scott to the South Pole in 1911 triggered bad feelings at London's Royal Geographical Society. Amundsen has no powerful organization with an investment in his immortality. And, unlike Cook,

Peary, and Byrd, he left no children to spread news releases on his anniversaries. To the contrary, he died at a time of strained relations with organized geography and bitter ones with his own brother. But should such factors determine the history one reads? To a large extent, it has unfortunately done so. Among major Polar explorers, Amundsen is relatively unknown in the English-speaking world today. That imbalance should now be righted in light of the Norseman's emergence here as the legitimate first attainer of the North Pole — and thus the discoverer of *both* Poles of the earth.

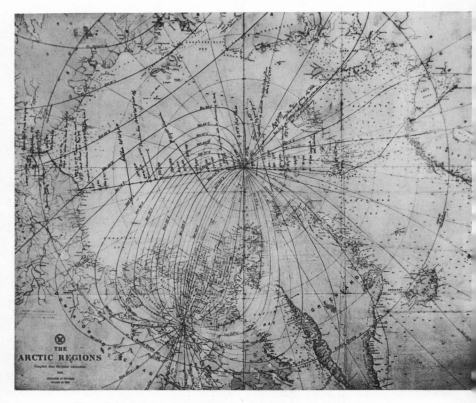

The original chart of the *Norge's* route across the Polar Sea.

Appendix

The Henshaw Ward Discoveries

Shortly after publication of my Naval Institute *Proceedings* analysis of Peary's navigational ice-follies of 1909, I received a letter (June 15, 1970) from Carlton Wells, Professor Emeritus of English at the University of Michigan. Wells had corresponded in the mid-1930's with the highly respected writer (and grammarian) Charles Henshaw Ward.

In 1934, Ward did a skeptical piece on Peary for the *American Mercury*. However, Wells informed me that Ward had written an entire book for Yale University Press on Peary's strange records and the associated "stories and the secrets and the hugger-mugger." But Ward died suddenly on Oct. 18, 1935; the *English Journal* noting, "The passing of a man who had affected American life as much by commercial or political activity as Ward did by teaching and writing would have been featured by the daily press throughout the country."

Yale never published the book, and Wells hadn't communicated with the author's widow, Florence Ward, since 1937. Ward would have been 97, so we entertained little hope that his widow was still alive. There were no children.

Nonetheless, on July 2, 1970, I wrote Wells back: "Ward's papers and typescript on the Peary case strike me as being irreplaceable (almost no one is now left alive who remembers the things he learned first-hand from participants). . . . How do you suppose we might trace their whereabouts? If you have any clues whatever, I think we should follow them up right away."

Wells made inquiries of Ward's major textbook publisher, Scott, Foresman Co., and an editor there, Giggina Pietrangeli, amazed us by supplying a 1967 address for Ward's widow. Wells quickly wrote her and soon received a letter dated Aug. 4:

My dear Mr. Wells:
I have been living in Ward's old home here . . . [virtually] ever since his death . . .
When [your letter] came, I went directly to the attic — an old garage long since too narrow for a car — where I keep THINGS. I salvaged the Peary MS without difficulty and looked through it with interest. It is decidedly worn and a good deal soiled.
. . . I'll send it along posthaste.
It is pleasant hearing from you. Ward has been gone for thirty-five years. . . . I am eighty-two now — fifteen years younger than Ward. Thanks to Giggina Pietrangeli . . .

The ms. was quickly multiple-copied for safety's sake. Florence Ward painstakingly catalogued and sent all of Ward's research-materials. A niece, Bobby Headley, copied and transmitted all polar-related excerpts from his private diaries (in her possession). The entire collection has been received by the U.S. National Archives.

Ward's readable ms. and correspondence may be consulted by specialists for details, but his three truly startling discoveries will be provided here.

The first of these arrived in Ward's mail unexpectedly (right after his own article) from Lt.Cdr. Valentine Wood, U.S.N. — providing a recollection reaching far back into Wood's memory (to 1913, though Ward wrongly thought it must be 1916). Of the general truth of the events described, there can be no reasonable doubt. Chester's oil deals are accurately recalled; and Peary's sole Explorers Club medal was indeed 1914. Wood was quite willing to testify in court for Ward if the need arose. The letter read:

12 Sept. 1934.

Mr. Henshaw Ward,
C/o The American Mercury,
750 Fifth Avenue,
New York City.

My dear Mr. Ward:—
Concerning your article in the American Mercury, "Peary did not reach the Pole," I would like to add the following anecdote to your collection.

In the Summer of 1913 after I had graduated from the U.S. Naval Academy I was stationed on the U.S.S. North Dakota at the New York Navy Yard. My father, Commodore M.L. Wood, U.S.N.(Ret) was then living at the Army and Navy Club on 43rd or 44th Street opposite the Elks Hotel.

One afternoon, when I was about to return to my ship after visiting my father he gave me a very dirty book, the pages covered with grease spots and many smudges. As I was to be aboard ship over the week end with the duty he asked me to examine the computations in the navigational work book.

When I had time aboard ship, I re-computed about half of the sights, which were for very low altitudes. Far lower than I had ever seen consistently used. The sights were very poorly worked out, full of errors and towards the last, I became fairly sure, faked. I told my father that I considered many of the sights "Gun Deck Sights" — that is sights taken below decks or false sights.

My father then told me that the book I had been verifying was Peary's work book. It was the book he presented to the National Geographic Society as a proof of his claims from an astronomical point. The Society had asked Admiral Colby M. Chester, U.S.N.(Ret) to check the computations. Admiral Chester had given the book a perfunctory look and stated the claims were confirmed by the computations. Later when the opposition developed in Congress the Society had asked Admiral Chester to again check the work book. Since Admiral Chester was about to leave for Europe to secure some oil rights in Persia, he asked my father to investigate the book and send him the result of his investigations.

My father wrote Admiral Chester that he believed the sights were for the most part false and that Peary never got near the pole.

About a year after this I was with my father in the New York Yacht Club when a friend came up and said, "I have two tickets for a very entertaining reception at the Explorers Club — don't you want to go?" My father said, "For whom is the reception?" "Why I forgot to tell you that the greatest explorer of them all is to be there — Admiral Peary." "HUMPH. No thank you" said my father, and that is for both of us."

I hope that this story of the actual investigation of the missing note book will be of some assistance in completing the rather complete chain of damnatory evidence you have so competently forged.

Very respectfully,

V. Wood, Lieut. Comdr. U.S.N. (Ret)

Wood and his father, Commodore Moses Lindley Wood, both taught at the U.S. Naval Academy and knew navigational mathematics thoroughly.

Wood's recollection of the size and condition of the convincingly dirty notebook he saw disagreed with Rep. Roberts' 1911 description of its cleanliness (and Rep. Dawson's 1935 memory of its dimensions — in an interview in Cincinnati just before Ward's death). This led Ward and Wood to the suspicion that Peary had cagily kept more than one set of "field-records." (The utter confusion about what form Peary's records were in is treated with scrupulous thoroughness in Ward's book.)

Ward's second find: Elsa Barker, in the spring of 1910, was using a copy of Peary's 1909 journal while ghosting his *Hampton's Magazine* series. Fortunately, her secretary, Lillian Kiel (later a Cook sympathizer) kept copies of the dictated Barker correspondence and in 1935 temporarily turned these over to Ward. His book quotes a number of 1910 Barker letters to Peary, including this one of April 1:

> I hope you will have sent me before this reaches you some of the data which I need for April 6th and 7th [1909 — the days that Peary supposedly spent at the Pole] . . . the climax of the story. . . . I hope you will have found time to dictate two or three words relative to those two days. Your eyes being so tired from the observations, *there are no entries in the journal.*

By 1911, Peary's allegedly original journal had been filled out quite nicely at April 6-7 for the Congressmen.

Peary's slow caution in setting down his "diary"-entries for these two days (ghost A.E. Thomas also had trouble in the spring of 1910 getting April 6-7, 1909 data out of Peary) is understandable, in the light of our theory that there was a serious clash here with events he knew were in Henson's journal.

This is one of a variety of indications that Peary's Camp Jesup story was in flux after his return. With so many documents hidden, nonexistent, or gone, one is left groping in the dark somewhat, and speculation is one's only recourse. (Eventual clarification of an occasional detail here shouldn't be confused with an answer to central mysteries.)

One notes that in September, 1909, Peary avoided saying that Henson was at the Pole with him. (And simultaneously, Bartlett reported that Henson stopped one march short.) And Peary's original "North Pole record" (as Helgesen saw in 1916 from diary excerpts transcribed during the winter of 1910 — original and copy gone since) differed from the published version's April 6 statement that the march to Camp Jesup was the 27th since leaving Cape Columbia; the first story (in Peary's own hand) was the 28th march. (Recall the length of this march varied greatly.)

Could it be that Henson's repeated public insistence that he was at the Pole, forced an awkward late alteration in the story Peary originally planned to tell? Perhaps all of this explains the repeating Hayes 1861 slip, when Peary refers in his other Camp Jesup "record" to his observations (see cairn record opposite page 13) on April 6 — though his final story has these only on April 7.

Also, Peary gave out no satisfactory sextant data or positional results from Camp Jesup (only) until August, 1910. This fact, along with Wood's testimony (and a 1911 rumor, possibly related to the latter, reported by Macon) suggests that Peary (like Byrd later) gave different stories to the NGS and the public.

Ward's third find was more critical than even he realized. As with the recovery of the Ward papers themselves, it is an archivist's dream/nightmare to ponder the thinness of the thread which led to this treasure and preserved it during capture.

In the spring of 1935, a member of the Peary cabal, evidently either slightly tipsy or imagining that the need for his anonymity had long since elapsed, did a little boasting at a dinner party. Ward lived nearby and happened to hear of it through mutual friends. He interviewed the man on June 11 — with a touch that proved just right in eliciting the most remarkable irrefutable inside information in the entire Peary affair. Ward's memorandum is here reproduced in toto.

The Talk With Hastings

This is my recollection of a talk with Hudson Bridge Hastings on Tuesday, June 11, 1935, typed on June 14. About June 1 or earlier I had written a note asking if he would appoint a time to see me and tell me the story of his visit to Eagle Island in the fall of 1909. This story he had told at a dinner in Loomis Havemeyer's house some time in April (?); McDonough told me about it when he called shortly after we returned from N.C. on the first of May. Several days after I wrote to Hastings he called me on the phone and said he was very busy, but would see me some time and would call me up and let me know when. On Tuesday, the 11th, I called him about 10 a.m. because I wanted to go to Washington, had been postponing the trip on his account, and needed to know whether I should go before or after a talk with him. He replied that he could see me that morning at 11. I was in his office on the dot; he greeted me with the utmost cordiality, had to take some papers to the registrar, returned, gave me a cigarette, lit a pipe, and began to talk within five minutes. I think the talk lasted about half an hour.

He told a narrative:

Some time in the early part of October, 1909, probably during the first or second week of October, Peary called the president of Bowdoin and asked if there was some instructor who was proficient in navigation. Other instructors declined for one reason or another, and Hastings was asked to go and see if he would do. Peary put him through a quiz for an hour and a half. At the end of the time he said, "You'll do. You have given the right answers to two questions that Bob Bartlett answered wrong."

Hastings was in the Peary home about a month and saw Peary every day. (I feel sure that "every day" was emphasized; probably it was repeated.) Hasting's business was to keep tab on all that the newspapers printed of Cook's statements. He computed for the observations that Cook said he had made and fitted together (I think he said something like "charted") Cook's outgivings to see what he was claiming and what his lies were. The idea was to be prepared to confute Cook if he should submit his data to the N.G.S.

I can't recall at what part of the conversation I asked the following question, but I think it was at about this point, when we had been talking for, say, ten minutes: "Is anything that you say to me confidential?" Hastings answered, "That would depend on what use you intend to make of it." I can't recall the reply I made, but think it was like this: "Well, it's understood that I will not quote anything you say until I have submitted the quotation to you and have your permission." I feel sure that I said such words, but am not sure that they fitted in as a reply at this point.

At any rate, he went on with his narrative, smiling and in the best of humor. He wrote out for Peary a connected account of the Cook material that he collected, and he kept a carbon of this. Peary, he said, was always magnanimous in his talk about Cook, speaking thus: "The poor fellow seems to have gone off his head. I doubt that he is deliberately lying. He seems to have got twisted, so that he really believes he did reach the Pole. He has hung himself. I don't want to publish anything against him unless I am forced to. He is down and out. I don't want to hurt him." Some two years later Peary asked Hastings to give back the carbon of his report, and Hastings did so.

Hastings said (I think in reply to a question of mine) that he

286

never saw the Peary record. Said he had always been glad that he had not seen it. For if he had and the fact had become known, people would have suspected that Hastings had helped to doctor Peary's record. He launched into a description of how Peary would put queries to him: "For instance, he once showed me a copy of the observations he made near the pole and asked me what positions these would show. I explained that an observation of the sun's altitude would not prove a certain position, but would only determine a circle, a great circle — no, not a great circle, but a circle around the earth — on some point of which the observer must have stood." Here Hastings began to sketch on a piece of white paper to show what he meant. His talk was rapid and technical. Of course I was lost in the details. But it flashed across me that Hastings had led me right up to the door of the only "proof" Peary offered — his two sets of observations near the pole; I was much excited at the thought that Peary could have been fishing for information from this hero-worshipping young Bowdoin instructor as to whether his observations would prove the position he wanted to prove. If this had been the case, Peary's claim of "observations" would have collapsed completely — and I had come to realize during the previous two weeks that he had absolutely no other proof.

I suppose my excitement showed in my voice when I asked: "Will you dictate to your stenographer what you have just said to me, and let me have it in writing, so that I can be sure of not misunderstanding and not misrepresenting what you have said?"

Then came the angry change in the conversation. It was as if (I am only guessing) the thought in my mind had occurred to him also. It is incredible that it should not have occurred to him; it is so simple and obvious. As I remember it — I am none too sure of the sequence here — he answered abruptly to this effect : "No, I will not do any such thing. For it could be twisted into a misrepresentation of what Peary was doing."

At some time — I think just about now — Hastings made some remark about "trying to show that Peary's proof was unreliable." It was in such a form that a reply was expected from me, and I thought I had best not conceal my purpose if he had not understood it. I remember clearly saying, "But that's my business — meaning "my business to show that Peary's proofs are unreliable."

From this point on Hastings two or three times spoke of my "attacking Peary's veracity." I replied (I think twice) that I was not attacking his veracity, because that cannot yet be disproved; but that I was only trying to show the insufficiency of the proofs. I made no impression. He had firmly lodged in his mind the belief that I was trying to prove Peary untruthful.

"Why, Mr. Ward, I am as convinced of Peary's veracity as I am that the sun will rise tomorrow morning. If you put into print anything that throws suspicion on Peary, I will fight you as hard as I can." My reply was, "Go to it. The harder the better." He was grieved and angered, as if he had heard blasphemy, and said, "Why, what you are doing seems to me the very worst form of muckraking."

The last minute of our talk I was standing up before his desk, trying to think of some way of concluding that would not be angry. There were silences. No hot words were exchanged. I walked out while he sat behind his desk, and I think not looking at me.

As soon as I got home I looked up the time of Peary's session with the N.G.S. committee. It was October 20. Since this date didn't jibe with Hastings's story, I wrote a brief note of inquiry: "Do you guess that you went to Eagle Island later than you thought, or is it more likely that Peary made a flying trip to Washington during your stay with him?" When I returned from Washington, his Jeremiad was on my desk.

So it turns out Peary had his own Captain Loose! — however unwitting the fellow's assistance. Peary also (again like Cook) had his own elaborate excuses for needing Hastings around the house. As if clipping agencies and anti-Cook math experts were not readily available outside of Eagle Island. Realistically, why should Peary require the availability of an M.I.T.-trained surveying instructor during the very month before the fateful November 1 appearance before the National Geographic with his data, in Washington? (Hastings' mention of Cook's public statements allows a check of his Eagle Island dates: Cook's *Herald* series wound up October 7; for lack of paying audiences, Cook had quit public lectures by the end of October.)

Interestingly, nothing of Hastings' visit seems to have been put into writing at the time as was discovered in 1935 by Ward's friend, Professor Albert G. Keller (of Yale's Social Science Department, to which Hastings also then belonged) via a letter to Bowdoin. However, the reality of Hastings' involvement was independently verified by the recollection of Bowdoin's President in 1914 — when it required an artful dodge by Hastings (obviously now sworn to secrecy by Peary) to seemingly deny any such thing. Hobbs' 1936 book mentioned Hastings' exam in a little footnote but without any specifics, and a Royal Geographical Society request to explain the note produced no response.

The significance of Ward's discovery of Hastings' role cannot be overestimated. Hastings' advice to engineer Peary was indeed not — like Loose's to the incompetent Cook — a direct invention of observations, since Peary's technical background rendered such gross assistance unnecessary. But the insurance of showing copies of his own inventions to Hastings was just as valuable for Peary's purposes in that it privately assured him in advance that his data were as consistent with his story as they needed to be for the upcoming November 1 National Geographic review (where the "original" records were first seen). He would thus have learned of any problems that needed ironing out well before they could cause embarrassment in Washington. As Ward rightly divined, this sneak preview renders worthless the purported value (on Nov. 1) of the "observations" as virgin corroborating evidence of claimed position.

Ward scrupulously did not mention the Hastings affair in his book because he was deceived by the National Geographic's public report's false exam date (October 20 vs. actually November 1) into thinking there was a problem of chronology where there was in truth none. (This is an ideal verification of all.) In fact, there survives a letter of October 29, 1909, from Peary to Peary Arctic Club Secretary Bridgman which serves quite nicely to pin down the time when Hastings left Eagle Island. Peary enclosed a four page analysis of Cook's tale, with Hastings' name on it, commenting only: "by a very bright young Professor of mathematics, who is also interested in Arctic matters, and who has been looking through the Cook story . . ."; no mention of anything else Hastings had seen, nor of his October residence, matters obviously best kept even from the Peary Arctic Club.

The near-loss of Ward's work forever is largely due to the clandestine machinations of one man, the geographer and academic socialite of the first half of the 20th century: Isaiah Bowman, a figure of international influence.

Director of the American Geographical Society from 1915 to 1935, Bowman then went on to take over as President of Johns Hopkins until 1949. In 1934, when Ward began major research into the Peary case, Izzy Bowman seemed one of the most likely people to approach. Ward did not at first know the sort of character he was dealing with. Bowman was in fact a man who could boast of burning a book, and who was to lead a notorious witch-hunt for Bolsheviki while President at Hopkins.

In response to Ward's October, 1934, written inquiries, Bowman said: "I wish I could talk as freely as I should like to about the Peary matter. . . . it is not a thing that can be written. So far as I am personally concerned, I wish to remain out of the discussion. . . . If this seems strange to you I can explain orally when we meet." Ward was not able to visit the AGS until May; and his private diary entry of May 18 relates that Bowman then told him that he could sum up his view of the Peary case in one sentence (which should interest those eminent figures here and abroad who still say they have always accepted the 1909 claim because the great Bowman assured them it was on the level). He had to admit to Ward: "As a human being, relying on hunches, I believe that he reached the pole; but as a scientist I have to say that there is nothing to argue about, since no evidence is accessible."

Bowman however did not tell Ward why the Peary records are not accessible, a fact that did not come out for a generation. Weems: "After Peary's death in 1920 Isaiah Bowman . . . suggested that neither the diary nor the observations be made available to the public in order to prevent Frederick Cook's supporters from possibly manufacturing refutations or otherwise twisting the contents to suit their own use." (Ward and Rawlins reject Cook but were still barred.)

On May 19, 1935, Ward wrote to ask Bowman to make public that one revealing sentence (which, in a rational community, would have sent the Peary claim into limbo immediately). But on May 20, Bowman responded: "I shall not enter the controversy except with proofs in my hands. . . ."

Additional Suppressive Items
relative to the Cook-Peary Affair

1. Peary himself was quite familiar with the craven streak running through the geographical societies — no amount of his private 1909 cajolery could give them spine; e.g., an October 26 Peary letter notes that the transparency of Cook's stalls "is known to every scientist . . . [here] and abroad. . . . And yet . . . no geographical organization has had the courage to come forward and make such authoritative statement. . . . the present 'National Disgrace' [Cook's Pole fake] . . . is due directly to the fact that the scientists and scientific organizations of this country, though knowing that Cook was a fraud and prevaricator in . . . [his 1906 claim] had not the courage to tax him . . . and insist upon his submitting satisfactory proofs."

2. In 1913, the Explorers Club officially urged its members not even to discuss the Cook-Peary controversy, as it was "disheartening to the good fellowship and harmony among the members." (Can one imagine such a directive from a society of physics, squelching discussion of the Thomson-Rutherford dispute of that day, relative to the structure of the atom?)

3. A member of the AGS Council reported to Congress in 1915 that he could not get his Society to consider reviewing the Cook-Peary controversy, adding his impression that "scientists . . . are very much afraid of it."

4. About 1916, it was feared that Cook might attend a Peary lecture at Ann Arbor. So Hobbs stationed Wolverine jocks in the crowd to throw out Cook bodily if he said a word.

5. In a 1923 letter, an explorer-geologist who later was President of the RGS (and of the British Association for the Advancement of Science) wrote Rev. J.G. Hayes regarding the latter's critical analysis: "quite a valuable contribution to Polar literature. . . . however . . . you are a bit too frank about old Peary. . . . it would be wise to

cut out that paragraph about the Nat Geog Soc & their support of Peary."

6. There is archival evidence that Peary was privy to Marvin's murder, though whether he instigated it is moot. In 1925-1926, the NGS and Bowman managed to suppress the news of the murder for over a year while their colleagues quietly went to Greenland to talk with the confessed killer.

7. Amundsen's 1926 doubts of Peary were not printed in any society journal (and none condemned his treatment by NGS), nor were the views of any other Norse veteran (Nansen, Sverdrup) of ice-conditions north of 85°N. Rather, an article by a Norwegian explorer who'd seen no more of central Arctic Ocean ice than Dr. Cook, was printed in *two* such journals, defending Peary's high speeds by comparison to his own sea-ice sledging — which he exaggerated by factors of up to *five*. Part of the article was plagiarized out of Peary's *North Pole* (a work itself partly plagiarized!).

8. In 1930, when Cook was up for parole out of jail, Hobbs organized among colleagues a letter-writing campaign to the parole board to keep Cook in jail.

9. In 1935, *Science,* the journal of the American Association for the Advancement of Science, published an article by Hobbs calling Rev. Hayes a deliberate liar for Hayes' statement that Cook's fictional Bradley Land had appeared on the map for Peary's *North Pole.* (It had.) *Science* refuses then and now to print a retraction.

10. Henshaw Ward's *Peary Myth* was set to come out through Yale University Press, when Ward died suddenly on October 8, 1935. The fate of the book was secretly turned over to Isaiah Bowman, who had repeatedly stated his desire to keep his name out of the controversy: "There is too much feeling abroad to permit one to say even 'boo' on the Peary question . . ." Unable to overturn any of Ward's facts, Bowman simply threatened Yale Press with a libel suit by the National Geographic. The Ward opus was dropped and the widow repeatedly advised against even seeking *other* publishers.

Bowman once referred to the reasons for his policy on Peary as "not a thing that can be written." His prejudices and love of association with glamorous heroes must have been crucial. National Academy of Sciences VP and AAAS President Bowman to Peary's daughter in 1943: "Dear Marie . . . I have a deep and abiding interest in the vindication of [your father's] work. . . . Our best to you and yours, as always . . ." Bowman in public (NAS speech, 1935): "today the threat to freedom in scientific inquiry [comes from gov't men. . . . more such] Politics . . . and the scientific approach is gone. . . ."

292

Isaiah Bowman was Geographer ne plus ultra in the first half of the 20th century in the U.S. In addition to the many posts already noted in passing: Bowman was, at one time or another, President of the Association of American Geographers, of the International Geographical Union, and vice-president and secretary of the Explorers Club.

11. In 1936, AAG President Hobbs fudged a figure by over 100 miles in his continuing effort to explain away Peary's speeds.

12. In 1939, Hobbs was caught doctoring, in a project funded by the American Philosophical Society, an Antarctic map (in an effort to cheat a British claim) and was exposed in the act by the head of the RGS.

13. In 1940, the APS *Proceedings* glorified Peary's work extensively and referred to doubters (none of whom were given space) as "irresponsible."

14. Plaisted's 1967-1968 trials with the ice convinced him that Peary's story was fiction and he frankly so stated publicly. Subsequently, as he sought funds for an Antarctic project, a close acquaintance of the President (Melvin Payne) of the powerful NGS wrote: "Mel . . . told me [Aug. 21, 1968] that the Society would have nothing to do with [Plaisted]. . . . he was inclined to discount [Plaisted's] accomplishments." The Antarctic venture died.

15. Today, NGS claims to possess no copy of Peary's '09 journal, though it is a matter of record that it once did. A 1968 request by the doubting opposition to see other documentary material undeniably in the NGS archives and freely shown to pro-Peary writers was not replied to. Nor was a request to see a specific rare book in the Society's library, though the NGS (e.g., during a 1967 Congressional push for special tax-breaks) boasts of the free access it allows scholars.

16. Letters (1968) to the NGS' President, Research Vice-president, and Geographical Research Chief, requesting a hearing for doubters, brought a reply which presumably represents a *genuine* first in the history of scientific institutions: "the case is closed."

17. This book, when under consideration for publication by a New York trade house, was vetoed by the Honorary President of a well-known exploring organization.

18. In 1969, the Explorers Club attempted to talk the Naval Institute into softening a 1970 article critical of Peary written by this author.

19. In 1970, a world-respected geographer-geologist and polar explorer (formerly AAAS President and Chairman of the Board of

Governors of the Arctic Institute of North America), a Life Member of NGS, declared the 1970 Naval Institute Proceedings analysis utterly wrong. A request for the reasons learned that he had not even bothered to read it because: "Some fifty years ago I was satisfied after being reassured by such people as Dr. Isaiah Bowman . . ."

20. In 1970, the American Philosophical Society, funder of Weems' 1967 Peary biography, refereed and voted acceptance (for the APS *Proceedings*) of a paper on the role of geographical societies in the maintenance of the '09 claim. But after NGS-Explorers Club complaints, APS chief George Corner arbitrarily refused publication. (The APS President is also VP for Research and Exploration of NGS.) A subsequent appeal foundered over the APS' specific insistence that all criticism of the modern NGS be deleted.

21. In 1970-1971, the RGS took five months to decide to reject an invited paper critical of the '09 mystery, on the excuse that the Peary Papers are "restricted" (a fact RGS had known all along). The Peary family was then (June 7) asked if "restrictions" were meant to exclude even major societies. No reply. So the RGS won't look, and the family won't show — the usual level of sanity. For perspective: can one imagine any normal society rejecting an invited critical paper on the ground that the party under scrutiny insists on hiding its evidence?

22. But recently, one geographer *has* been honest about the reasons for the long blackout of U.S. society articles exposing the skeleton in geography's closet; AGS editor Wilma Fairchild refused to publish admittedly "convincing" and "fascinating" analyses of Peary's prank mainly because this would upset the National Geographic Society and thereby "set off a train of incalculable consequences."

In the Peary context, one understands Peary Arctic Club Secretary Bridgman's 1923 despair (regarding the Cook hoax):

At this late day . . . it is wholly unlikely that any of the societies whose silence compromised their honor will take steps to purge their records and show the world that they really know the difference between truth and falsehood. . . .

Notes and Source Citations

(Page numbers are set in bold face type, line numbers are preceded by an asterisk and followed by a half-parenthesis, and source abbreviations are identified in the Bibliography.

Chapter 1.
7*3+)SPH302,WP267;Curiosities:midnight-start schedule of these days bad for eyes & steering, Apr. 5 sight would surely include longitude, actually no obs. at all on Apr. 5, "direct course" should be in compass-terms, "other" 5 mi. absurdly precise dead-reck., 2 mi. ahead of is worse, "Pole at last" vs. position not known before 6 A.M. Apr. 7 **9***3)Mars' poles long observed,RST1784:260*17+)PHm25:295*35+)HSG2 **10***11)MH291*18)NYT9/11:1:2*24+)WR194,182,LG250,CM518,601*31+)NYT12/22:3:1,10:1 **11***20)e.g.BAC4006 **12***F)PHm25:173(B24,285);24:19(NYT9/26:5:2.4)
Chapter 2.
14*1)e.g.SGe2:44*13)NGM137:526*19)ME233*30)KH22 **15***1+)VB77,84*10)VBlxvi+*14+)VB195+*27+)HN28,147+ **16***1+)HN ccxii,117+,115,SHe2:2*4+)HNi,145*11)KH30,33;SA55+*15+)VB 77*20)EB1961:11:859*26)RGJ15:121,HNv-vii,145n2*29)HN12 (31°20′),16n2*31)HN15-16(no 7 Isl.)*33)RGJ15:125 **17***1+)HNxlix, 9n1,RGJ15:126+*12+)MT64,PV17+*26+)VM78(vs.KH37,ix!) **18***1)MNxi*14)PV43,64(MV25?)*16)PV92(considering relative rewards and relative ease of determination, a general rule is: a longitude error usually proves innocent; a record-breaking latitude error is highly suspicious)*18)PV20*23)KH53*25+)FP170+,381,248,NH **19***1+)VM112+*27)RAM2:91*35)PP115 **20***1+)RAN7:175)vs.e.g. SA596)*6+)KH93+,146+,157+(vs.VK38?)*23+)VM147*29)KG 162*34)KH163 **21***4)KG516+,VK78*10)RJG23:141*20)GF19+, B240*36)FLixn **22***2)NYT'56/3/17:2:3(FL204;106)*5)CK167*8) KA2:388*13)KA2:404,CK261*17)80°26′N.from writer's analysis of hitherto-rejected(SK43)longitude   obs.(KA2:383,57°26′.8;RKU) *23)RJG28:272+*28)NAM-148:234:137:6,VK190(puts C.Jef. N. of 81°17′N.)*29)actual farthest well-known within 1 mi. for century (NNmap) vs. CK258+*35)VK149vs.CK167*38)VK190vs.KA2:310 **23***1)KA1:307+,464*4+)CK166,ECJ48:2:78,80vs.VKch.#1,RJG23: 136*11)VK25+;CK290n4false*13+)VK77+*20)HJ27+*27+) ECJ48:2:79vs.VK160+33+)KA1:393+ **24***1)VK150*7)VK32,173, 185*8+)LW58,VK170*16+)HJ347(likeB49-17+),355+*28)HO349,

351,359+*30+)CA39,HO374*34+)CA24,38,CK258,273;RJG37:cx
25*2)WA134*3+)HO351,HAG8:31*15)mapsSHvs.SK*17)20*24+)
HO351vs.HAG8:31(like F12,B108-2+)*35)HAG8:29-30*38+)SPM
#367/13/2vs.MS90,ML299,MR83+   **26***3)HO454*11)LW239,58;
WA103*15)TD148*20)LW323+,TD162,NSR'73:300+*31)NYH
'73/5/21:5:1+*32)DP603*34)LW344 **27***1+)BH,LW297+*12)
PF310+Payer's mismappings could have been fatal for Nansen in
'95(NF1:580,2:167,190,226+,268+) RGJ10:190 (single-limb),236+,
336,11:439;N.pt. of F.J. Land was neither reached nor seen by Payer,
who (ignorant of Hall's '71 work) believed his nonexistent C. Fligely
would become a record North land reached *31+)NN1:155,158,377
(map:compass-var.100°W.± 2°, uncertainty measure of magn.
field's weakness) **28***4)GS53,165*7+)VM159*17+)DJ573+,589+,
HJ83+*31+)GR120 **29***9+)GT1:335,2:317*17)TA244,284+,NYT
9/21:2:4*20+)GR148*32)PY325 **30***F)KA2:57;RGJ20:483,NGM
13:460

Chapter 3.
31*5+)HP7,15,23,PON9:31,LG228,WP8,16*21+)WP3   **32***3+)
WP49,65 **33***12+)NGM1:315"a region which has interested the
thinking world for more than 3 centuries"*21)NC3*25+)WP99
*35+)HP84 **34***5)WP117*9+)FC22,28*14+)WP122,PG1:296
*24)WP164*31)PG1:xxxv,279(vs.2:524,PY113;vs.HJ168*34)SA
596+*35+)PG1:283,MH130,157 **35***3+)SPH313*10+)WP48
(105;WR29)*24)NS1:5(DJ880+)*25+)NF1:14+,29,59;40*32)
NS13:9-11*36)NS6:xx+*37)NS6:70+,7:1+   **36***7)NS6:115*12+)
NF2:529,589*18+)HP177*26)GP166*28)FC64,HP197*35+)HP
192,478 **37***10+)FB69(PG2:574n1) **38***4)PG2:372,384*9)WP308
*21)HP197,WP174*27)MG181+(no mention WP309) **39***5+)
HP198*19+)WP175,PY296*25)ECA'98/1/29*27)PY301vs.ECA
'99/8/28:5*29)PY296*34)ECA'98/1/29 **40***6+)ECA'98/1/29
(PY296),RD120*16)NAM#T369-4*22)seriously!HP207,LG227,
249,WP282(no mention of Jesup Land)*25+)FaS27 **41***29+)WP
176 **42***1+)FaS63+,21,39*16+)PY301-305*23)WR229*29+)
RD124 **43***36+)WP181 **44***9)WP180*13+)HP214 **45***1)HP199,
206*3+)FaS40*28)PY312 **46***2)WP183*4+)PY321+*23+)WP187
*32)PG2:618,WP125,310(irony NGM4:206)   **47***5+) PY327+,
TMJ9:140,RR38+*20)WP196(94!)*23+)WP197*29+)HP242,
WP198,PY336 **48***1)FC71,271*2+)HP243+*9+)PY340+*18)
PY345,118,123,144*25+)PY344,TMJ9:140*32+)WP200 **49***2+)
WP201*9+)WP201,199*13+)RD157*17+)NGM14:29(like   A24-
16+)HP255 **50***3)PY314,AGB35:509,SAR'03:438*10+)HP215
51*3)e.g.NGM13:388*6)F30*17)RGJ21:481n vs.NGM20:461   **52**
*3+)ECA'99/8/28:16*10)RGJ22:648*16+)PY212,202*20)NGM19:
668*22)PZ295*37+)WP190   **53***10)WP205*12+)ECA'02/10/15
*16+)WP204*30+)ECA'02/11/15,21 **54***2+)ECA'02/12/6:26,29;
'03/1/18,23*15)GP145*21)BL202*23)MP'05/7/23,24;'08/7/17

*25)NYT9/15:2:1,BL161,181,FC99,RD168,GP358+(WP46),SPH
298,B72-2+,77-4*27+)WA138,408,HP478   55*1+)GR59,102+,
157*6)MG236*16+)ECA'02/10/23;'03/6/26 56*10+)ECA'03/
6/26vs.GR334*13+)GR300,GHiii*21+)RW147*27)GiHn57*30+)
PY285+,355+*35+)HP259 57*4)WP203*5)NAG5062:11*6+)
FC80+,HP260,WR44,WP306*F)AGB31:380 58*F)PGB'04/1
Chapter 4.
59*6)WP183(B294-i20)*14+)NYT9/3:2:4,4:2:3*19+)OTL142:
218*26)WP233(&WRxiii,36;ECA'02/10/21,CA176,C52A:839;
NYT'69/1/30:37?)   60*2)WA135!*5)FAr411,I'71/4/15*15+)NYT
'26/5/10:4:5(MH285)*20+)BSU'23/11/25ed.(ECA),B294*31)
B189   61*4)PG1:476*15)e.g.ATH1864:375*16+)e.g.Trevor Hall's
writings(&TIME'73/3/12!);Kane's mistress was a Founder of Spiri-
tualism(FL,CK)*24+)RGJ35:523(530&FaL131;ix,15+,133,171;
Fawcett & Doyle both believers)*32)RMSapp.6,8,RE136,139,SPH
322,WR187,WP288*33)RPP'68/8/27*35)RG181,215,Reeves   met
many ghosts(190)but nary a dishonest medium!(195)*39)WPM116+
(WORLD'14/6/7)   62*1)AMERICAN WEEKLY'61/10/1:14*3)
NGM135:448,138:535*6+)ARC17:219,19:209(vs.23:288),RPP
'69/1/16*9+)SPR16:164*19)even in the 1970's in the"best-edited
geographical journal in the world"(AGR63:5;&it is),one winces at
inability to handle high-school math (61:573+);also in the J.Air
Pollution Control Assn.(who has the embarrassed author secretly
referee criticism)*31+)MR80   63*1)WA3*7)RPP'68/10/9*8+)
RGJ12:382,McH141,RG47*19+)RGJ124:91*33+)AGR41:19,30,
WA152(14) 64*6+)SB192,I'71/4/1*11+)WA52,55,57*16+)Lauge
Koch (BPJ'37/3/15,NYT'37/3/10;HP484!)*21)RPP'70/5/27vs.
NYT'71/12/19(I'72/1/11),2 days aft.StN;SQpref.*26)MR186,
DNB4S:464*32)OTL142:218*35+)NYT12/22:3:3   65*12+)
NS6:113+;A137-7*25+)LP2:442+*29)NGM10:362*30+)LO50+,
LP2:478,490*34)LP2:515,520vs.478,488;A137-7 66*1+)CG271+,
NM57,147*7)AGB35:228*F)NGM14:330
Chapter 5.
67*5+)SM4,MP'05/8/5(7/20)*8)MP'05/8/2,4,6*9+)MP'05/7/27,
30*13+)PY44*18+)MP'05/8/14-16*8,9)*27+)PY98+,109,HP
274+   68*54+)PY117,119+,126+,PHr350*16+)PY129-131
*31+)PY134 69*7+)PHr340vs.PYmap (paths also differ)*11)
CM542(PHr350,HP277,WP217)vs.PY134(A25-24+)*17)B117
*23)PY134-174(likeHO365+)*25+)NYT12/25:3:2*28)PHr500vs.
PY148*31)RL5/26,30*34)BL163*35)e.g.PY132,203(xiii) 70*2)WP
339 (like B80-28)*5)PY183*12)NGM106:525*15+)PY329;147;
280;112,HP257*32+)PY174,HP284 71*2+)PY169,189-190*11+)
NGM19:668*27+)PY215;240,HP293*36+)RL4/19 72*2+)GP
338,NYT'10/2/25:5:2*5)GR219+*7+)BL171+*23)NGM15:256,
MF88,412,SF523*29)WR173(186,221;227, actually'07/7NGM) vs.
PHr340,PY map *32)FC80 *33+)PY202(6/24)   73*1+)PY207

(6/28)*12+)MF80 *16+)MF83+,RR49n34 *18+)MA180+(MF
92),FAd229 *29+)NYT'14/11/26:14:2 *34)PY201-203 (excerpts
from 6/24,28 used) *35)CM542 74*2)NYT'10/12/26:4:2('07:PZ
69,117) vs. C54A:54,59 (vs.WRxi) *6)WA138,HP478,WP339 *16)
ECA,NGM17:638 *19)PY280 *21+)NYT'06/11/24:5:2;12/13:
2:6 *35)PHr (no name), PYmap 75*3)HP296+(289) error from
caption PHr507(GN86) vs. HP290+,NGM106:521,GN86,PY196+,
201-203(Capes Colgate&Hubbard confused; so no 6/24 record)
*4)vs.PY329,PZ334 *5)HP290+ *7)F77 *12)PY207&219 vs. 210
*29+)F77 76*1+)PY168*12+)PZ299 *24)MP'08/7/27 *25)HP461,
478 *30)BL181,206(GP321,PZ291n) 77*4)NYT9/15:2:1,A54-25
*6+)PT169vs.BL166,NGM17:643 *F)HP292+,ARC8:15 78*F)
fromPYmap
Chapter 6.
79*7+)DS286(vs.e.g.WB113,115)*24)AS1:19+,AM26+,74+ 80
*1+)FC80,NGM15:460(C54A:63)*3)FC92*6)NGM14:405*7+)
FC88+*13)NYT12/25:3:2*14)CT180*15+)FC89,CM523*21+)
CT191, NYT12/25:3:2-3 *26)FC91 *28)NYT10/16:2:1 (like A70-2)
*29)A69-25+*30+)StA102+*32+)WCU,LIFE'56/8/20:86(9/10:
15),AAJ10:49,NYT10/15:4:2*35)CT233*37)CT227+vs.239+
(192+;WCU,Mt.#8450); see WCU photos 24&28, 22&29(23,A.J.)
81*1+)FC88-93,182-183,CM524,BrC70(NYT10/15-16,*7+)ECA
10/26*17+)FC92*22)CM523*25+)CD53,CM29*34)CM542(FS247)
82*1+)FC92,PYvii*11+)CM542*18)CM542,A76-25*20)B89-12+
*26)FS98,277+,284,SD238,PSc217*28)RPP'70/8/11(&A25-38+)
*30+)FS245-248 83*6)B189*11)FC103vs.C54A:46*21+)FC130vs.
137,161*30)BW250,NYT9/26:5:6*34+)GA46,NYT9/23:2:1,RER
40:445-448 84*1)CM244+(246;AGR5:141!)*4)NYT12/22:3:1*5+)
RER40:436-438(FL204)*19+)ECA10/12*22+)NYT9/3:2:6,3*36+)
HP372 85*23+)FAr32*33+)FC197+,CM580,538(vs.FC198,but no
chronometer times in NYH story!) 86*2)DS93,NYT12/10:4:2;9:3:
3;10:3:5-6*19)HP382*21)CM245n*25+)RE135n11,26 87*4+)
B166(FC149+,170+,196+)*25+)PZ276,MH185 88*6+)B130-25+,
34*21+)HP382+,NYT12/23:1:7*31)FC205*32+)NYT12/22:1:7
89*10)NYT9/20:2:6*12+)SD99,WRxiii,FC101,NYT9/8:2:2*15+)
NYT9/5:1:5,4:2:3,9:1:1,BoN4:151*27+)FC158*32)OTL93:338
90*1+)FAd55*10)GA49,54*11)NYT12/22:3*12)OTL93:625*14)
NYT12/26:2:2*15)NYH9/11:3:6-7*19+)WP284*24)NYT'26/1/25:
20:1*25+)B254-27+*34)FC216,AGR5:140,HP484,RPP'68/6/5,
ARC23:289 91*19)CM290+,NYT12/9:3:4*22)SS124*26+)SF
517+,SP272*31)RDpref., HA4*34)F94,GSC59,69,79,SNmap
92*14)DS93,98,139*15+)FU13(Cook was not expelled from the Explorers Club in '09 for exploration-fraud, since there was no Club
rule against this,NYT12/23:2:2),RPP'70/10/15*19+)AGR5:140,
BoN4:151*29+)ECAclip(nd;1919?),WP323,LTD79:10:10*32+)
FC249,256+,LIFE'56/8/20:92 93*1+)TV2:285(140,252,260)

*16)also   T.Bridges,NYT'10/5/2:6,CN97!(120),BU228,239,533,
FC213*21)ECA11/9 94*F)NYT10/13:2
Chapter 7.
95*2+)PZ192,9,PYxiii,A54-25*16+)PY127*23)BT144,WP239,
PZ259(201vs.171,233,249,270,281,303,306,316)*26)NYT9/20:2:4
96*1+)BNG19*4+)LG226,BL183,PZvii,MP'08/7/9*16)WP239
*19+)MP'08/8/16,9/14,PZ21+,77,130,BT23*28+)MP'08/8/30,
9/2,PZ113,115*34+)PZ120;130;MP'08/9/12,BoN4:37 97*6+)
MP'08/9/10;11/22(PZ160)*25+)PZ17,170,MH164   98*3)HA4vs.
BL190*8+)MH164*20+)BT145*28+)BL191,MH168,BT146*36+)
PZ215   99*7+)NYT'06/12/9:7:1*14+)PZ267,285(HP396)*29+)
PZ4*37+)BL192   100*6+)PZ4(HP344+)*19)NYT'06/11/29:7:1
*23+)PZ4(B137-33)*31+)PY281 101*5+)PZ215*12+)PZ218,
221*18)BT153*21+)PZ224+*23+)BL194,BA941*27+)PZ226vs.
MH179*33+)PZ232,WP251   102*2+)BoN2:101vs.PZ236,MH188
(date?MA97+),B107-17*4)MH192,PZ325*6+)BA942*8+)BT178+
*15+)BT192*25)PZ214,234,245,253*26)PZ246*28+)BA943   103
*1+)PZ249+,351+,F134*4+)B292(i6)*11)PZ260,BA944*14)
PZ262vs.338*15+)RRnH(&NGM140:519A)*25+)PZ265*34)
B107-36+   104*6+)PHm25:170(PY106,PZ240,PS52;MFded.)
*24)PY98,PZ234*28)PZ248(208),PS263+,C53A:1630-1631(vs.HP
279!)   105*1+)NYH9/22:4:1-2*27+)PZ266*34+)SPH312   106
*16+)RG79*19+)SPE181:240*21+)PZ272,RDpref*26+)SPH311
(vs.BL201!)   107*11+)NYT9/15:1:7-2:1*17)A102-2+;cheap:WP
132,ECA'05/7/24*23+)BT48;131*31+)MH181;233vs.161*36+)
PZ273,360,SPH305,B117-7+ 108*2+)PZ359vs.360&BL193(1
single-limb vs. plural, again;A25-24+,69-7+)*11)HH113*F)NAP
Chapter 8.
109*2)NYT9/16:2:1,NYH10/17:5:3(HW12836vs.HA4)*4)SPH
303*7)PZ275(SPH302)*8)PZ266,BA945*10)NYT'35/4/21VI:17
*12)PZ360vs.Marvin 3/25 certificate "the going good and improv-
ing each day"F134*14+)PZ279-284*24)HE129*26)PZ274*27)
HE131   110*3)HW12835&HA4*5+)HW12836*17)HW12837,HA4
*20+)PZ285;vs.Scott's speed continuity(SL503) 111*8)BA942*15)
PZ205(258,259,BA944;3/27)*16)F134*21)PHm25:170,BA944*23)
PZ264,303*25)HW12836*26)SPH302(vs.e.g.PZ310!)*28+)NYT9/
11:1:5-6*30)PZ267*36)PZ271*38+)HA1-2vs.HE129(Stokes);
AHI1:2:46,WR167,RPP'70/11/12-14,WP303,B292(i6) 112*6)
BA944-945*17+)PZ194   113*9)NS6:115('95/4/7-8)*14+)NF2:168
(4/5-6)*18)B217*20)PZe.g.265,302*21+)PS291*26)NGM104:478
*37)PZ212,HP344+(SPH319) 114*8+)F134*13+)PZ269,274+
*26+)SPH301*37+)SPH302(WP267)vs.AS1:135   115*1+)HA1,4,
HW12837vs.SPH302*77+)HW12837*12+)HA1*20+)HW12837
*34)NYT9/16:1:7   116*2)PZ285,362*3+)HA1,4vs.PZ289+*20)
HE134*33+)PZ290vs.HW12837*35)B28-20   117*7+)PZ273*10)
A103-25+*13)BT181*15)PZ270,SPH299*25+)PY118,PHr498

*29+)PY144 **118***1)PY143*9+)PY145*15+)PS55*19+)PY146,168 *22+)PHm25:170,PZ264*27+)PZ303 **119***3+)PZ307*10)vs. B295*19+)SPH302,RD206*33)PZ362,SPH302*34)PZ225,232*36) vs.PZ224 **120***2+)GP306*12+)PZ302*35)A73-16+(actually, new moon worse in '09) **121***13+)PHm25:285vs.PZ307*34+)PY143 **122***3)PZ303*5+)HE141*9)PZ188*13+)PZ282*19+)NYT'26/9/ 25:2:8,B292(i6)*23)HE143,PZ318+*25)FAd71+*27)AHI1:2:49; polar explorers involved in shootings or struggles for firearms: Franklin, Kane, Hayes (CK291n3,200,164),Hall(LW215),Greely (TA243),Shackleton(PSc217) **123***1)WR30,WP105*4+)PZ283(HP 325)*16+)PY135;344*30+)B150-16&A76*35+)NYT9/11:1:7 **124***2+)HE140*5)PZ315(glacial fringe before midn.)*7)PZ168*F) NAP

Chapter 9.
125*2+)BNG19*12)A124-7 **126***10+)NYT9/8:2:,C52A:336,GP 304,RR36n35*31+)AS2:125,SL424,RGJ103:168,173 **127***6+) WR179vs.WP175,192-200(194),PY130*10)PZ10,A126-10+*17+) NYT9/10:3*21)RD7*25+)NYT12/25:3*27+)PZ236,242*33+) A104-28 **128***1+)PY149,142*8)HA2,LG238(NGM21:72)*14)HE4, 110,114,124*19)PZ351+,F134*20)NYT11/4:4:1,SPH295*32)WR 217,HB39*34+)SAR'12:701,AGR21:194+,A125-31+ **129***4)SPH 311,315*13)A125-5*15)PZ338(232 not obs.)*20+)PYx,281*23+) SPH315(two 1000 fathom lines&one 2000 f.)vs.RGJ36:142,146 (RR38)*25+)A35-32*27+)MH200,217,227*33+)PZ210,SPH298 **130***3)PZ304*5+)PZ338,SPH298*25+)RR36n34,A88-6+*34) TMJ9:140,PY117,344*38)MH215(184,194) **131***3+)Ladies Home Journal'05/3:58*10)BoN4:140*15)PZ211,276,294n(MH185,NYT9/ 16:2:1)*16+)PZ232(SPH299,310)vs.B137-7*28)PZ288n **132***3) HP467 *11)CD58,NYT9/20:2:6(PZ289n); for how to, RR35 *19) NYT12/23:1:7-2:1,SPH322,RR42*29+)NYT12/26:2:1 **133***F) RN37(from NAV'11/2:9,HP422,HRR4) **134***F)PZ356+
Chapter 10.
135*13+)PY129,142,149,MH187*19)PY106,111*20)PY98,101,105, 110*21)PY117 **136***1+)BT141+*4)BT174,arccos(1/1.3)=40°*5) RGJ136:512n,arccos(1/1.75)=55°*6+)HE111*28+)e.g.PZ228, 238,294n*34)SPH298,307*37)SPH316-318,302;PZ269 **137***7)all magnetic figures treated herein as standard are extrapolated from USNO Chart H.O.1706-N,Magnetic Variation,Epoch 1965.0 Arctic Regions(N.of 55°N.)*15+)PHm24:784(bowdlerized:PZ211- 212)*25)HA2*30)A100-23+*33)PZ232,276vs.MH169(PY102) *35)PZ288+ **138***1+)NNmap,vs.GSC340,560*4+)GPr8-9*10) PZ215,221,238,257,259(vs.237);HE128,NYT9/16:2:1*13)e.g.PZ 256,284,294n,BA944,MH177,A1-7*13+)MH185(vs.PZ232)*21) SPH319*21+)SPH319;BOW'62:623-624,161 **139***5+)HH 135,PY117*9+)StN51vs.A121-34+,123-1,4+*15+)HP20*36) B231-4,A137-15+ **140***2)RR35(4.35mi.)*3)(4.35/413)radians

=0°.6*5)AS1:212,2:117,125,401,RGJ103:174*20+)A139-9+*23)
PZ274,BT316,MH185(NYT'34/2/1:19:4)*26)ECA'99/8/28,B
286*31)F12vs.A136-34*37)arctan(20+/50)exceeds20° 141*1+)
A101-4,15+*10)e.g.PS302vs.244,263*15+)SPH294*25)PZ287
&362,290&292vs.StN51*26)SPH308,326*28)(4°+/360°).2π.413
mi.=c.30mi.*35)RN36 142*17)F12(A68,69);both c.35mi.*29)
PZ203*36)BL193 143*6)RPP'70/6/19*9+)GP275,HP278,483,
NYT'26/1/24:2:6(MH197)*20+)B298-6+,227-7*30+)NYT9/11:
1:7,PHm25:174,PZ284,SPH302*35)HW12837,HA1,4(HE129-132,
A111-38+)*39+)SPH317 144*6)B150*14)HA1*17)PZ268(359
has 2 mi. error, RN35;F134); also WP341n40*22+)SPH299vs.302
*25+)B231*35+)NYT9/11:1:6-7 145*3)SPH324*5)SPH309,
324*6)SPH302*7)PZ359,362*9)WR152,A86-25+*13)HA1,2,HE
129*14)HA4*15+)SPH302 146*F)PHm25:11
Chapter 11.
147*22)the chance of 13 sextant data consistently placing a man at
his goal of 23 years, just be accidental error, is effectively zero;
"when you have eliminated the impossible, whatever remains, *however improbable* [a priori] must be the truth" DH118*24)e.g.B254-1
148*30)DH10,904*34+)DH204,896(85) 149*23)A114*31+)also,
had the Sun's path not seemed at least roughly level, Henson would
have noticed 150*2)B156-1*16)or the public's,PZ291n*27+)A143
vs.114;SPH302*33+)MDA692+,RGJ90:165 151*26+)HA1-3
152*37+)HE135 153*15)HA3(2)*24)WR216*34+)A85 154*28)
SPH294*35)SPH298*37+)SPH314,317 155*7+)C53A:275(SPH
301,312-313)*19)BL163*25+)LTD39:1121 156*1)PZ288n!(June vs.
MA99);RN37*2)most of the Earth's surface is deeper,EB'61:16:
684*5)A35-32*8)RGJ30:584+*10)RR38n37*16+)SPH309*21)
MF76vs.SPH315*35+)C46:2715,HP418,WR175 157*25+)HA3
*30+)HA2-3;HW12834,HE122+*38)PZ315vs.SPH305 158*2)
HP344+*7)RGJ136:512n*10)SPH303*38)HC49,HP477,RRnJ
159*4+)HP344+*10)SPH299,PZ306*13+)A118,119*18)HP344+,
PZ303*32+)PZ315,SPH305vs.197*37+)BL196vs.MH217,BT316
160*9+)PZ316,WP342*20)BL197
Chapter 12.
161*6)SPH312,A160-20(MH214)*10+)HE153;ECA'62/7/26*18+)
MH216vs.A127*26)MH278,WP276,PZ334 162*1+)PZ327*6+)
PZ325+(HE155)*15)MH234*20)A70*22)PZ331(1st delay) *28)
BoN4:148*33)WP275,BT302,MH277*35+)MH277(why not more
northern Hopedale?,as in '06,NGM17:638) 163*3+)GP309*7+)
FC153,BoN4:20(7P.M.)*12+)NYT9/7/3(6vs.WR130,WP276,
343n84*16+)WP276,MH278,FC153,NYT9/7:3:1+*32+)WAP9/
7:2:5 164*15)FC155(vs.HP373?)*21+)NYT9/8:1:7*34+)NYT9/8:
1:6,FC156+ 165*5)BoN4:24*9)NYT9/11:1:4+*10+)BL205*20)
A162,FC166*24+)MH284*28+)FC167+ 166*9+)orig. written
story(pre-Sept.'09):"most of my instruments were intrusted" to

Whitney, no mention of data, NYH10/7:4:4;early Sept.:all orig.
data with Whitney,FC150;near equinox:Cook&Whitney both have
complete sets of data,NYT9/22:1:7-2:1;finally:most of data with
Whitney,now lost,FC198,CM244n*12)NYT9/18:1:7,22:2:1,23:1:4,
2:1*13+)HP377(actuallyN.F.),NYT9/26:1:4,27:1:1;10/17:1:7
(9/26:5:6),A87*20+)FC171,WP284*29+)McH120,WR143,FC170
(9/30) 167*F)NAP 168*F)NAP
Chapter 13.
169*9+)NYT9/8:3:4,IND67:572*14+)NYT9/13:2:5(&12:1:7
ECA10/7)*25+)NYT10/7:1:1   170*3+)SPH294*10)NYT10/2:3:3
*13+)ECA9/22,29,10/7n,NYT9/29:1:3,10/7:1:1*32+)SPH294
171*12+)NYT   10/13:8:6,WPP'35/7/10(GP326)*20)B189-21+,
190-25+*23)B191*30)WP287,B285   172*1+)HP378*6+)WP287,
A171,B191*8+)NYT11/5:1:1,6:6:1,FC195*22+) NHT11/6:6:1,
HP378,386,FC197,WP286 173*1+)FC198+207,RPP'67/12/15
*16+)GP327,SPH295*28+)SPH295,C45A:78-79,NGM20:921,
1008,PZ363   174*30)&SPH295,324   175*1+)SPH324*14+)NYT
10/21:2:3,11/1:5:4*30)SPH295,325*35)NGM20:921 176*3+)
FC193*12+)NYT11/2:1:3*18+)SPH295,WP231,312,A175-1+
*24)NYT10/21:2:3*24+)SPH295vs.173-28+*29+)SPH295,NYT
10/14:4:3,ECA10/19   177*2)A164*5)HP392vs.FC207*6+)WP295
(vs.ECA)*24)B182,HP418*32)NYT11/2:1:3 178*2+)SPH314,
294,296,325   179*4)NYT11/2:1:3   180*2+)NYT11/2:1:3&SPH
294vs.A173,174*7+)SPH296,NGM21:72*12+)NYT11/4:4:1,3:8:1
(&9:1)* 20+)A173-28+ 181*7+)FC177,160*26+)NYT9/3:2:3
182*3+)SPH296,B216*F)PHm24:5
Chapter 14.
183*1+)FC207,WP298,345,NYT'10/1/6:20:3,HP406*15+)GN
147,PZ364*22+)NGM17:205,18:281,58   184*4)NYT9/8:4:1,SPH
308*18+)B186,CM544*26+)ECA10/26   185*4)NGM26:613*6+)
SPH296vs.ECA10/27(&opinion) 186*1+)NGM21:72*4+)SPH
294,295,A173-28+vs.C53A:270 187*1+)NYT'23/4/22II:6:2,
VIII:1:1;FRP'21:2:919(fraud)+*12)B238*21+)HP478,PY290,
NGM19:668,WA408;DAB10:62,AMJ12:129   188*7+)NYT9/8:1:6
*10)NGM18:51,HP193(actually Councillor AGS)*19+)NYT12/22:
3:3   189*1+)BL248,WP283*21+)NYT'20/2/22:10:2(vs.'06/12/9:
7:1,but shows GG's priorities)*32+)NGM106:531*35)PG1:350
190*1+)NGM18:51,281,19:447,661,21:75,NYT9/8:4:1,FC160
*25+)GN51*35)176 191*NYT11/2:1:3*5)NYT9/15:2:1,A189-21+
*8)RPP'68/10/15*10+)ECA10/12,13*24+)A176,172*30+)ECA11/
6*33+)SPH295 192*F)KeA
Chapter 15.
193*8)Cook"must be stamped out"ECA10/7*9+)NYT9/28:2:3,
HP378,A80   194*1+)FC38,99,137,C52A:332,837,HP192,DNB1S:
398*15+)NYT9/3:2:2,4,4:2:3,7:1:3,8:1:5,7,3:2*35+)NYT9/7:1:7
195*5)FC144*14+)FC91,159,175NYT9/2:3:1,3:2:4,4:2:3,5:1:5

196*11+)NYT9/15:2:1vs.RRnM*24)FC156*24+)SPH310,307
*35)SPH309,NYT11/4:4:2,BNG28,30,63,65,66,69,NAG5062:17
197*1+)NYT9/8:4:1,SPH307*27+)A173,86,92-15+*35)WR187
198*1+)HP426*12+)A8-35+,PZ294
Chapter 16.
199*1+)NGM21:71*9+)LH38:55*15)WP285,325   **200***3+)NYT
'26/1/25:20:1,A182*15+)FC152,165,210*22+)WP239,FC196*33)
C52A:838,B213-34 **201***3+)WR182*12)WP282*21+)WP189
202*4+)HP240   **203***1+)LIFE'68/2/9:30*5+)RPP'68/7/18*10)
FAd131+,125*16+)WP193+,ECA'02/11/26,12/15;10/27,31
204*1+)WP338n21,WPP'34/12/12*6+)BJ194+,44+,54+,DAB4:
331,CY132*26+)WP234*35)PG2:404+,1:509;394,495,500;510
205*17)NGM124:561(14:44)vs.GN27(37);39*35+)PZ30,PY12+
(PG1:511) **206***3+)WPviii,26,46,47 **207***9+)WP76,91,101,GP229,
282   **208***7+)SPH307,PZ76,WP238,239,284,HP314*34+)WP274
(B271)   **209***6+)WR176,C46:2712;53A1628(PZ24),PS74,77   **210**
*F)PG1:500;NAP
Chapter 17.
211*1+)C45:1417,1426,2145,B213-38(one degree honorary)*10)
GP330vs.WP290(312);B221*16)B213-24,221-4*18+)A36;57,B228;
225,GN53,147   **212***1)ECA11/23,NYT11/25(13:3*3+)PZ51,202,
WR172,WP156,C46:2712,B240*21+)ECA'02/11/21,12/25*30+)
HP308(some wording lifted fromNYT'10/2/9:1:3) **213***1+)FC209+
*9+)NYT'10/2/23:5:4*17+)C45:1628,1752*30+)HP410,GP357)
WP290,310,A200-33*38)C45A:1953,2194   **214***1)BDC789*21+)
WAT'10/2/18:13vs.C45A:78*26+)NYT'10/2/25:5:2,HP418
215*6+)C46:4224,GP338,BDC466*17+)NAL'10/2/27;S.6104
(retro to '09/4/6,HP424) **216***20+)B238*23+)SPH293 **217***20+)
MH184*34+)SPH294   **218***18+)SPH295-297   **220***1+)SPH297-
298*10)WP343n6,FC207*12)B229*15)SPH298*25)NGM21:276
(SPH320)*28)NYT'10/2/17:5:1*31)C45A:82   **221***4+)B227-20+
*15+)C45A:78-81   **222***33+)NGM21:276,A218   **223***1+)HRR7,
46:2702,B239,OTL94:596*13+)SCA102:294*26+)255,A214
*33+)HP401+,479,SPH297   **224***1+)SPH326*6)HP399+,WP288
*7+)A194(&HP389)*11)C45A:75*15)SPH326*21+)A183-1+,
PZxv+*26)PZ288*32+)HP417
Chapter 18
225*1+)HP420;C52A:837*13)GP337*15+)SPH298(vs.C46:4226),
300   **226***6+)SPH299   **227***20+)SPH303,309(324)*26)GN110
*30+)SPH310   **228***13+)SPH312*20)BNG22,SPH306*27+)SPH
312   **229***14+)SPH312*26+)SPH313   **230***2+)SPH314(300)
*24+)SPH317   **231***14)PZ278   **232***11+)B297)PZ211*18+)SPH
318 **233***16+)SPH319   **234***16+)SCA104:404,NAV'11/2;10,GP
336,HP421,WR182,WP290*31+)RST16:564,C54A:52,BOW'62:62-
3 **235***4)SPH323(294,B219) **236***1+)SPH325*24+)B220,218*31+)
SPH322 **237***7+)RGC8:172,RE136*14+)SPH326*33+)RPP

238*8+)SPH327*19)e.g.C46:4226+,HRR22vs.WR222(vs.WPP
'27/2/5,suppression of suppression of suppression)*24)C52A:836,
WP288*26)NIP'59/4:69*27)HRR1*38NYT'11/1/28:1:4 **239***15+)
C46:2701+ **241***23+)B175,178,236(SPH324)*37+)C46:2712+
242*16)C46:2723*20+)C46:4225+,HP425*30+)WR191,HP424
*37)GP337

Chapter 19.

243*4+)C53A:285*17+)CD51,58,64,66,500,NYT'10/12/17:5:1,
24:16:2 **244***1+)C52A:336(vs.334:mudsplattered Cook puckishly
abbreviatedCivil Engineer to just Engineer Peary)*7+)WP294,
HP409*11+)A200*22+)OC448*32+)CM601 **245***1+)CM601
246*7+)CM18,552;WP198*17+)HP410*22+)FC237+,CM602+,
BNG87 **247***14+)A203,LVA274:31%24+)HP425,WP311;C51:
7475,11007,52:3616,52A:39,157,330,670,53:5558,9479,54A:42
*31)C52A:670+*31)WP311,347n11,NYT'16/9/29:8:6,C52A:158,
333,674,HH442+*34)e.g.C52A:331*36)C52:2756"this, of course, is
the greatest generation of all time...;but....We are largely in the
hands of fakers,principally on the outside of Congress." **248***1+)
C52A:482,838,658,834*7+)C54A:43,FC240*10+)C53:1033(WR
200,WP310)*13+)C53A:268+,1626+*22)C53:12013*26)HP426
vs.C54A:42+*31)A247-31*33+)WP311+ **249***5+)WP319+,HP
447+*F)KeA **250***F)KeA

Chapter 20.

251*3+)FC241+,LTD79:10:10*10+)FC247+*23+)NYT'26/1/
24:2,25:4:1,20:1,3/4:18:2,5:23:6 **252***15+)NHT'26/3/4:18:2,
MG231,AM115+*26+)NYT'26/3/7:4:4;AM225(227vs.74),MH
283,WR178 **253***16+)GiH12,98*25+)RPP'68/11/25*34+)RGJ11:
239,NGM14:432 **254***1+)ML357(v),RGJ35:303,IND115:442,
MAC'15/5/27*10+)HP412+C53A:1645*15)HP418,GiH87,NYT
'26/1/24:2:7*16)C52A:333,NYT'20/2/22:10:3vs.HP485*18)WP
128,PZvii,HP485vs.405*20)NYT9/8:1:5,FS279*27+)NYT9/12:1:7,
12/23:1:7,24:1:7(SD236) **255***1)HP405*2+)FS442,SD240*6)
RPP'68/6/5*7)HR2,HC49*8+)B236,MRvi,175*17)NAT'34/12/8,
WPP'35/1/20*18)NYT'25/4/26:2:5,28:20:8,29:20:6*19)SPM'35/
1/6(Hayes to Mill)*20)ShA28*21)WPbk,cv.,B295-7*22+)HP481+
*25+)SCI56:8(CHR48:209);A64-16+;NAV'11/2:12;A60-5;FAd
217*27)NGM112:36 **256***F)courtesy Ralph Plaisted

Chapter 21.

257*5+)AO6+,AF17*12+)AO106,150(10,AF13)*22)AF96+*25)
AO45,108 **258***1)A68,AO290(12)*2+)AO109*5+)AO106+,136,
168,176,345+*10+)AO177+*12+)AO76,124vs.106,134,79+338
*22+)BS142+,GN30*31+)C66:1013,BS149,HL66 **259***4+)BS141
vs.DB305*9+)GN38+*13+)NYT'25/8/21:7:1vs.NGM48:477
*20+)NGM48:520 vs. 475 (&'25 map "Arctic Regions") *32)BS163
*38)AF14 **260***3)A252(Jan.23)*9)FRA'26/1/26("a few days ago"),
NYT'26/1/31:1:5,NAB95(Feb.4,8)*10)NGM50:381(379Navy),

NAB83:19*12)GN92(exceptionally;there were anonymous donors,
BS332)*14)BS167*15+)AM234,CA173,AF14+,128,109,NM30
*34+)NM20,AF65,112+,160+*36+)AF78,NM31　261*3+)BS168
(aloft "for a certain reduced distance" on 2;NYT'26/5/17:4:1=2)
*7+)BS167*10+)AF52,BC20,36,BS180*17+)NYT'26/5/6*20+)
BS181*27+)BS175,183,NYT'26/5/10:2:3*31)NYT'26/5/10:1:7,
NGM50:363vs.385,BC43,BUR2,*34+)AF120,LD591,NM50
262*2+)NYT'26/5/10:2:3*5+)RGJ68:63vs.AF118-120(15h10m,
local times) *7)BUR6 *9+)RGJ68:63,LD590,BC66 *18+)BS172,
177,319-333,BUL*22+)BS183,332*37)NGM50:376　263*2)I'71/4/
14(tested only ½ hour before embarking)vs.BS168(NYT'26/1/31:1:5
SecNavy)*4+)NGM50:376,378*16)NYT'26/5/10:1:5=6,17:1:3=4,
30:3:2,LOT'26/5/29:9:6*27)NGM50:373(A258),NYT'26/5/17:1:3
=4,6/24:2:3,26:3:3vs.5/11:1:7=8*31+)NGM50:373,MG230,A101(-
RGJ68:67,NAB83:26ch.)　　264*6+)NYT'26/5/11:1:7=8*19)NYT
'26/5/16:4:4=5*20+)BS197,182*27)BS139!*34+)LD　265*7)HL22
*16+)HL125*29)RGJ68:68*37)A252　266*1+)HL126*26)NGM50:
384,378,A238*33)NGM50:377　267*4)HRR17*9+)NGM50:384
(no date)*29)NGM50:377　268*2+)RPP'68/6/19*13)NYT'26/6/
30:5:2vs.NGM50:385(SFv:"that genius in editorship")*16)NYT
'26/6/11:1:4-5,NGM50:382*22)A180*28+)NYT'26/6/23:3:6,24:1:
8(NAB95:28;17 out of order)*33+)BC55;NAB95:18,20(25?),28;
NYT'26/6/23:1:1,HL126(A267-9"Prior")　269*1+)NYT'26/6/24:
1:5,3:5,2:5;3:1;2:2*16+)RGJ68:68(62)*27+)NGM50:386,388
270%1+)RPP(RE138)*4+)RPP'68/6/19;7/23m10/15*11+)BUR6
vs.A261-34+(NGM50:376,BS200)*14+)NYT'26/6/17:4:3=4,NGM
50:376,BS200*19)NGM50:387*20)BUR6*22)Nat.Geogr. report also
avoided specifying the moment of return,NGM50:385+*23)A261-
34+*25+)NYT'26/5/17:4:1=2,5=6,NGM50:383;BS102+*31)
A259*35+)HL139　271*4)SB190vs.NGM50:383(A208)*6+)SB192,
232,201+,198 *16)SPM'32/10/31 (to Mill) *21)GN147 *23+)MO
289+　　272*2+)MO47*5+)MO126,291,261*19+)AF199,135,271
*21+)AF127+,225,NM54,57,77*30+)AF202*35+)AF202+;138,
140　273*2+)AF180,206+,C68　:4824,NM57*5+)F280,AF138+,
206+*23+)AF207,309 274*15+)AF142+*29+)A273-5+*35)
A72　275*2+)AF215+*10+)TIME'26/5/17:36,AGR16:664,AF144,
218,240+*22)NYT'26/5/16:3:8*25)A252,257,260(AO 12;likeHC68)
*31)AM214,CG20*35+)NGM52:215(further glories of fascism,70:
362,71:140,178,325)　276*6+)CG19*9+)NM107+,145+,265+,
CG284+*18)CG264+,A66*20)NM198*23+)CG106,VM245*27)
NM215*29+)CG286,FAd301*37+)AN224　　277*2)PL12*5+)PLii
(15,31,40)*21)I'71/4/15*25+)CS62+,144,184+　278*3+)F256,
A126*13+)RGJ136:511,HT265+　279*1)KuA109*4)BC26,36,A261
*6+)AS1:42+,A251*10)A107*21+)AM,ARC12:221*37)MR175,
AM72,PSc307　280*4)AM114*F)KeAApp.

Appendix
281*1+)RPP'70/6/15,'34/12/26(ENG.J.'36/1:70),'70/7/2,17,22,
28,8/4+   **282***28+)A187,HP480,YPW1:4   *31+)WPP'34/9/12
284*1+)WWW4:1040,WPP'35/1/15*4+)WPM148E,WPP'35/8/10
*9+)WPM133+ *15)C52A:331,675 *19+)WPM113 (Ward's
emph.) vs. SPH302 *30)A115-4 *38+)NYT9/11:1:7-2:1,17:2:1;
14:1:7 *41+)C53A:1628 vs. SPH302;WP342n66,RPP'70/11/19
285*1+)PZ296 vs. C53A:1628(A145),NYT9/26:5:2 *5)NYT9/16:
1:7-2:1 "we went no distance beyond the flags" *8)F12,A25 *11+)
NYT9/11:1:7p2:1 vs. PHm25:176 *13)C46:2705 *14)A270 *27+)
WPP'35/6/14   **288***20+)A85-33+ *30)A166 *32+)WPP'35/8/8,
C52A:40,HP400n12,RGJ89:257   **289***20+)ECA10/29 *32+)QT
952,1'71/4/2,GoR103 *42+)WPP'34/10/24,WPD'35/5/18
290*14+)WPvii *20+)WPP'35/5/19,20   **291***1)ECA10/26(7,30)
*12)ECM1913 *18)C52A:671 *22)WR193(Hobbs was the campus
Hun-sniffer,RPP'70/11/13) *25)WPP'32/7/23   **292***3)BoN2:101
vs. BT174 (publ. by Stokes, like PZ,HE);(PG1:507,2:398;RPP
'70/11/25,12/2);A111-38+;FK6(ECA copy, Fiala note),C53A:
1641 *8)AGR19:132 vs. SN2:295,PZ285(C53A:1641) *18)FC255
*20)SCI81:362 (vs. WR186), REAL AMERICA '36/1,RPP '69/
11/17('70/9/30:when Rev.Hayes died of cancer in '36,Hobbs "actually rejoiced")*25)WPD'35/6/11,WPP'35/5/20(A289),YPW'35/12/
23,26,'45/7/24;WPP'34/10/24,BPJ(Biogr.)'49/1/31,(Stafford)'43/
2/10vs.SCI82:532   **293***7)HP363n12(vs.SCM40:394),cited AGR16:
102*9)RGJ94:311,316,BPJ(Wordie)'39/6/29"Hobbs' attack re-
minds one most of the great literary forgeries, but I doubt if there
has been anything quite like it in the history of exploration"*13)
APP82:921*16)Assoc.Press(Montreal)'68/5/10(KT124),RPP'68/8/
21*23)RPP'68/7/8,8/5,10/15;11/12vs.WR221,C113:11369*31)
RPP'68/4/15,22 **294** *3)RPP'70/9/30,10/27 *6)WPviii,RPP
'70/5/19;'71/3/25;5/21('70/6/29,7/2,'71/5/7),'73/1/23;I'70/6/23,
7/13*14)RPP'71/5/18(RE138),6/7*23)RPP'71/10/8,11/12

Glossary

altitude: celestial body's angular distance above the horizon
apparent noon: moment when sun crosses one's meridian
artificial horizon, reflecting: level reflecting surface (e.g., pool of
  mercury) for use with sextant when horizon not smooth; ½of
  angle measured between actual and reflected celestial object = its
  actual altitude

azimuth: true direction, angle taken on horizon (from north thru east, conventionally; e.g., southwest = 225° azimuth, or 135° azimuth west of north)

chronometer: timepiece; accuracy critical to longitude determination

colatitude: angular distance (on earth's surface) from the North Pole; colatitude = 90° minus latitude

cross-staff: simple pre-telescopic instrument for measuring altitude

declination: celestial body's angular distance from celestial equator; tabulated in the *Nautical Almanac*

double-limb observation of sun: altitude of upper and lower limb of sun each observed, average of the two yields the altitude of sun's center

fathom: common unit of depth measure, equal to six feet

latitude: angular distance (on earth's surface) north of equator

lead: a wide, watery rift in sea ice

longitude: angle west (or east) of Greenwich meridian

meridian: a line of constant longitude; or a plane including the observer, his zenith and nadir, and the north and south points of his horizon

mile: *all* miles in this book are "nautical" unless otherwise stated; a nautical (or "geographical") mile = one minute of angle on the earth's sphere and is c.15% larger than the common "statute" mile

noon observation: altitude of sun's center, taken via sextant (or theodolite) presumably at local apparent noon; latitude or colatitude then obtainable by arithmetic: colatitude = altitude minus declination

order of magnitude (ordmag): nearest power of ten

reduce: convert raw data into quantities sought (e.g., solar altitudes and chronometer times into latitude and longitude)

refraction: bending (by earth's atmosphere) of light from celestial object, apparently raising it (this correction is tabulated in the *Nautical Almanac*)

sextant: a common device for measuring angles (e.g., altitudes)

single-limb observation of sun: only altitude of upper or lower limb of sun is recorded, and then corrected (to find altitude of sun's center) for the solar semi-diameter (tabulated in *Nautical Almanac*)

theodolite: a common surveyor's instrument ("transit"); measures altitude and azimuth

transverse: left-right, lateral, or cross-wise — en route to the North Pole, transverse motion would correspond to change of longitude

Bibliography and Reference-Key

A	Above (internal cross-ref; e.g., A52-31 = above, p. 52,1.31)
AAJ	American Alpine Journal, Amer. Alpine Club (AAC)
AGB	American Geographical Society, *Bulletin* of
AGR	*Geographical Review,* AGS, New York
AHI	*American History Illustrated*
AMJ	American Museum of Natural History, *Journal* of
APP	American Philosophical Society *Proceedings,* APS, Phila.
AF	Amundsen, Roald et al., *First Crossing...,* Doran, NY, 1927
AM	Amundsen, *My Life...,* Doubleday, Garden City, 1927
AO	Amundsen et al., *Our Polar Flight,* Dodd, NY, 1925
AS	Amundsen, *The South Pole,* Murray, London, 1913
AN	Anderson, Wm., *Nautilus 90 North,* World, Cleveland, 1959
ARC	*Arctic,* Journal of the Arctic Institute of North America
ATH	*Atheneum*
B	Below (internal cross-ref; see A)
BC	Balchen, Bernt, *Come North with Me,* Dutton, NY, 1958
BL	Bartlett, Robert, *The Log of...,* Blue Ribbon, NY, 1928
BA	Bartlett, "Peary's...Attainment...", 1940, APP 82:935
BH	Bessels, Emil, *Physical Observations...,* Washington, 1876
BDC	*Biographical Directory of...Congress,* G.P.O., Wash., 1961
BoN	Borup, George, "Notes..." (1908-'09 diary), AGS archives
BT	Borup, *A Tenderfoot with Peary,* Stokes, NY, 1911
BPJ	Isaiah Bowman Papers, Johns Hopkins Univ., Baltimore
BU	Bridges, E. Lucas, *Uttermost Part...,* Dutton, NY, 1949
BSU	Brooklyn *Standard-Union*
BJ	Brown, W.A., *Morris Ketchum Jesup,* Scribner, NY, 1911
BOW	*Bowditch Navigator,* Secretary of the Navy
BW	Brady, William A., *Showman,* Dutton, NY, 1937
BAC	British Admiralty Chart
BrC	Browne, Belmore, *Conquest...,* Riverside, Cambr., 1913, '56
BNG	Bur.Navig.Gen.Corr. 1903-13, Natl Arch., RG24, file 1438
BS	Byrd, Richard, *Skyward,* Putnam, NY, 1928
BUL	Byrd letter to Alfred Collins, 11/6/26 (copy Natl. Arch.)
BUR	Byrd, "Navigation...", 11/24/26 (carbon copy Natl. Arch.)
CHR	*Canadian Historical Review*
CS	Calvert, James, *Surface at the Pole,* McGraw, NY, 1960
CA	Caswell, John Edwards, *Arctic Frontiers,* U. Okla., 1956
CY	Comstock, Anthony, *Traps...Young,* 1883 (1967, Harvard)
C	*Congressional Record* ("A" refers to volume's Appendix)

CD	Cook, Frederick, "...Own Story," 1/4/11, *Hampton's* vol.26
CM	Cook, *My Attainment...,* Polar,NY 1911; Kennerly,NY 1913
CN	Cook, *...First Antarctic Night,* Doubleday, NY, 1900
CT	Cook, *...Top of the Continent,* Doubleday, NY, 1908
CK	Corner, Geo., *Dr. Kane of the Arctic Seas,* Temple U., 1972
CG	Cross, Wilbur, *Ghost Ship of the Pole,* Sloane, NY, 1960
DB	Davis, Burke, The Billy Mitchell Affair, Random, NY, 1967
DP	Davis, Charles, ed., *...Expedition...Polaris...,* Wash. 1876
DJ	DeLong, George W.,*...the Jeannette,* Houghton, Boston, '88
DAB	*Dictionary of American Biography* (original vol.-nos.)
DNB	*Dictionary of National Biography* ("S" ref. to Supplements)
DH	Doyle, A.C., *Complete Sherlock Holmes,* Garden City
DS	Dunn, Robert, *Shameless Diary...Explorer,* Outing, NY, '07
EB	*Encyclopaedia Britannica,* Benton, Chicago
ECA	Explorers Club Archives (Explorers Club, NY)
ECM	Explorers Club Minutes (Directors' resolution)
ECJ	*Explorers Journal,* Washington (journal of Explorers Club)
F	Figure (internal cross-ref.; see cited page-number)
FaS	Fairley, T.C. *Sverdrup's Arc. Adv.,* Longman, Toronto, '59
FaL	Fawcett, Percy H., *Lost Trails, Lost Cities,* Funk, NY, 1953
FK	Fiala, Anthony, *Kodak at the North Pole,* Rochester, c.'10
FS	Fisher, Marg. & Jas., *Shackleton...,* Houghton, Boston, '58
FB	Fitzgerald, Charles Galt, "Log...1897" (copy at Natl. Arch.)
FRP	*Foreign Relations...Papers...,* U.S. State Department
FL	Fox, Margaret, *Love-Life of Dr. Kane,* Carleton, NY, 1866
FC	Freeman, Andrew, *Case...Cook,* Coward-McCann, NY, '61
FAd	Freuchen, Peter, *Adventures...Arctic,* Messner, NY, 1960
FAr	Freuchen, *Arctic Adventure,* Farrar, NY, 1935
FP	Friis, Herman, *The Pacific Basin,* AGS, NY, 1967
FU	Friis & Bale, Shelby, *U.S. Polar Expl.* Ohio U., 1970
GF	Gardner, Martin, *Fads and Fallacies,* Dover, NY, 1957
GSC	Geological Survey of Canada maps, 1970 (Index Sheet nos.)
GiH	Gibbons, Russell, *Historical Eval.,* Ohio Northern U., 1954
GA	Gibbs, Philip, *Adventures in Journalism,* Harper, NY, 1923
GS	Gilder, William H., *Schwatka's Search,* Scribner, NY, 1881
GoR	Goldman, Eric, *Rendezvous with Destiny,* Knopf, 1958
GPr	Gordienko, P. et al., *...Oceanogr. Res...,* DRB Canada, '61
GH	Greely, Adolphus W., *Handbook...,* 5 ed., Little, Bost., '10
GR	Greely, *Reminiscenses of Adventure...,* Scribner, NY, 1927
GT	Greely, *Three Years of Arctic Service,* Scribner, NY, 1885
GP	Green, Fitzhugh, *Peary...,* Putnam, NY, 1926
GN	Grosvenor, Gilbert H., *Nat.Geo.Soc. & its Mag.,* NGS, '57
HH	Hall, Thomas, *Has...N.P. Been Disc'd.?,* Bader, Boston, '17
HB	Hattersley-Smith, G., "P's NP Jny," '61, *Beaver* 292:1:36
HJ	Hayes, Isaac Israel, *Arctic...Journey,* Brown, Boston, 1860
HO	Hayes, I.I., *The Open Polar Sea,* Hurd, NY, 1867

HAG	Hayes, I.I., unpublished manuscripts, AGS archives, NY
HC	Hayes, James Gordon, *Conquest...NP,* Thornton, Lon., '34
HR	Hayes, J.G., *Robert Edwin Peary,* Richards, London, 1929
HW	Henson, M., "Negro...NP,"4/'10, *World's Work* 19:12825
HE	Henson, *Negro Explorer at the North Pole,* Stokes, NY 1912
HA	Henson,"Real Story...," Bost. *American, 7/17/10 (#by col.)*
HT	Herbert, Wally, *Across the Top...,* Putnam, NY, 1971
HSG	*History Speaks* :phonograph discs), Gotham Records, NY
HP	Hobbs, William Herbert, *Peary,* Macmillan, NY, 1936
HD	Hoehling, A.A., *'Jeannette' Expedition,* Abelard, Lon., '67
HRR	House of Repr. Report #1961, 61st Congress, 3rd Session
HL	Hoyt, Edwin P., *The Last Explorer,* Day, NY, 1968
HN	*Henry Hudson...Navigtr.* (G.Asher, ed.); 1860, Hakluyt 1:27
I	Interview
IND	*The Independent*
KA	Kane, Elisha Kent, *Arctic Explorations,* Childs, Phila.,1856
KG	Kane, *The U.S. Grinnell Expedition,* Harper, NY, 1854
KeA	Kershner, Howard, Air Pioneering, Nat. Amer. S., NY, '29
KH	Kirwan, Laurence, *History of Polar Expl.* Norton, NY, 1960
KuA	Kugelmass, J. Alvin, *Roald Amundsen,* Kingston, Chi. 1955
KT	Kuralt, Charles, *To the Top of the World,* Holt, NY, 1968
LD	Liljequist, Gosta, "...'Jos. Ford'...," 1960, *Interavia* 15:589
LTD	*Literary Digest*
LVA	*Living Age*
LH	Titus Livius, *History of Rome*
LOT	London *Times*
LW	Loomis, Chauncey, *Weird & Tragic Shores,* Knopf, NY, '71
LG	Lord, Walter, *The Good Years,* Harper, NY, 1960
LP	Luigi, Amedeo, *Polar Star,* Hutchinson, London, 1903
LO	Luigi, *Osservazione Scientifiche...,* Hoepli, Milan, 1903
McH	MacDougall, Curtis, *Hoaxes,* 1940, rev. Dover, NY, 1958
MN	MacLaurin, Colin, ...*Newton's Discoveries,* 3rd ed., 1775
MA	Allen, Everett, ...*Life of Donald MacMillan,* Dodd, NY, '62
MF	MacMillan, *4 Years in the White North,* Harper, NY, 1918
MH	MacMillan, *How Pry. Reached...Pole,* Houghton, Bost., '34
MAC	Albert Markham Collect., Nat. Maritime Mus., Greenwich
MS	Markham, Clements, ...*50 Yrs....RGS,* Murray, Lon., 1881
ML	Markham, C., ...*Lands of Silence,* Cambridge Univ., 1921
MT	Markham, *Threshold...Unknown Region,* Low, Lond., 1873
MV	Martens, Fred., *Voy. to Spitzbergen*; 1855, Hakluyt 1:18
MP	Marvin, Ross, diaries, Chemung County Hist. Soc., Elmira
MR	Mill, Hugh, *Record...RGS 1830-1930,* RGS, London, 1930
MDA	Mitchell, H & Duvall, C. (& Hubbard, T.), *Acts* IGC10:682
MG	Mitchell, William, *General Greely...,* Putnam, NY, 1936
MO	Montague, Rich., *Oceans,..., & Airmen,* Random, NY, '71
ME	Morison, Sam., *Eur. Disc. Amer.,...N.Voy.,* Oxford U., '71

NF Nansen, Fridtjof, *Farthest North,* Harper, NY, 1897
NC Nansen, *1st Cross. of Greenland,* Longmans, London, 1896
NS Nansen,...*Scient. Results,* Longmans, London, 1900-1906
NN Nares, George,...*Voyage to...Polar Sea,* Low, London, 1878
NAB National Archives, Gen. Corr., '97-'26, R.G.80, file 29455
NAG Natl. Arch., Gen. Records Navy Dept., Record Group 80
NAL Natl. Arch., Legislative Correspondence re Peary bill
NAM Natl. Arch., microfilm collection
NAP Natl. Arch., Gift Collection...Polar Regions, R.G.401
NGM *National Geographic Magazine,* NGS, Washington
NAT *Nature*
NIP Naval Institute *Proceedings,* U.S.N.I., Annapolis
NAV *The Navy,* Navy League
NSR *Annual Report of the Secretary of the Navy*
NYH New York *Herald*
NYT New York *Times*
NM Nobile, Umberto, *My Polar Flights,* Putnam, NY, 1961
NH Nordhoff, C. & Hall, J., *Bounty* Tril. #2, LB, Bost., '32-'34
OC Osbon, Bradley, "Cook & Peary," 9-11/10, *Tourist,* vol. 6
OTL *Outlook*
PL Papanin, Ivan, *Life on an Ice Floe,* Messner, NY, 1939
PP Parry, Ann, *Parry of the Arctic,* Chatto, London, 1963
PF Payer, Julius, *New Lands..Arctic Circ.,* Appleton, NY, 1877
PHm Peary, Robt., "Disc. N.P.," 1-9/10, *Hampton's,* v. 24 & 25
PHr Peary, "Nearest the N.P.," 2-3/1907, *Harper's,* vol. 114
PY Peary, *Nearest the North Pole,* Doubleday, NY, April 1907
PZ Peary, *The North Pole,* Stokes, NY, September 1910
PG Peary, *Northward Over the "Great Ice,"* Stokes, NY, 1898
PS Peary, *Secrets of Polar Travel,* Century, NY, 1917
PGB Philadelphia Geographical Society *Bulletin*
PV Phipps, C. & Lutwidge, S., *Journal,* Newbury, London, 1773
PON *Polar Notes,* Stefansson Collection, Dartmouth College
PSc Pound, Reginald, *Scott of the Antrc.,* Cwd-McC., NY, 1967
QT Quigley, Carroll, *Tragedy & Hope,* Macmillan, NY, 1966
RE Rawlins, D., "Evaluating...," '72, *Norsk Geogr. T.* 26:135
RN Rawlins, Dennis, "Peary & the North Pole," 6/70, NIP:3,32
RPP Rawlins Papers U.S. National Archives, Washington
RR Rawlins, "Retrospective Critique...," 1970, PON 10:24
RKU Rawlins, "Ulysses of the Polar Seas," in press
RG Reeves, Edward, *Recollections of a Geogr.,* Seeley, Lon., '35
RMS Reeves, unpubl. ms defense of '09 claim, 1910, RGS archvs.
RER *Review of Reviews* (American Edition)
RD Robinson, Bradley, *Dark Companion,* Fawcett, NY, 1967
RFA Rockefeller Family Archives
RL *Roosevelt* Log 1906, Chemung Co. Historical Soc., Elmira
RAM Royal Astronomical Society *Memoirs*

RAN	Royal Astronomical Society *Monthly Notices*
RGC	Royal Geographical Society Council Minutes
RGJ	*Geographical Journal,* RGS
RJG	*Journal* of the Royal Geographical Society
RST	Royal Society *Philosophical Transactions*
RW	Russell, Bertrand, *Why I Am Not a Christian,* S&S, NY, '57
SH	Schott, C., *Phys. Obs....Hayes,* Smiths Cntr. #196:1867
SK	Schott, *Phys. Obs....Kane,* pt.3, Smiths Cntr, #129, 1860
SCI	*Science,* Amer. Assn. for the Advancement of Science
SCA	*Scientific American*
SCM	*Scientific Monthly*
SL	Scott, Robert Falcon,...*Last Expedition,* Dodd, NY, 1929
SPR	*Polar Record,* Scott Polar Research Institute, Cambridge
SPM	Scott Polar Research Institute archives
ShA	Shackleton, Edward, *Arctic Journeys,* Hodder, London, '37
SHe	Shackleton, Ernest, *Heart of the Antrc.,* Lipp., Phila., 1909
SS	Silverberg, Robert, *Scientists & Scoundrels,* Crwl., NY, '65
SB	Smith, Dean, *By the Seat of My Pants,* Little, NY, 1961
SAR	Smithsonian Inst., Annual Reports, G.P.O., Washington
SPE	*Spectator*
StN	Stafford, Edw. Peary, "Peary & the N.P....," 12/71, NIP:44
SPH	*Statement...Peary...House...* :"Peary Hearings") C53A:293
SD	Stefansson, Vilhjalmur, *Discovery,* McGraw, NY, 1964
SF	Stefansson, *The Friendly Arctic,* Macmillan, NY, 1943
SA	Stefansson, *Great Advntrs. & Explrtns.,* Dial, NY, 1952
SG	Stefansson, *Greenland,* Doubleday, NY, 1943
SP	Stefansson, *Problem of Meighen Island,* Robinson, NY, '39
SPC	Stefansson Collection (Dartmouth), Polar Controversy file
SM	Stowell, James, *Tragedy...Arctic,* Chemung Co. H.S., 1954
SGe	Strabo, *Geography*
StA	Stuck, Hudson, *The Ascent of Denali,* Scribner, NY, 1914
SQ	Sullivan, Walter, *Quest for a Continent,* McGraw, NY, '57
SN	Sverdrup, Otto, *New Land,* Longmans, London, 1904
TMJ	*Terrestrial Magnetism, Journal of*
TV	Thackeray, William, *Vanity Fair,* Estes, Boston
TA	Todd, A.L., *Abandoned,* McGraw-Hill, NY, 1961
TD	Tyson, Geo. & Blake, Euph. V.,...*Drift...,* Harper, NY, '74
VB	Veer, Gerrit de, *Three Voyages...;* 1874, Hakluyt 1:54
VM	Victor, Paul-Emile, *Man...Conquest...Poles,* S&S, NY, '67
VK	Villarejo, Oscar M., *Dr. Kane's Voyage...,* Univ. Penn., '65
WPD	Henshaw Ward diaries
WPP	Ward Papers, U.S. National Archives, Washington
WPM	Ward, *The Peary Myth,* 1935 (unpublished)
WCU	Washburn, Bradford, unpubl. ms on Cook-McKinley, AAC
WAP	Washington *Post*
WAT	Washington *Times*

WP	Weems, John Edward, *Peary...*, Houghton, Boston, 1967
WR	Weems, *Race for the Pole,* Holt, NY, 1960
WWW	*Who Was Who in America*
WA	Wright, John K.,...*the AGS 1851-1951,* AGS, NY, 1952
WB	Wright, Theon, *The Big Nail,* Day, NY, 1970
YPW	Yale University Press, correspondence file on WPM

See also the generally excellent bibliographies of Weems and especially Gibbons.

Index

313

315

317

319